THE
GOSPEL OF PEACE
ACCORDING TO
GURU-GRANTH SAHIB

THE WORLD GOSPEL SERIES 8

THE GOSPEL OF PEACE ACCORDING TO GURU-GRANTH SAHIB

Based on a new translation of the Japji and many portions of the Guru Granth of the Sikhs, with explanatory notes and a historical and biographical Introduction

DUNCAN GREENLEES

THE THEOSOPHICAL PUBLISHING HOUSE
Adyar, Madras, India • Wheaton, Illinois, USA

First Edition 1952
Second Edition 1960
Third Edition 1968
Fourth Edition 1975
Fifth Edition 1994

ISBN 81-7059-236-4 (Hard Cover)
ISBN 81-7059-237-2 (Soft Cover)

Printed at the Vasanta Press
The Theosophical Society
Adyar, Madras 600 020, India

The World Gospel Series

Gather us in, thou Love that fillest all,
Gather our rival faiths within thy fold;
Rend each man's temple-veil and bid it fall
That we may know that thou hast been of old.
Gather us in; we worship only thee:
In varied names we stretch a common hand;
In diverse forms a common soul we see,
In many ships we seek one spirit-land.
Each sees one colour of thy rainbow light,
Each looks upon one tint and calls it heaven:
Thou art the fullness of our partial sight—
We are not perfect till we find the seven.

G. MATHESON

APART from a few scholars and devotees, the modern public are unwilling to spend time reading through the whole of the lengthy scriptures of the world. This little series is planned to offer them, in a cheap, handy and attractive form, the essence of each of the world's great scriptures, translated and edited by one who has a deep and living sympathy for each of them.[1]

---

[1] It is however obvious that the writer does not thereby pronounce his own personal convictions.

It is based on the inevitable conclusion of any fair student that all the great religions and their scriptures — the authentic Word of God to man — come from the one divine source, in varying degrees of purity of transmission, and according to the needs and capacities of those to whom they are addressed.

It is hoped that the series will form a useful little reference library of the world's religious literature which has done so much to mould the thought and culture of today, even though few, perhaps, in each of the communities have been able to reach the ideal laid down in their holy books.

DUNCAN GREENLEES

The Gospel of Peace (Guru-Granth Sahib)

SIKHISM is the religion taught through Guru Nanak in the forms of the Ten Gurus, and now through the *Guru-Granth Sahib* and the whole community of disciples. It is a practical way of life that does not involve itself in verbose theorizing but leads a man straight to his goal.

There is one God, absolute, eternal, infinite, beyond all human comprehension, yet revealed through creation, and through grace to one prepared by the practice of devotion and the virtues. This God never limits himself to one form by taking birth, but sends his messengers from time to time to lead his creatures towards him.

God alone is of himself altogether true, eternally real. His whole creation is real only because he pervades it and can be found through it; in the absolute sense it is like a dream which arises from and eventually disappears again into his infinite person. As no final happiness can be found in perishable things, God's creatures reach their end only by union with that eternal Lord from whom they came. Ensnared in a world of change which should have been a playground but has become a prison, caught up in a wearisome round of births and deaths resulting from its own act in identifying the self with its physical body and environment, the creature can be freed and admitted into that union only by a whole-hearted choice of God as the guiding principle of its life. Regarding worldly things as shadows, the aspirant gives his whole life to God and thereafter looks on himself merely as his instrument or servant, relying on him at every moment for guidance and strength.

Such a life is possible only when the soul is thoroughly disillusioned with the instability of other things and filled with an intense longing for the Eternal. Made ready in this way by the supreme virtue of surrender, she receives God's grace in the society of a saintly teacher—the Guru. She is now able to realize God as ever present with and in her, and to pass every moment in harmony with his known will. This blessed soul is then called to the inner chambers of the heart where, through the mystic way, she is made perfectly one with her One Beloved, and thenceforth lives the divine life on earth and in the inner planes.

To tread this path there is no need to renounce the world or to adopt the robes or way of life of the ascetic. God pervades the whole world, including man's homes; he is in the heart itself, and can be found equally in any environment. As he is equally in all his creatures, none should be despised, injured or unkindly treated for such contumely is against the Lord himself and falls back on the head of the offender, throwing him once more on the tortuous paths of incarnation in our dark physical world.

To protect the young community of disciples (*Sikhs*) that had become subject to persecution, the sixth Guru converted it into a semi-military brotherhood, arming it with outward insignia and sacraments, and thus subjecting it to the purifying fires of martyrdom, which instilled the necessary courage and resolution in its heart. The Sikhs should therefore have a great place in the future of their country, as so pure and spiritual a religion as theirs has already a great place among the religions of the world.[1]

---

[1] I am immensely indebted to the well-known Sikh scholar, Bhai Jodh Singh, M.A., Principal of the Khalsa College, Amritsar, for reading through the manuscript of this book, making frequent suggestions and several emendations. He was good enough to write to me as follows:

'I have read the manuscript sent by you ... and have gone through it very carefully. I have noted certain historical inaccuracies that I have found and given the correct facts. ... I have not made any suggestion where the original text could bear your interpretation. ... Yes! From the doctrinal point of view your account is accurate. ... I congratulate you on the industry that you have put into this work.'

I must thank also the friends of the Sikh Cultural Centre in Calcutta who pointed out several slight errors in transliteration and printing and, of far greater importance, threw light on the life of Guru Gobind Singh which was unknown to the authorities consulted by me earlier. At the same time I must apologize for being unable to accept every suggestion they made; the volumes of this series are for the general public, not for Sikhs alone, and pedantry has been avoided in transliteration; it is better to use a system which will help ordinary readers to pronounce the words with reasonable accuracy.

This is also the time to thank good Sikh friends all over the world for their kind reception of this volume and for their eagerness to make it even more authentic as a statement of Sikh faith, practice and history.

D.G.

Preface

IT was in early 1947 and I was in Adyar. A Sikh Theosophist who had served in the Indian National Army heard of *The Gospel of Islam* in this series and that I was writing other volumes; he asked me if I had ever read the *Guru-Granth Sahib* of their Guru Nanak. I had heard of it, of course, but knew of no English translation and was ignorant of the dialect of medieval Punjabi in which it is mostly written. But he assured me that I would find it easy, knowing Hindi, and that I would certainly love the book when I read it. I then added the title to the projected series.[1]

Three years passed, and I had made the first selection of passages from Macauliffe's great work;

---

[1] My grateful thanks are specially due to Principal N.B. Butani, to Sri K.C. Advani, advocate, Bangalore, and to Sri Bhagwan Singh B. Advani, president of a Gurdwara in Bombay, for the gift of the **Sri Guru-Granth Sahib**, to Mrs Butani for the inspiring portrait which presided over my work and now appears as frontispiece to this volume, to several Sikh friends for encouragement, to Dr Srinivasamurti, Hon. Directior, Adyar Library, for three times lending their Macauliffe's volumes and condoning long extensions of the time limits!

Sikh friends from South Kanara, Bombay and Bangalore sent me a fine copy of the Holy Book, and a Sikh lady sent me her own portrait of Guru Nanak. But until volume seven had gone to press I found little time to work at all seriously on this volume. When I did so, I was appalled at the difficulty in tracing the selected passages; Macauliffe, like almost all Sikh authors, satisfied himself with merely referring to the *rag* and the *mahala* (author) — no chapter, no verse number! It took me more than a month to trace all the passages; but this proved useful work for it gave me a certain familiarity with the book and a delight in its inspiring thoughts and musical language. The more I dug into its pages, the more I fell in love with them — my Sikh friend was justified in his prophecy! Among the world's scriptures few, if any, attain so high a literary level or so constant a height of inspiration.

When it was time to select new passages to fill in logical gaps, to make certain rearrangements, to undertake a complete retranslation of the whole, the non-existence of a Gurmukhī-English dictionary proved a serious handicap, although the Hindi of Tulsīdās, Sūrdās and their contemporaries helped me out. At times, though, I had to take my authorities on trust and merely shaped their English in harmony with that employed throughout. Principal Teja Singh's English renderings of a few great sections of the *Guru-Granth Sahib* proved helpful in conveying the spirit of some hard passages. Professor Sahib Singh's excellent works gave me all confidence in their careful accuracy and scholarship; I soon had cause to give his versions preference over all others because of his deep knowledge of the grammar. Here and there other renderings also threw light on dark places, but in a few I had no means of going behind

Macauliffe's version, as for instance in the narrative extracts used in § § 2 and 53.

In this volume, as in the case of *The Gospel of Zarathushtra*, I have felt it desirable to include a second part. This is a direct and unbroken version of the *Japji*, Guru Nanak's great poem, which may well be classed with the *Gītā*, the *Gāthās*, and a few other spiritual masterpieces. It is held to give an outline of Sikh philosophy; it is the morning devotion on rising from bed; it is the most loved of all the Guru's hymns. Puran Singh says of it: 'The hymn *Japji* is the burden of the whole *Guru-Grantha*. The day of the disciples begins with *Japji*. The melody breaks forth in our inner ears with the strain of the first dawn of creation. Our eyes close and, as if in a dream, we stand listening to the music that rings through eternity. We are the children of *Japji*. Its music is our motherland. It comes to us with an intimacy as close as if it were born of the hidden seat within our soul. The maker of this hymn is so filled with its beauty that he, himself, the master of its music, is entranced with it. Every morning, since its birth, in its chant we have the mingling of a myriad holy voices — the voices of the disciples. I feel at times that with *Japji* I am as one transported to the land of immortals. I am as one apart from the body, listening in wonder to a Voice reciting *Japji*. In my reverie, I feel that the singer has hands that touch my soul. Then I realize that *Japji* is the Word. With such visions I do not feel lonely. ... When the world beats us and breaks us by the weight of its matter we go to *Japji*. The sore melancholy of our hearts and minds is made whole by *Japji*.'

The Guru's hymns are the very life of the Sikhs. The Sikh community is not among the largest of the world's religious groups; there may be about five million baptized Sikhs, and perhaps twice as many more who have preferred to hold their worship secret in their hearts. But their importance in India's religious life is out of all proportion to their numbers; as a strongly martial people, stationed for the most part on the uneasy north-west frontier of the land, they are its guardians, and on their happiness and loyalty must largely depend the safety of the whole of India. Such was their name in the past that General Sir John J.H. Gordon wrote: 'None have fought more stoutly and stubbornly against us [British], none more loyally and gallantly for us, than the Sikhs' (*The Sikhs*, p.3). When the British ruled India they indeed provided 'the flower of the British Indian Army'; today also the Indian Army, Navy, and Air Force are filled with these brave men, and they will give as good an account of themselves in the future as in the past, when they almost made a hobby of collecting Victoria Crosses. Even in the eighteenth century, when subjected to a most brutal persecution for many years, they stood firm; they stood firm again during the tragic days in Punjab which followed the partition of 1947; they will stand as firm in any future dangers that may threaten India. The heroic spirit of the warrior saint and scholar, Guru Gobind Singh, is still alive among his 'lion' disciples. And those who have tasted the comradeship and kindliness of the Sikhs of today will not easily forget the experience.

A religion which combines the most passionate

mystic devotion and love of God with heroic conduct in daily life, and just and reasonable social customs, is certainly worthy of study. I trust and believe that a few of my readers at least will be urged to study the Holy Book itself, and then to share the fruits of their study with us by giving us a complete, accurate, sympathetic and literary translation of what is — apart from its great religious importance — certainly one of the world's masterpieces of poetry.

Perhaps a word on why in this volume the Introduction is largely devoted to biography and history may not be out of place. The Sikh religion has never been a philosophy of books, of theorists, but as Mahtab Singh says it is a 'discipline of life', an ideal of brotherhood inspired by passionate devotion to the highest, guided by the example of the Guru's own life and interpreted in the life of the Guru Khālsā-Panth. Sikh history cannot be divorced from Sikh philosophy; it is its very life-blood. Of course, none but a Sikh in union with the *Khālsā* can truly write that history; my attempt is a sort of presumption, but I trust that my goodwill may compensate in some degree for my inadequacy and that Sikh friends will permit me to offer this fruit of happy labours at the holy feet of Guru Nanak.

Contents

PART ONE
SIKHISM

CHAPTER ONE
The Perfect Teacher

1. The Coming of a Teacher, 2. The Call of Nanak, 3. The Humility of Nanak, 4. The

Introduction

1. INDIA BEFORE THE GURU

1. The Hindus

DIVIDED over petty dynastic and personal quarrels, the peoples of India — Hindu, Buddhist, and Jain — put up a very poor defence against the ruthless, hardy and energetic invaders from the Muslim dominated Middle East. In each province, a few battles, a few secret betrayals were enough; indigenous rulers were replaced by Muslims, temples by mosques, the Purānas by the *Korān*. This was on the national scale, but of course millions of Hindus retained their own religion, at a price, and under the shadow of the conqueror lived lives which were little more than slavery.

They practised their rites and social customs on sufferance and were liable at any moment to have them interrupted and forbidden on pain of death. Many, whose names history has not recorded, died rather than turn false to the faith of their fathers; millions more embraced Islam and, in later years, covered the name of that noble religion with shame by the atrocities they committed on their brothers who stood firm.

Hinduism, as it was then understood, taught non-resistance, directed the eyes of its believers to a better existence in *svarga,* and so led them to indifference to the miseries of life on earth. Only the Brāhmans were allowed to study the scriptures, which were written in Samskrit, and they neglected their duty of teaching the spiritual realities to the masses who sank into the most pitiable slough of superstition and materialism. For them, religion became a mere matter of special ways of eating, drinking, bathing, painting the forehead with caste-marks, marrying, and disposing of corpses. Where the local Muslim authorities were tolerant — or contemptuous — enough, they were allowed to worship their idols and perform their pilgrimages, giving liberally to the ignorant and lazy Brāhmans who presided at these functions. Where they were permitted to do so, they rebuilt their temples and went in procession to holy places such as Kāśi or Paṇḍharpur. The Brāhmans themselves were satisfied with learning their mantras by heart so that they might earn a living by reciting them; they cared little or nothing for the meaning nor did they attempt to live according to their precepts and ideals. Thus the people were ignorant and indifferent, and their priests selfish and careless; both alike were imprisoned in meaningless rites and superstitions, and spirituality was buried deep under the outer forms of different sects. Many found it useful, while secretly keeping a certain sentimental attachment to their ancestral religion, to conform outwardly to the ways of the conqueror. They adopted Muslim dress, attended the mosques and repeated the Muslim creed in public so as to secure immunity from poll-tax and persecution, and to open the door to their own social and financial advancement, for it was all but impossible for a Hindu to gain worthy employment at that time or to hold offices about the court.

As the Muslims treated them, so the upper castes in turn treated the Śūdras and untouchables; they were not permitted to carry swords nor had they the right to slay, but they murdered them with hatred, contempt and social exclusion. Even such a man as Tulsīdās was not above referring to Śūdras as men whom even the highest virtues could not raise; other saintly men like Ravidās and Kabīr accepted their own upliftment in social life as exceptional, and made little attempt to raise others of their caste along with themselves. So utterly were the Hindus degraded that they were the prey to self-abasement and servility; they had lost all self-respect and faith in their gods, and most of them, being deprived by caste-rules of the right to bear arms, had all but lost that natural manliness which alone could promise a better future. One half even of the higher castes was also subjected to contempt and dislike, for women were held to be definitely inferior and could not attain to salvation or enter heaven until they had been reborn as men. They were considered to be sensual, the natural tempters and spoilers of men's spiritual life, the first condition of which was their total renunciation. It was natural, then, that the few who still looked for spirituality turned away from society and entered the forests or took to purposeless wanderings; a few may have 'meditated' during their travels, but most were idle tramps who fell into evil ways and indulged in many vices.

It was indeed an unhappy age for the heirs of the Buddha and Śaṁkara, and the devotees of Vishnu. Politically, the state of the people was miserable almost beyond belief. The emperors at Delhi cared little or nothing for their welfare; most of them held that Hindus were created to be the slaves of Muslim believers and that their households might be freely broken up to satisfy the demands of lust. Nanak tells us that in his days 'the kings had become butchers and cannibals, officials dogs that licked the blood and devoured the flesh of the people in their power; there was none to protect the honour of the weak or of the women. All was falsehood, and religion had flown away from such horrors as it beheld when Bābar came to India.' Most people sank under the burden of their misery into pessimistic resignation, but it stung Nanak even into challenging God for tolerating such brutalities. (cf. N. *Āsa* 39:1-2)

Nor did things improve under the Mogul rule. There may have been great splendours at court; lovely buildings like the Taj Mahal may have been built that delight the eyes of later tourists; but they were built with mortar moistened with the blood and tears of the people. There was ruthless taxation, the land was farmed out to contractors who fleeced the people to the utmost so as to get enough for their own profits and for the heavy bribes which secured their privileges for the future. Corruption and disorder were rampant everywhere; the country was a prey to brutal murderers and robbers, and desolated by cruelty, wastefulness and vice; honours and places were freely bought and sold; the rulers were sunk in luxury and vicious debauchery. Terrible famines swept the land, like that of 1630 which destroyed Tukārām's family; irrigation was totally neglected; dynastic wars and rebellions were incessant; travel was unsafe and perilous. Such was the life Hindus lived under the Afghan and Mogul tyrants.

2. The Muslims

The rulers were intolerant and fanatical to such an extent that Alauddin would allow Hindus to keep only enough corn and coarse cloth for six months. Nor were the Muslims themselves much happier. The common folk were totally ignorant of their own religion, for their mullās were in no way more spiritual or religious than the Brahmins, and they ignored both the principles of the *Korān* and all the humane laws of the Shariat. They throve on the self-assertion which their own brutality had made possible for them; they regarded the non-Muslims as existing solely for their own pleasure as slaves, or worse, and so they themselves degenerated swiftly. Indeed, they looked upon their own women as playthings for their lust, as little better than toys or animals; intense distrust of them made them imprison them in rooms away from sunlight and fresh air, letting them go out only under escort and covered with the enveloping black veil or *burqā*. When a daughter was born to a family it was looked upon as a dreadful calamity, and so infanticide, strictly forbidden by the *Korān,* became common among them and it is even said that the practice of *satī* was not unknown among them in the days of Jahāngir. Their few holy men imitated the Hindus in withdrawing from society, for the most part into the forests where they could live in peace undisturbed by the cruelties which devastated the 'world'.

3. Religion in the wilderness

When Elijah complained that he alone was faithful to God he was told that there were yet many, unknown to him, who had not bowed down to evil. So even in those dreadful days there were still men—albeit a few—who withdrew from a society which they felt to be incurable, in order to live lives of prayer and of dedication to God. Such a life was all but impossible in the towns, save for the very few who were strong enough and brave enough to fight at every stage. But to the gloomy picture we have just seen we must not forget to add the sunlight which came from Maharashtra where the holy men of Viṭṭhal, followers of Jñānadeva, Nāmdev and Ekanāth, kept the saffron flag aloft; from Gujarat where, in 1481, Narasingh Mehta was just finishing a glorious life of devotion to God; from Bengal, where Chaitanya (1485-1533) was about to be born in a saintly family into a life which is still the inspiration of millions of Hindus everywhere; from the plains of Ganga, where Kabīr had begun to stir the masses with a new feeling of devotion, hope and love; from Andhra, where Vallabhāchārya (1479-1531) was awaiting the time to be born and to carry the flame through western India.

So even before Nanak raised the standard of hope there were great stirrings of aspiration and desire. Advaitāchārya, in far Navadwīp, was praying daily for an *avatāra* of God to save the people from the vanity of godless philosophers, the tyranny of rulers, the slough of despond into which they had fallen. Here and there in forests and lonely places, in little-known valleys in the mountains, there were hermits and bands of seekers after God who encouraged one another with hymns, and strove by various yogic ways to realize the truth. Nanak himself in his youth met many such and delighted in their company, which he could not have done had they all been hypocrites like the majority. God was, it seems, preparing the Revival, and because the country was so vast that no one man could do the whole work, he was sending teachers to each part of India. Men they were, not gods or *avatāras,* though their followers naturally called many of them that; they were human like us, but tempered of a finer steel, purified by the fires of steady devotion lit with the torch of faithfulness and effort. To the Punjab, when the hour was come and all was prepared, God sent Guru Nanak.

4. Nanak's task

Out of this wretched, misery-trampled, hag-ridden peasantry Nanak had to build a nation of self-respecting men, devoted to God and to their leader, filled with a sense of equality and brotherhood, eager, indeed ready, to die as martyrs for their faith when opportunity allowed, and yet prepared to fight tyranny with its own weapons in defence of the weak and to protect the righteous. The naturally law-abiding and peaceful Hindus had to be filled with courage, disciplined, and trained to use the sword and musket where these were required; yet the Gurus never fought save in self-defence, never raised the sword in anger, never forgot the noblest ideals of chivalry while fighting. They looked to the future with hope and faith instead of despairingly accepting the effects of karma from earlier lives. We are told that Nanak himself smelted the Hindu ore into steel by burning out the dross of hypocrisy and superstition; then out of that steel, Gobind Singh forged the sword.

Nanak began the work by ridiculing superstition and outer show, by tearing caste prejudices to pieces, by teaching and living a life of brotherhood with his Sikhs and so leading them to extend that relationship to a wider field. He set out, in short, to awaken the demoralized people from their superstitious dreams and to give them new hope, bringing religion into their daily lives, filling the home itself with the constant thought of God as a personal friend, and thus giving them a motive for holding to their own faith instead of falling into Islam out of cowardice or worldly ambition. By persuasion and personal attractiveness he also did all that he could to win the fanatical Muslims into a more humane — a more Muslim — way of life. Like Kabīr he opposed idolatry and formalism in religion, and he was even more uncompromising in his rejection of caste and all its implications, of the notion that woman was inferior to man, and of timid retreat from the world to the easy security of *sannyāsa*.

Other reformers, prophets and saints strove elsewhere, each in his own way as taught by his own Master, but in the Punjab, Guru Nanak, through the ten lives he devoted to his labour, built a nation, brave, proud and strong, upright and self-respecting instead of prostrate on the ground, and taught men and women how to love God as a most beloved and intimate friend. That was the spirit he infused into the Sikhs, and it transformed the whole of society in the north of India.

2. THE VAISHNAVA DEVOTEES

When Guru Arjan compiled the holy book for the Sikhs, he included in it certain of the hymns and poems of the lovers of God who had preceded Guru Nanak or who were even then singing to God in India. Muslims and Hindus alike were thus honoured, provided their songs did not offend against the fundamentals of the Guru's doctrine, and the hymns of Kabīr, Farīd and Nāmdev were especially drawn upon to enrich the *Guru-Granth Sahib*. Since the present 'Gospel' contains passages from nearly all the *bhagats* who were thus represented in the *Guru-Granth,* it will be of interest to see a little of who each of these was and something of what he did.

1. KABĪR (1440-1518, though Sher Singh almost alone holds the earlier date, 1398-1443) was born near Banaras of uncertain parentage and brought up by a Muslim weaver whose craft he practised throughout his life. His life was full of miraculous stories, but what is known to be historical is miraculous enough in itself. He, a weaver, a Muslim who lived at Banaras, became the personal disciple of the Brāhman Saint Rāmānanda. Later he preached to Muslims and Brāhmans alike, was uncompromising in his teachings, became the guru of many distinguished disciples, and left behind him a sect now numbering more than a million adherents. This, in such an age, was indeed a wonderful thing.

While he worked at the loom, Kabīr sang his songs, which his friends wrote down. They are homely, direct and penetrating in their style, in the simple Hindi of the age but inspired with the deepest vision of spiritual truth. He never retired from the world but lived a normal married life and is said to have had a son and a daughter. He, too, made fun of formalism in religion and the absurdities of the yogis of his day. He taught God as the Lover, the Player, the Musician, impersonal and yet truly personal, 'ever distinct from and yet ever united with' the soul. It was natural that at last in 1495 he should have been banished as a heretic by the Emperor Sikander Lodī. He took to wandering here and there among the cities of the Gangetic plain until he died at Maghar near Gorakhpur. The same story is told of him as of Nanak, how after his death Muslims and Hindus both claimed him as their own and nothing was found of his body save a heap of flowers, of which each took a share and burned or buried according to their custom. Kabīr's songs still inspire devotees of God today wherever the Hindi language is spoken.

2. SHEIKH FARĪD. Farīduddin Mas'ūd, son of Jamāluddīn Sulaimān (eldest son of Sheikh Shu'ib) and Bibi Marīam, was born in 1173 near Dipalpur and by the age of five knew the whole *Korān* by heart. At sixteen he made the pilgrimage to Mecca and had a vision of the Prophet, who promised to spend nine hours every fifth day of Muharram at his tomb. Farīd then studied theology at Kābul under the saint Khwājā Qutubuddīn Bakhtiār, after which he went with friends as far as Bukhara to meet other holy men and so came in touch with Shahabuddin Suhrawādi. He returned to his guru, where he was a co-disciple of the Sultan Shamsuddīn Altamish, himself a former disciple of the famous Sūfī saint, Hasan Chishti. When his guru died, Farīd himself became a famous saint, his great disciple being Nizāmuddīn Auliya. He married the daughter of the Emperor Nāsiruddīn, and after him Farīdkot is named; he had six sons and two daughters, the eldest son, Sheikh Badruddīn Sulaimān, succeeding him when

he died of pneumonia in 1266 at the age of ninety-three. His tomb at Pākapattan, where he lived after his guru died in 1235, is a place of Muslim pilgrimage.

A later 'Sheikh Farīd' (Ibrahīm), a remote descendant of the Khālif 'Umar and of Farrukh Shāh, the King of Kābul, reigned as Pīr in the eleventh generation after the founder, from 1510 to 1552. He was a scholar of Persian and Arabic, and a man of true realization; in his company the Guru spent delightful hours. He had a collection of the hymns by the original Sheikh Farīd. His burial-place is at Sarhind.

3. NĀMDEV (1269-1295) was one of the greatest of the Maharashtra saints and a personal friend and companion of Jñāneśwara, being about five years his senior. He was born at Paṇḍharpur and as a small child spent his time in the temple of Viṭṭhal. From seven years of age he delighted in dancing and in singing to God to the music of his cymbals, treating God as his playmate and friend. He neglected his studies, food and sleep for this blessed occupation, and had many wonderful adventures that showed him God's loving care of him, even when his neglect of business led him into serious trouble with his father. He met Jñānadev when about twenty, and was persuaded by him to go on pilgrimage round India for about five years; this helped to widen his view of God beyond the limits of Viṭṭhal's form and shrine at Paṇḍharpur. The story is told how he was driven to find a guru and was taught by Viśoba Khechar that God was everywhere. It was he who, seeing God in the form of a dog that had stolen his chapatti ran after it to give it some butter also. He was present when Jñānadev took *samādhi* at Ālandi. We have still about

four thousand poems believed to be from his pen. Nāmdev, too, was a householder; his wife was Rājābai, and he had four sons and a daughter. He was buried at the door of Viṭṭhal's temple opposite the Harijan holy man, Chokamela. Nāmdev's servant maid, Janābai, was almost as famous a saint as himself.

4. RAVIDĀS, or RAIDĀS (fifteenth century), another of Rāmānanda's disciples, was a tanner and cobbler who used to give away shoes to God's lovers and once made an image of God out of hide. A holy man gave him the 'philosopher's stone' which he carelessly left in the thatch of his hut for over a year, explaining that he wanted only God's Name and not such useless wealth. One day he found five gold pieces and spent them all in building a temple and a hostel for the poor. He used to cure lepers, and even Brāhmans came to him. Others harassed him when a queen of Chitor became his disciple, and God showed a cobbler sitting next to each caste-proud Brāhman at their feast. It is said that Ravidās lived to be one hundred and twenty years old; he left many poems of devotion and there is a sect of Vaishnavas, the Raidāsis, called by his name to this day.

5. JAYADEVA (twelfth century) was a poet at the court of Lakshman Sen. He tells us that his father was Bhoideva and that his mother was Bāmadevi; he was born at Kenduli near Birbhum. For a long time he would not even write down the beautiful Samskrit songs and music that flowed from him. Nor would he at first agree to marry Padmāvati when his God bade him do so, but persisted in his life of an ascetic. He put up a hut with a shrine in it and here he wrote his second great book, the

immortal *Gīta Govindam*. His two other great books were *Rasana Rāghava* and *Chandraloka* on the graces of literary style. But neither of these came up to the *Gīta Govindam* which, in lovely words, tells of the divine love of Rādhā and Krishna — the soul and God — and is, as Macauliffe says, the world's one great popular poem in what was already a dead language. It won immediate fame, and even Muslims delighted in it. Jayadeva went to Brindāvan; at Jaipur he was attacked by thugs and mutilated. Karaunch, King of Utkala, saved him and when the thugs came disguised as *sannyāsis* Jayadeva called them his brothers and defended them from suspicion. When Padmāvati was falsely told of Jayadeva's death, she herself died at once, illustrating what the Guru was to tell us later is the only real *satī*. The story goes that Jayadeva raised her to life and that they both returned to Kenduli where they served devotees and adored the One God.

6. RĀMĀNANDA (c. 1360-1450), a follower of the sect of Rāmānujāchārya (1017-1137), was born at Mailkot, a son of Puṇyasadan and Suśila. Sent to Banaras for his education, he met Swami Rāghavānanda who initiated him and, at his destined hour of death, saved his life by putting him into a trance. He went on a long pilgrimage and on his return declared that it was no longer possible for him to keep all the customary Vaishnava dietary and other rules. This led to a breach with his guru and Rāmānanda broke away and formed his own sect, abandoning caste-exclusiveness and recognizing human equality. His verses show his teaching: *Jāti panthi pūcchai nāhi koi; Hari ko bhaje, so Hari kā hoi* (Let no one ask of caste or sect; if he worships God then is he

God's). He had twelve disciples who transformed the face of the Hindu religion. Two were women, one a barber, one a cobbler, one a weaver, one a Muslim soldier, one a peasant. He became famous for his love for God and for his kindness to man, opening the way to God for all through the use of the Name. He died in Banaras.

7. DHANNĀ, a Jāt farmer's son born at Dhuān in the state of Tonk near Deoli. He was illiterate and could not read the scriptures but was full of love for God even from childhood, thanks to the *sādhus* who used to visit his father. At the age of five he saw a Brāhman *sādhu* worshipping a *sālagrām-stone* and persuaded him to let him copy this act even with a common black stone in which the child saw God's image. He now gave all his time to the worship of God through this stone, offering all his food to it first and thus quickly increasing in devotion and intimacy with the Lord. He would not eat until the Lord ate first a little of his chapattis before his eyes, nor did he dream that this was no usual experience. Krishna used to go with him to the fields, milk the cows at his side, and play with him. It is said that when he grew older he once gave away all the seed-grain as alms to some *sādhus*, and then ploughed the field as usual. Even though no seed had been sown, God made the field yield a heavier crop than any other in the village. While Guru Nanak was on one of his long journeys he visited this saint who must, by that time, have been very old if, as Macauliffe says, he was born in 1415.

8. PIPA (born in 1425) was the king of Gagaraungarh and was always kind to saintly men. He was sent by

Durga in a vision to Rāmānanda, who at first would not receive a king; he went home, sold all his possessions and gave to the poor, returned as a fakīr, and was even ready to drown himself in obedience to the guru. He was accepted and sent home to serve devotees for a year, after which the guru took Kabīr and Ravidās to visit him. He left his throne and went with his wife to Dwārakā. From there, they fled from their growing fame as saints, and his wife was with difficulty rescued from some Afghan soldiers. Then they went to the North-West Frontier region, and whatever they received they at once spent on the poor. Pipa converted King Sursen and turned him into a hermit. When thieves stole his buffalo he gave them the calf also, and they restored the animal; when others stole his wheat he gave them money to buy cooking vessels, so they also gave back the wheat they had taken.

9. SADHNA (late thirteenth century) was a butcher at Sehwan in Sind; he used to sell meat of animals killed by others, weighing it with his *sālagrām-stone*. A Brāhman rescued the sacred stone from such mean work, but it refused his worship and demanded to be taken back to the poor butcher who then became a great devotee of God. He suffered much from the false accusation of a woman and his hands were cut off; he was finally walled up alive. His tomb is at Sarhind in East Punjab.

10. BENI, of whom nothing is known save that he may have lived about the twelfth century. His writing is archaic in language and very hard to understand.

There are other Vaishnav holy men whose writings were included by Guru Arjan in the *Granth-Sāhib* but are not included in this text.

SAIN (c.1390-1440) was a barber in Rewa who acted as a surgeon, a matchmaker and a story-teller. Because he devoted himself to serve *sādhus* rather than care for his own interests, God once took his place at his master Rājārām's court and saved him from great trouble.

BHIKKAN (died 1573) was perhaps a disciple of Kabīr; he lived at Kakori, and Teja Singh tells us he was a learned Muslim.

SŪRDĀS (born 1528) was a Brāhman named Madanmohan whom Akbar made Governor of Sandila near Hardoi in Awadh; he spent all the revenue on *sādhus* and fled before the accounts were inspected. When he refused to appear before the emperor he was jailed for a time and, on his release, devoted himself to serve *sādhus* in all humility and then retired to the forest.

PARMĀNANDA, a Brāhman disciple of Rāmānanda, lived at Barsi near Sholāpur. He had many visions of Krishna within and without; he used to prostrate seven hundred times daily and was always in tears of love and ecstasy.

TRILOCHANA (born 1267) went to Paṇḍharpur and served *sādhus;* when too many came he sought a helper; Krishna himself came under the name of Antarjāmi and served them for thirteen months until Trilochana's wife grumbled at having to look after him also upon which he vanished.

These honoured men, and many more like them, enriched the spiritual life of India during those dark days of foreign rule and interior decay of spirituality and faith among the masses.

3. ONE IN TEN—GURU NANAK

1. Guru Nanak I—Humility

1. Early Life (1469-1507)

In the simple village of Talwandi, about forty miles from Lahore, lived a Kshattriya farmer and village official named Mehta Kalu and his wife Tripta. Kalu was the son of Sivarām and Banārasi, and the family had come to the village from the Amritsar district some years earlier. They were worthy people, honest and hard-working, with the normal share of piety. Early on the morning of Saturday 15 April 1469, their hearts were gladdened by the birth of a son whose glory was destined to shine out through the centuries. They called him Nanak and the astrologer who attended his birth foretold that he would rule both Muslims and Hindus and would worship one only God.

At the age of five little Nanak began to talk about God, and his prattling words were admired by all. At seven he was sent to the village school under one Pāndhā[1] and learned all that his teacher knew; he is said to have often embarrassed the poor man by his penetrating questions into the reality behind all things.[2] When he was just eight his elder sister, Nānaki, was married to Bhai Jairām, the revenue collector for the

---

[1] Gopal Pāndhā is said to have taught him Hindi, Pandit Brijnāth to have taught him Samskrit, and Sayyid Hasan other things.

[2] He is said to have demanded the esoteric meaning of the first letter of the alphabet, just as Jesus does in The Gospel of the Mystic Christ. Such children are very difficult pupils!

2

Nawāb Daulat Khān of Sultanpur, and Nanak was left alone with his parents. Next year, 1478, they insisted on investing him with the sacred thread to which his caste in Hindu society entitled him, though for a long time he rejected it and asked for a 'real thread', spun from mercy and contentment, which the pundit could not bestow on him. At school he had acquired a sound knowledge of the current Hindi dialect; in order to succeed his father one day as village accountant he learned Persian also, and we have an acrostic in that language said to have been written in his childhood.

In those days he spent much time in the fields grazing buffaloes, and we are told that the shadow of a tree under which he rested used to move round against the sun so as to keep him always in the shade.[1] His heart was already seeking God; he found no interest in the secular work his father put him to—digging in the fields, working in a little shop, and the like. He sought every chance of slipping away into lonely places where he could feel the unity and beauty of nature and reach out towards that great God who, out of his own love, wove this infinite pattern of loveliness. At times he gathered together a few friends, and they sang hymns to the glory of that Creator whom he had begun to love with fiery yearning.

All this piety in their son did not please his parents, for he was their only son and they looked for him to carry on their worldly avocations and to support them

---

[1]God's chosen ones are one with Nature, and she exists to serve the devotees of her lord.

when old age drew near. They thought him ill, and sent for the village doctor; in vain he prescribed his remedies, for none could cure the boy's feverish thirst for God.[1]

Then they got him married, on 1 April 1485, to divert his mind from such unworldly thoughts; the girl chosen was Sulakhni or Kūlamāī, the daughter of Baba Mūlaji of Batala, near Gurdāspur, but this, too, was unsuccessful, for his poor wife could do nothing to turn his mind. Once when his mother, in understandable exasperation, bade him leave his endless meditations, he lay down for four days unmoving, saying that he would die if the Name were taken from him.[2] He now took to meeting *sādhus* and yogis in the dense forests, giving them food from his father's fields, and talking with them about God and the spiritual path. Seeking their company more and more, he must have gained much encouragement in his own search for the one Truth, and it is probable that in this way he confirmed those ideas he shared with Kabīr and the great Vaishnava devotees of his age.

In 1497 his elder son, Srichand,[3] was born, and three years later came Lakshmidās, but Nanak paid little heed to his family. He meditated much, became more withdrawn from the world, and found his greatest creative joy in singing the hymns he composed. From the *sādhus* he also learned how to speak and to express his views persuasively so as to convince others, though it seems

---

[1] cf. *GGS* 6: 2-3.   [2] cf. *GGS* 32:5.

[3] Afterwards founder of the sect of *Udasīs* or mendicant Sikhs

certain that these views welled up from the depths of inspiration in his own heart and owed little or nothing to what he received from others, either through books or through their words. The family had enough land to support them so they were never in want, but Kalu again and again tried to induce his son to till the fields and give up his useless dreaming and poetry. He also tried to engage him in business at Saiyidpur and Lahore; while he was working at Chūharkāna, his father sent the lad twenty rupees to buy goods for trading but he gave them all away to some wandering ascetics.

In 1504, Bhai Jairām visited his relatives at Talwandi and agreed with Rai Bular, the village zamindar, that Nanak could well be employed with him at Sultanpur. The idea of his son getting government employment delighted Kalu, and he sent him off gladly with his brother-in-law. Jairām introduced Nanak to Daulat Khān, who appointed him storekeeper, and the young man devoted himself to his duties with honesty, zeal and efficiency, delighting everyone. Unlike most petty officials of the time, he was totally free from corruption and would not even improperly hold a pie of another's money for a day. He also gave away most of his own salary to the poor.

At this time Mardana, a minstrel, came from Talwandi and joined Nanak as his personal attendant. They loved each other from the start, and used to delight each other at night singing sweet hymns to God, Mardana playing the rebec to accompany his friend. A certain Bhai Bhagirathi also came from Mailasi, near Multan, and stayed for a while with Nanak as a sort of disciple. Nanak's life as a teacher was beginning.

2. *The Call of Nanak (1507)*

On 20 August 1507 came the day of destiny. After his morning bath in the river, Nanak sat for meditation and heard God's call to give his life for the upliftment of the world and to guide men on the path to Him.[1] He at once resolved to obey; after three days he returned to the office, resigned his post, gave away all he had to the poor, and prepared to set out on foot. The Nawāb did all he could to persuade him to stay, being deeply distressed at losing so good and so winning an employee, but others thought he had gone mad.

One day, towards the beginning of September, he put on the Hindu *kāshāya* robes as a *sannyāsi*,[2] and declared to the local Muslims, 'There is no Hindu, no Mussalman!' Then he attended the mosque prayers with the Nawāb and the local Qāzī; when all prostrated at the call, he remained standing. This gave some offence, so he pointed out to the Qāzī, in whose face he had laughed direct, that none of them had yet begun to pray, for the Qāzī's mind had gone off to a filly of his, while the Nawāb was thinking about buying horses in Kābul. They had both humbly to confess the fact! When Nanak again spoke in public to the Muslims, he taught them what a true Muslim is,[3] and they declared that he spoke as a real prophet. The Nawāb's storehouses were found to be full, so Nanak got the good man to give away everything in them freely to the poor.

---

[1] cf. *GGS* 2..

[2] From the start his dress was peculiar and did not conform to that of any sect.

[3] cf. *GGS* 28:1-2.

3. The First Missionary Journey[1] (1507-1515)

After a brief and apparently uneventful visit to his parents at Talwandi, Nanak went with Mardana, dressed as fakirs or *sannyāsis*, to Aimanabad. Here he was welcomed by a rich fellow-caste man, Malak Bhāgo, and invited to a feast; but he began his public ministry by deliberately breaking caste, going to the house of Lālo, a poor Śūdra carpenter, and spending the night with him in *bhajans*. When, next morning, Bhāgo protested at this, the Guru told him that the bread of the rich was full of the blood of the exploited poor. He then took a loaf from Bhāgo's house and one from Lālo's; when he squeezed them, from the one came blood and from the other the milk of human kindness. Thus he showed that the coarse food of the poor offered with love is purer than the finest the rich can give in their pride. Bhai Lālo later became a distinguished Sikh.

The companions went together on their way to Hardwar for the Vaisākh full moon festival. Seeing the Hindus there throwing water to the east for their ancestors, Nanak turned round and began to throw water in handfuls to the west. When asked what he was doing, he replied, 'I am watering my dry fields at

---

[1] I have used these words to translate the Punjabi *Udāsī*, in order to stress the fact that the Guru's journeys were not in search of truth but to propagate the truth he already knew. Macauliffe has entirely altered the life of Guru Nanak, I think without justification, in pursuit of the idea that the recorded itineraries are unlikely. In my own reconstruction I have used the outline given by Sahib Singh, filling in details from Macauliffe and other writers as seemed most probable. I see no reason to reject the early evidence cn the Guru's three great journeys.

Talwandi.' They mocked him as a fool, until he pointed out that if their water could reach their ancestors, his could certainly reach his fields which were much nearer. Thus he made fun of certain superstitious rites, but he told others who were chanting God's name together, 'It is true that if you take the Name with love you will not be damned.' He took fire from where a Brāhman was cooking food, and when they protested that this had defiled the meal, he replied, 'It is already defiled by the evil thoughts in the Brāhman's heart.' Some of the Brāhmans there tried in vain to win him back to the Hindu fold.

On the road to the south-east the two travellers met a party of yogis to whom Nanak taught the true religion,[1] and they acclaimed him as a knower of the Real. Near Pilibhit he sat under a withered pipul tree and its greenness was restored. They visited Ayodhya and Prayāg, and so came to Kāśi (Banaras), where the Guru argued with various sectaries against idolatry and induced Pandit Chaturdās to give up worshipping the *sālagrām*, making him, too, a Sikh. At Gaya he showed the foolishness of rejoicing at the birth of a child when in a few days the laughter turned to tears at the infant's death. The Brahmins asked him to offer the usual *piṇḍa*[2] to his ancestors, but he refused to do any such thing, telling them what the real *piṇḍa* ought to be. He stayed for four months at Patna with Salas Rai Jauhari, and then visited Gorakhpur, where Kabīr was perhaps at the time — he died at Maghar nearby. After this they

---

[1] cf. *GGS* 30.

[2] Oblation of food

moved off into Assam in the far north-eastern corner of India.

Somewhere in this region, at Kāmarūp, Queen Nurshāh made several attempts to entice him into worldliness by her wiles, but was herself converted for her pains. We are told that, in a lonely spot, Kaljug, the evil spirit of worldly desire, tempted him to give up his mission: 'I possess everything,' said he. 'Say but the word and I will build you a palace of pearls, inlay it with gems, and confer upon you the sovereignty of the East and West. Take whatever pleases you!' (M. I:79) But what could the Guru do with wealth but give it away? It might only lead him to forget God's Name, and that would be death for him! These two incidents seem to be connected, and both may well be allegorized versions of temptations of the heart such as those that came to Jesus and Zarathushtra.[1]

At a village in Bengal the wanderers were met with insults and driven away; on departing, Guru Nanak blessed the village with all prosperity. Another village welcomed them with loving hospitality, and Mardana was amazed when his Master said that that village would be destroyed. When asked to explain, Nanak said, 'When these people are scattered abroad they will save hundreds besides themselves by their piety.'

They travelled down the Brahmaputra, and then took ship for Puri, whither Chaitanya Mahaprabhu had not yet come. When all stood for the evening *ārati* in the great temple, Nanak remained seated and sang his own

---

[1] cf. GMC 22 and GZ 29.

hymn telling how God is fitly adored by the whole of nature. (*GGS.* 18) A certain Brāhman was boasting of his clairvoyant powers, so Nanak playfully hid the man's waterpot and all laughed while he vainly sought it everywhere.

They went on by sea and land to Rāmeśwaram; Nanak was wearing wooden sandals, and a rope twisted round his head for a turban, a patch and streak as caste-mark, and carrying a staff in his hand. He defended himself from the criticisms of the Jains of the south and then satirized them mercilessly and, by a short poem now in the *Āsa dī Vār*, converted the brutal ruler of an island on the way. From Rāmeśwaram he crossed the sea to Śri Lanka. Here he made the garden of Rājā Śivanabha blossom miraculously[1] and wrote his mystical treatise *Prānsangali*, leaving it with the Rājā who vainly tried to detain this mysterious yogi at his court.

Returning to India, the companions wended their way along the west coast to the banks of the Narbada, where the Guru composed the *Dakhani Omkār* at Śiva's temple and converted a party of thugs. They moved further west, visited Somnāth and Dwārakā, where Krishna once

---

[1] The miracles ascribed to the Guru form a difficult problem, for it is not the claim of Sikhs that he based his teaching on such childish things. Indeed many say with Kamla Akāli: 'Guru Nanak had no miracles. If he had, it was not his own, it is that of the True Name.' Guru Har Gobind was sternly opposed to such acts that appear to transgress the laws of ordinary nature, and Guru Gobind Singh definitely denies that his father ever stooped to them. Yet the lives all include stories like this; so we are free to give them some meta-phorical sense if we prefer, even those of the raising of the dead by several Guru-forms.

reigned as king, and returned homewards through Bikaner. Probably it was on this desert journey that Mardana was distressed by thirst. The Guru said, 'We must refresh ourselves with God's Name. Take your rebec and let us sing some hymns.' But Bhai Mardana protested that he was far too thirsty to sing or play. Nanak produced some fruits for him, but told him not to eat them yet; Mardana disobeyed, eating some behind his Master's back and at once fell down unconscious so that Gurudev had to restore him by a miracle. Then Mardana made two conditions for future travel with his Master: that he should feed him as he fed himself, and that he should never notice what he was doing. Nanak agreed!

They came to Ajmer, and then visited the great Vaishnava devotee Bhakta Dhannāji at Pushkara; after this they came to Mathura, and so to Brindāvan. Here they watched the 'Krishna-līla', with its actors dancing wildly with simulated emotions, and the Guru satirized the hypocrisy of such a show got up as a means for collecting money from the devout.[1]

At Delhi he raised a dead elephant to life, but when the Emperor Sikandar Lodi bade him repeat the miracle for his amusement he let it die again, saying, 'It is God alone who destroys and brings to life.' At the tomb of a Muslim saint in Panipat he was greeted with the usual *'Assalām 'aleikum!'* (The peace be upon you!) but at once replied *'Salām Alekh!'* (Homage to the Unseen!) The Sheikh at the tomb at once went to meet this

---

[1] cf. *'Āsa di Vār'* Pauvi 5, *śloka* 2.

unusual visitor and heard with great respect all he had to say.

He came to Kurukshetra in time for a great fair, where he shocked the orthodox pilgrims by solemnly cooking venison in their very midst. When they expostulated, he pointed out the absurdity of such superstitious regard for the food of the belly[1] and added that those who preached *ahimsa* often drank human blood in their rapacious greed. He taught them that hermit or householder would reach God through the Name if he followed one of the four paths—the company of a saint, honesty and truth, humility and contentment, and self-control.

On the homeward way Nanak visited his sister and her husband at Sultanpur, and then drew near his native village of Talwandi. First he sent Bhai Mardana to ask if his father were still alive, telling him not to speak of his return. But Tripta at once guessed the truth and asked Mardana for her son, weeping; she followed him back to where the Guru was waiting. Once more she begged him to please her in her old age by living at home and taking to some trade, but he even refused the food and clothes she brought him in her motherliness, saying, 'God's word is food, and brooding on him is raiment!' Then Kalu arrived with a horse to take the wanderer home in order to show him the new house, but Nanak would not do this; for it was not right for a *sannyāsi*, having once gone out, to re-enter his family house. His father even tried to tempt him with a new wife, but he replied that

---

[1] cf. *GGS* 37:4.

God's choice of Sulakhni was best and that that tie would endure until death. Then Tripta ordered him to come home and earn a respectable living, while Kalu reproached him for neglecting them for twelve years; he sent his parents home alone, telling them that they would soon be consoled.[1] And so they were when they saw that their son had become the guru of thousands of men and women of every class.

Nanak then went to Lahore as the guest of the rich Dunichand for his father's *śrāddha* ceremony, and took the occasion to discourage all such rites and to convert the ruler to the Sikh way of life.

At Pathāndi he converted many Pathāns, and then he visited his wife and sons at Batala on the Beas River; to his uncle he foretold that Bābar would shortly conquer the Pathān kingdoms in India. At last, after eight years of constant wandering, and at the age of forty-six, he settled on the site of Kartarpur in January 1516, and consoled his old parents by bringing them to live with him there quietly for nearly two years.

4. *The Second Missionary Journey (1517-1518)*

The travellers resumed their wanderings late in 1517 by crossing over to Uttarkhand, where the Guru argued with a group of *siddhas* and yogis, describing for them the meaning of true yoga. Then they paid a short visit to Kartarpur, to visit his parents, and after visits to Pasrur and Eminabad they went up to Sialkot.

---

[1] The Guru's mingled firmness and sweetness with his parents may be well compared with Chaitanya Mahāprabhu's attitude to his mother, and that of the Buddha's to his family after his enlightenment.

Here a certain Pandit Brahmdās visited the Guru, with a pile of Samskrit books in hand and an idol hanging on his breast, and upbraided him for wearing leather and a rope and for eating meat. Nanak made no direct reply but burst into an ecstatic hymn to God and the Guru and the wonders of creation. The pundit was pleased, but his pride kept him from surrendering so soon. The Guru sent him to four fakirs who would show him a guru to his taste; these sent him to a temple where a woman gave him a sound beating with her shoe. This, the fakirs told him, was his real guru, and her name was Māyā, worldliness! Cured of his pride, the pundit hastened back to Nanak and made a full surrender at his feet.

The Guru then visited Srinagar and crossed the mountains to Mount Sumeru where he had a certain mystical experience among the great *siddhas* of that remote Himalayan summit.[1] They welcomed him among them as one of their own. Returning to Sialkot, he sent Mardana to purchase a farthing of truth and a farthing of falsehood. He found there an old friend, Mūla Khatrī who said, 'Life is a lie and Death is the truth.' When the Guru came to Mūla's house his wife hid him away, saying that he was not at home, fearing that he might be converted and join the pilgrims. As he lay hidden there in the house, a snake bit him and he died. Death was indeed the truth for him!

At Mithānkot they visited Sheikh Miān Mīthā, a

---

[1] This seems to have been something like the initiations which we are told take place beyond the Himalayas on inner planes from time to time; see C. W. L. *The Masters and the Path.*

noted Muslim holy man, and the Guru had a verse contest with him convincing him that God alone is true and no prophet or saint can be named along with him. As the Sheikh fell at his feet in reverent delight, Nanak fell into a trance of ecstatic love and uttered one of his divine hymns. From here they returned home to Kartarpur.

5. The Third Missionary Journey (1518-1521)

Wearing blue robes, the Guru set out on his last long journey with Mardana, and went straight to Pākapattan, the abode of Sheikh Ibrahīm, the heir to Sheikh Farīd and himself also a great Sūfi saint. The Sheikh scolded Nanak for wearing secular clothes while living as a fakīr, to which he replied, 'God is all I have, and he is everywhere, even in these clothes!' The two then competed in verse, gradually leading each other up to the sublimest heights of philosophic beauty, and so they passed the night in delightful spiritual companionship. In the morning a peasant brought them milk, and when he took away the bowl it had turned to gold and was full of golden coins. Nanak was pleased with this holy man, and as he went his way punned on his name, saying 'Sheikh Ibrahīm, God [Brahm] is in you!' Before he left Pākapattan, the Guru made a copy of Sheikh Farīd's *ślokas*, many of which are now included in the *Granth Sahib*.

By way of Tulambha the pair moved on through south Punjab towards the State of Bahawalpur. Perhaps this was when the Guru visited a notorious robber who thought he would be an easy victim. But by a few verses Nanak showed that he knew his murderous intention, and the robber begged pardon. The Guru replied,

'Forgiveness in God's court is gained only after an open confession and full amends done for the wrong.' The robber at once confessed his many murders and dacoities, gave away his illegal gains to the poor and, under the name of Sajjan, became a famous Sikh missionary in those parts.

They went to Surat and from there took a pilgrim ship to Jeddah, and thence went up to Mecca, the holy city of the Muslims. There, Nanak was roughly awakened from sleep and well scolded because his feet were pointing towards the holy Kaaba. He apologized quietly and asked the man to turn his feet in any direction where God was not.[1]

He often gave the call to prayer here, and used to play with the children in the street, being followed about by them much as the Prophet Hazrat Muhammed was in his time. People noticed that there was always a cloud shading his head during the heat of the day.

From Mecca, the two went on to Medina where the Guru vanquished the Qāzīs in argument. They proceeded to Baghdad where Guru Nanak, acting as muezzin, gave a new call to prayer, changing the words of the creed. When asked to what sect he belonged he replied: 'I reject all sects, and know only the One God, whom I recognize everywhere. I have appeared in this age to show men the way to him.' Then we are told that he repeated the *Japji* to them, and when the high priest challenged the reference to 'many heavens and underworlds' he gave him a vision of some of these. (We

---

[1] The same story is told of one of the Mahratta saints.

must remark that the Muslims of these parts seem to have been surprisingly tolerant; such a thing could hardly occur in our own days.)

Crossing the Iranian plateaù, they next went to Balkh, for many years the home of the Prophet Zarathushtra, and then on to Bukhara in Central Asia. So they worked their way round by Kābul to Peshāwar where the Guru argued with yogis at the temple of Gorakhnāth. Descending to the plains at Hassan Abdal, a noted Muslim centre, he was forced to dig a small well for himself, and this drew away the water from a rather selfish wonder-worker, Bawa Wali, who lived higher up. Wali threw a hill at Nanak, who protected himself with his right arm and left the mark of his hand, *panjā sāhib* on the hill.[1]

By way of Bhera Shahu and Dinga they came to Eminābād[2] immediately after Bābar's invasion of the Punjab. All was in confusion; Pathān and Hindu houses alike were robbed and burned to the ground, women were driven away shrieking and weeping. Nanak made a pathetic poem about their sufferings. The pair were imprisoned under Bābar's officer, Mīr Khān, and made slaves. Nanak had to carry loads on his head, Mardana to sweep with a broom or lead a horse. The officer saw the load floating a cubit above the Guru's head while Mardana played the rebec and the horse quietly followed him. He reported the wonderful sight to Bābar who came to see it for himself. He found Nanak feeding

---

[1] Here we surely have a piece of folklore; it reminds one of the legends of St Michael on the Tor at Glastonbury. The print of his five fingers on the hill was long shown as a relic of Guru Nanak.

[2] Also known as Saiyidpur

corn to a handmill and singing a hymn while the mill turned itself. Bābar prostrated before the Guru and offered him a boon; Nanak asked only for the release of all Saiyidpur captives, but these would not go free unless he too joined them. Then when they all got home they found that everyone had been massacred; in a trance, Nanak sang a doleful lament, being deeply moved by the sufferings of the poor people. He went boldly back to Bābar's camp and sang to the prisoners there; Bābar offered him a drink of bhang, often used by 'yogis', but he fell into ecstasy and his whole body began to shine. On his request Bābar set all his prisoners free and even clothed them in robes of honour, in return for which generous act the Guru promised that his empire would remain for a long time. He stayed three days with the emperor, but refused to accept anything for himself and firmly refused even to think of embracing Islam. When Bābar asked him for advice, Nanak told him to rule the people with justice and mercy, and this in fact he did during his short reign. Thus Guru Nanak saved India from much misery which the invasion must otherwise have caused her.

After this long journey in foreign lands and his useful contact with the Mogul conqueror, Nanak settled down quietly to live in peace at Kartarpur, almost for the whole of the rest of his days.

6. Ashram Life at Kartarpur (1521-1539)

A rich convert founded a new village with a Sikh temple at Kartarpur and disciples began to emigrate there from wherever Guru Nanak preached his message. The Guru occupied himself largely with vigorous work in the fields. He also wrote down many of the hymns he had sung elsewhere and which no doubt Mardana had committed to memory. Thus the *Mālār* and *Mājh Vārs* were written out while Mardana still lived, and the *Japji* and *Āsa dī Vār* soon after them. When Mardana died in 1522, he was succeeded as chief minstrel by his son Shāhzāda.

The Guru now put off his strange costumes and dressed himself as an ordinary ·householder. He regularly preached to the great crowd that came daily to see him, teaching them to live in the world and work, thinking of God always, and praying for nothing but His grace. His strong personal attractiveness, his lovable ways and playful sense of humour, his persuasive words and the simplicity which came from his own all-embracing love went straight to the hearts of his hearers; he seemed especially to draw the poor and sorrowing to his presence. He taught them to drop meaningless outer forms and complications, to cling to the simple essential truth, to abandon caste and all other forms of egoistic pride, and to seek refuge only in the Name. His great courage in so boldly speaking out in open criticism of Islam and Hinduism wherever he went shows us that he was a true predecessor of that great hero, Guru Gobind Singh. As Puran Singh said his lively speech 'radiated love and faith and attracted men as light gathers moths. Wherever he went the hearts of the people were gladdened and they began singing his *Song of Silence,* which is not written on paper but on the hearts of his disciples, and there it still sings as of old.'[1]

---

[1] Much of the spiritual strength of Sikhism comes from this conviction that Guru Nanak still lives in every true disciple, and the fragrance of his presence seems to flow round them when at prayer.

Though always quietly firm for the truth, in his own person he was the very essence of humility. In spite of his vast influence he never claimed any extraordinary greatness for himself, deeming himself a mere man among men, mortal and sinful as they were, though conscious of his union with the almighty Lover of souls. Nor would he hold anything for himself even after settling down to worldly life again; whatever came to him he at once spent on building almshouses and providing food for the poor.

A shopkeeper convert, who had lived with him for three years, sold his goods, took the Guru's blessing, and went to Śri Lanka where he converted that same Rājā Śivanabha who had been the Guru's host long before. To this man, as he left, Guru Nanak promised: 'Whoever bathes in cold water and for three hours before dawn repeats God's Name with love and devotion shall receive nectar at God's door and be blended with Him who is unborn and self-existent.' (M.1:146)

One morning the Guru noticed a little boy of seven years of age who came daily for the dawn prayers and slipped quietly away immediately afterwards. Nanak asked the lad why he came and was delighted by his wise and pious answer. This was Bhai Budha who later installed the first five of the Guru's successors. In those days, early in the morning, the Sikhs repeated the *Japji* and *Āsa dī Vār* in the Guru's presence, following these with more hymns, the Guru freely explaining them and answering questions until about nine-thirty. Then followed the *arati-prayer* taught at Puri, and after that came breakfast, all the Sikhs taking food together as one family. More singing and preaching followed, with manual labour, and after the *Rahiras* at sunset they had dinner together, followed by more songs. At about ten o'clock they sang the *Sohila* and then all slept, though a few rose for prayer in the night.

Some time about the end of 1531 the Guru wrote his exquisite mystical poem on the 'Twelve Months', its theme being the loving union of the soul with God. One day, in 1532, Lehnā, the priest of Durga in Khaḍūr, was led to the Guru, and he saw the goddess whom he adored worshipping at Nanak's feet. He surrendered to Nanak at once and became his favourite and most faithful disciple. Once when his friends congratulated the Guru on having so many converts he replied that he had, in fact, few real disciples; he then assumed a terrible form and many ran away from him at once, others stopped only long enough to pick up some money; only one yogi, two other Sikhs, and Lehnā remained. The Guru asked these to eat the flesh of a stinking corpse, and only Lehnā was ready for this; he found himself chosen as the Guru's successor and the carrion turned to sweetest *prasād*; Nanak's own two sons had already proved themselves to be not perfectly obedient. On Lehnā's intercession the deserters were forgiven and recalled to their Guru's side.

Early in 1539 Nanak attended the Śivarātri festival at Achal Batala where huge crowds saluted him with deep reverence. Here he wrote the *Sidha Goshti* which is believed to be a report of a discussion held there with certain yogis who followed Gorakhnāth. He went on to Pākapattan and called again on Sheikh Ibrahīm; the old man rose to receive his great visitor with great respect. The two embraced, and spoke of God to each other in verse all that night; they were most loving to each other and each was thrilled by the sayings of the other. Nanak visited Dipalpur and went as far as Multan on this his last journey, and then returned home through Lahore. He did not leave his ashram again while in that body.

On 2 September he had Bhai Budha formally install Lehnā—later Guru Angad—as his successor, laying before him five pice and a coconut as offerings. The crowds began to sing, and for five days a festival was maintained, a sweet feast of song. Nanak fell into an ecstatic trance; his *gaddi* he had given to Lehnā, the Name as heritage to his two sons. They sang the *Sohila* and the last *śloka* of the *Japji;* the Guru covered himself with a sheet, uttered the Divine Name of Vāhigurū once, and passed into the Being of the Beloved Lord, his light being transferred to Guru Angad. It was the 7 September 1539, and next day when the Hindus and Muslims disputed the right to dispose of the holy body they found only flowers beneath the sheet.[1] The two *samādhis,* Hindu and Muslim, were later washed away by the river Ravi, so that men could not make them into idols and so betray the teacher they loved.

2. Guru Nanak II (Angad)—Obedience

1. Early Life (1504-1539)

Bhai Lehnā, whom Guru Nanak found worthy to carry on his work, was born four hours before daybreak, on 31 March 1504 at Matte dī Sarān, near Muktsar in the district of Ferozpur. His father, Bhai Feruji, was a trader and a village priest of the goddess

---

[1] The same story is told of Kabīr who died at Mahar near Gorakhpur and of several other saints. Sai Baba also united in his own person the two great faiths.

Durga; his mother was Daya Kaur. When the village was sacked during Bābar's invasion the young man went with his father, his wife Khivi, two sons Dasu and Datu and a daughter Amro, to the town of Khaḍūr and settled down there. After two years at Khaḍūr Bhai Feruji died in 1526 and Lehnā became the head of the family.

One early morning in 1532 he chanced to hear Bhai Jodha chanting the hymns of Guru Nanak and was so charmed by their beauty that he went at once to Kartarpur to see the renowned teacher. He found Nanak hard at work in the fields, cutting grass with his own hands, and at once began to serve him, carrying bundles of the muddy grass on his head. That evening he saw his family goddess doing *pādapūja* to the Guru, and he knew that his life was settled for him by destiny. A short visit home was enough for him to wind up his domestic affairs for good, and he settled at Kartarpur with the Guru to serve him and enjoy his sweet company. Lehnā's humility and voluntary poverty, as he busied himself in sweeping the visitors' quarters, washing their clothes, and doing all kinds of other menial work, won the heart of the Guru. Daily he used to bathe long before dawn and then sit before the Guru for three hours of rapt meditation. Again and again he was tested for patience, endurance and obedience; always he came triumphantly through the tests. In 1535, after three years, he was sent home to his village where the Guru visited him twice. On the second visit he changed the name of this faithful servant; embracing him he called him *Angi-khud* (Angad, of my own limb) and added: 'Hereafter there is no difference between you and me!' He then took him back to Kartarpur.

On the 2 September 1539 Nanak bade Bhai Budha put the *tilak-mark* on Angad's brow and proclaim him the future Guru by seating him on the *gaddi* or royal throne. But the Guru's sons, Srichand and Lakhmidās, were vexed at this, so the Guru sent his beloved disciple home to Khadūr where, for six months, he lived in silent intense meditation, taking daily only a small pot of milk and seeing no visitors. The Sikhs were distressed at his absence, but for a long while no one could find out where he was until Bhai Budha used his clairvoyant powers. With three companions he went to the place, and when Angad opened to them they saw his face shine like Nanak's as he agreed to be their teacher in obedience to his own Guru's will.

2. Guru Angad (1539-1552)

Guru Angad's was indeed a fine character, of sterling piety and unflinching devotion, so that he lived in an ecstasy of serving love. He was fond of playing with children, took part in sports and enjoyed watching them, and was always reverent to the common people. All that came to his hands went at once to the poor, while he himself lived in extreme simplicity, earning his living by twisting coarse yarn and string. After his morning bath, singing of hymns and meditation, he would heal sick people, including lepers; and then he preached to all who came to him, expounding the great hymns of the Guru and often explaining them with couplets of his own. After the common meal the children were called for their instruction and then they watched wrestling-matches and other sports. The Guru taught all who came to the *āshram,* irrespective of their caste or apparent fitness for his teaching.

Like his own Guru, Angad wanted to raise Hinduism from within in order to expel superstition; he modified the script of the Punjabi language so that it might be more easily learned by illiterates and the hymns be more widely known. This Gurumukhī script did much to break down the exclusiveness of the Brāhmans who had enjoyed almost a monopoly of literacy and learning for so many years. From his own memories and those of Bhai Bala and other disciples, Guru Angad wrote the first *Life of Guru Nanak,* and this was the first published work of Punjabi prose.

Angad organized more fully the free kitchen, personally seeing to the needs of the poor who came there, and with great kindness supervising their meals which were taken along with devotees and other visitors, caste being thus broken by all in the *āshram.* This *langar* proved a powerful publicity for Sikhism, besides being also a noble field of charity and a bond of union among the disciples who were being gradually welded into a distinct group. Though still holding many Hindu ideas and customs, the Sikhs shared a simple, strong and zealous faith, purified from superstition and lit by devotion to their common Guru.

One day Emperor Humayun came to the *āshram*; he was told that he must wait for an interview with the Guru who was then absorbed in deep ecstasy. The emperor was annoyed at this rebuff and angrily drew his sword; when the Guru received him he prophesied that Humayun would wander for some time in exile but would later regain his throne. And this, indeed, took place.

The coming of Amar Dās to his *āshram* brightened the Guru's last days, though he was once driven away from Khaḍūr by an ascetic because the rain had failed. But as the ascetic himself failed to make rain, the people drove him away and called Guru Angad back.

He passed away with the name of Vāhigurū on his lips, on Tuesday, 29 March 1552, after very nearly completing forty-nine years of life and after installing Amar Dās as Guru in his place because he deemed his own sons to be unworthy. Thus light of Guru Nanak moved into the already old body of Amar Dās.

3. Guru Nanak III (Amar Dās) — Equality

1. Early Life (1479-1552)

Amar Dās was born on 5 May 1479 in Basarke, a village of Amritsar district, at the time when Guru Nanak was a boy of ten. He came of a good Kshatriya family, staunch in Vaishnava principles and regarding with loathing the eating of meat; his parents were Tejbhān and Bakht Kaur. Impelled by the traditions of his faith to seek a guru even in his old age, this kindly simple-hearted man one day heard Amro, his nephew's wife and daughter of Guru Angad, singing the Guru's hymns, and he was so charmed by the lovely melody and words that on learning these were the songs of the guru of the singer's uncle he at once sought out the *āshram* at Khaḍūr.

Realizing at once his visitor's Vaishnava preferences in food, the kindly Guru Angad offered him dhal with his bread. Amar Dās, however, did not want to be treated differently from other devotees, so he made a complete break with his past and asked them to serve him meat along with the others. This moral courage and readiness to change delighted the Guru so much that Amar Dās became his favourite disciple. As for Amar Dās himself, one glimpse of the Guru was enough; he knew at once that here was his soul's divine teacher, the raft whereon he could cross over the stormy world-sea to the haven of liberation. After that, he could hardly bear to look anywhere save on the Guru's face, so that once he walked backwards all the way from Khadūr to Goindwāl in the dark in order that his eyes might be towards the beloved form. So wholly devoted was he from the first that he forgot himself altogether and people thought him crazy, but his Guru understood that madness, which is love divine, for he himself knew it also.

At that time a disciple, Govind, was building at Goindwāl a new city for the Sikhs to live in together; Guru Angad tested the obedience of Amar Dās by asking him to help in the work there. He had to sleep there at night but he returned daily for his *darshan*. Later, the test became more severe for his Guru bade him stay there altogether. Amar Dās did not waver for a moment; his humility and obedience were absolute and won his Guru's hearty blessing. Soon afterwards he was afflicted with a sore foot, but that too did not shake him at all; in fact, he was glad of it because the pain kept him awake at night so that he could remember God all the time. During the day his old body laboured constantly in the Guru's work; nothing made him more happy than to undertake some new duty when already worn out.

Such was Amar Dās. His Guru saw so great a contrast between his own sons' indifference and this aged disciple's tireless zeal that he did not hesitate to choose him for his successor, enthroning him with the usual gifts of a coconut, five pice, and the *tilak-spot* on his brow. On 29 March 1552 the spirit of Guru Nanak passed over to the already aged body of Bhai Amar Dās, and he became Guru in his turn.

2. Guru Amar Dās (1552-1574)

For a while the Guru observed a retreat in lonely and silent prayer and then assumed the responsibility of his high place; he was at this time seventy-three years old. He, too, insisted on the middle way, rejecting alike Baba Srichand's asceticism and the world's luxurious frivolities. He made the Guru's kitchen still more famous, serving all castes together in it and letting no one see him before taking food there and so breaking caste restrictions. Personally, he still lived in the greatest simplicity; save for one single set of clothes he gave away all his other possessions.

Once Angad's unworthy son, Datu, drove Amar Dās from Goindwāl, where he had established his *ashram,* and set himself up as Guru at Khaḍūr. Amar Dās quietly withdrew to his own village of Basarke and immured himself in one room of a peasant's house; he sought no power or prestige for himself but, like other saints, gladly welcomed all who came to him as the will of his beloved God. But others would not tolerate the usurper; none would have him as Guru, so after a while he took everything he could find in the place and went off home again to Khaḍūr. On the way there he was robbed and wounded; though saints do not defend themselves, those who injure God's chosen must expect to suffer.

No one knew where the real Guru had gone, so they asked Bhai Budha, and he followed his mare's leading and she brought him to the village retreat. They broke down the wall and persuaded Amar Dās to return with them. He at once forgave Datu, as he forgave all other enemies and traducers, for he himself lived out his own advice to others: 'If one treat you ill, bear it three times, and God himself will fight for you the fourth time.'

Once he went to the forest for a brief period of solitude. Being ill-received by the Governor of Kasur, he foretold that one day a Sikh State would arise there. Another successful prophecy he made was when little Arjan, his grandson, stole some food from his plate and he playfully said, 'Come, heir to the plate, will you have it?' and people rightly took this as a sign that Arjan would one day be the Guru.

Twice he raised the dead; with a little water, a touch of his foot, and the holy words of *Japji*, he restored a dead boy, and his own grandson was brought back to life by the Name of God and a touch of the Guru's foot. Some of his bath water cured the leper Prema, whom he made into a worthy man, renamed him Murari, and married him into a good family. With a mere look or a few kind words he turned Sikhs and Muslims into righteous men; one day he called his elder son Mohan 'crazy' and this at once drove him mad with love for God.

One day, Māidās, a strict Vaishnava, came for *darshan* but could not bring himself to take food in the Guru's free kitchen and went away disappointed to Dwārakā. There he met Sri Krishna in a forest; the God fed him and told him to return for more of such divine food to the Guru at

Goindwāl. Maīdās at once obeyed and was lovingly welcomed by the Guru. When Maīdās left later, he had become a perfected man. And this was how the Guru made saints.

Amar Dās divided the whole area over which Sikhism had spread into twenty-two districts (*manjā*), each under a pious leader who taught and organized the *sangats* (assemblies) where the Sikhs gathered to sing the Guru's hymns and to enjoy each other's virtuous company. He also trained and sent out ninety-four men and fifty-two women as itinerant preachers to various parts of India; two went to Delhi and founded the first Sikh temple there. He chose three days for Sikh assemblies every year: Diwali, and the first days of Vaiśakh and Magh. Everywhere he taught gentleness, forgiveness and self-control, stressing a holy life and showing the futility of caste pride.

His fame spread in all directions. Once on his way to Lahore the Emperor Akbar came to see him and treated the coarse rice of the Guru's kitchen as the holiest of nectar, behaving before him with the utmost reverence. But vain were his offers of villages as an endowment; the Guru would have none of them and gave them at once to his daughter, Bibi Bhani, with Bhai Budha to look after them, and their income went entirely in charities to the poor.

Some orthodox Hindus complained to Akbar that the Guru was extorting funds from them to maintain his own 'court', but Akbar at once scouted the absurd tale. Then they protested against the breaking down of caste, and the defiling of religion by using the Punjabi vernacular instead of the holy Samskrit for teaching about

God. The broad-minded Akbar, who wished to be fair to all his subjects, asked the Guru to explain his position, and he treated with all respect Bhai Jetha whom Amar Dās sent to Delhi as his representative. Akbar was convinced that the Guru was in the right. Having failed in these charges, the accusers next hinted that the Guru was secretly plotting rebellion and collecting funds to that end, but Jetha was able to convince Akbar that this was also untrue. Jetha got permission from the emperor for the Guru to take, free of all charges and dues, a large pilgrimage party to Hardwar and thus show that he was not opposed to Hinduism as such. A great crowd availed themselves of the chance to travel free; all of them claiming to be Sikhs of the Guru's party! The Guru taught all who gathered there, boldly condemning *sati* and advocating the remarriage of Hindu widows.

Once in a vision he saw the first Guru, Nanak, and was bidden by him to dig a reservoir for water at Goindwāl to which Sikhs might go on pilgrimage instead of to the Hindu shrines. It was then that he dug the *bavali* at that city, a site which is still one of the chief places of Sikh worship. A perfected yogi once came to him imploring that he might be reborn in the Guru's family; Amar Dās foretold that this soul would come as the son of Mohari, his own younger son; when the child was born he sang the lovely hymn, *Anand,* which is still used on all festive occasions. Once, watching his Sikhs feasting, he remarked, 'Whatever the Sikhs eat nourishes me too, for there is no difference at all between us.'

The Guru was a truly simple man. He once earned his living as a carrier of goods from village to village, his pony being then his only property; he would never use the public funds provided for the Guru's kitchen, but to earn his keep he used to carry fresh water from the river—a distance of four miles each way—for the old Guru, Angad, to bathe in. When other disciples twitted the old man as a homeless beggar, Guru Angad replied: 'No, Amar is not homeless, but the home of homeless ones; and he who will follow him shall find his home with the Lord.' It was this blessing which made his life so fruitful.

In his turn, as Guru Angad had done with him, he severely tested his son-in-law Jetha in order to prove his worthiness, and then installed him as Guru Nanak's true successor. At a great feast in Jetha's honour, Amar Dās announced his own immediate departure. Next day, when they had recited the *Japji*, amid joyous shouts of God's Name from the Sikhs, the old Guru covered himself with the sheet and passed away, his light blending with God's; it was ten o'clock on the morning of the full moon day of Bhadron, 1 September 1574. The deserted body was cremated with royal state on the banks of the river Beas, and Guru Rām Dās (Jetha) reigned as Guru Nanak.

4. Guru Nanak IV (Rām Dās) — Service

1. Early Life (1534-1574)

At Lahore lived Haridās, the son of Thākurdās of the Sodhi clan; he and his wife Anūpdevī (Daya Kaur) worshipped the one God by repeating his Name and serving his devotees. They had prayed long for a pious son and at last, on Thursday, 24 September 1534, the son was born, saintly, kind and generous as themselves. They called him Jetha.

One day, when he was still but a young lad, Jetha met a party of Sikh pilgrims on their way to see their Guru. He joined them and had his first *darshan* of Amar Dās to whom he at once surrendered mind, heart and body, becoming a serving devotee at the Guru's *āshram*. After a while Amar Dās, who saw into the future, gave his own worthy daughter Bibi Bhāni or Mohani, as wife to the devoted young man, and then sent him home for a short visit to his parents. On his return Jetha became a humble personal attendant of the Guru, serving him day and night with tireless energy and devotion. One day Amar Dās put a precious jewel around his neck calling him 'the Guru's own image, dearer to him than life', thus preferring him to his own sons Mohan and Mohari. But when a ragged beggar asked Jetha for the jewel he gave it to him without a moment's hesitation, so little did he cling to worldly things.

It was Jetha who convinced Akbar that Amar Dās was innocent of oppression, anti-Hinduism and sedition, and cleverly arranged for the famous pilgrimage to Hardwar, free from the usual taxes, as a compensation for the nuisance caused by these false accusations. The publicity derived from this pilgrimage spread the name of Sikhism throughout India.

Soon after this, Jetha was bidden to dig a reservoir at a place twenty-five miles away where Guru Nanak had often camped beside a pool — a site that had been given to him by Akbar. Around it grew up a flourishing centre of trade among the Hindu peasantry that in later times grew into the city of Amritsar (nectar tank), the name that Jetha had given to the new tank. Amritsar (founded in 1577) became the unquestioned religious capital for all Sikhs. From the beginning it brought in a steady revenue for the Guru's funds, and Sikhs eagerly competed for the honour of digging and building there with their own hands. Seven times the Guru made Jetha break down and rebuild a certain platform, proving by his humility, obedience and loyalty, his worthiness to sit on Guru Nanak's *gaddi* and to receive his spirit within him.

2. *Guru Rām Dās (1574-1584)*

But when Jetha was enthroned as Guru under the name of Rām Dās, his predecessor's elder son, Mohan, refused to acknowledge him, holding that the title should be hereditary, as in Hindu monasteries. Neither of the brothers helped him in the work at Amritsar, so for some time he worked there alone. One day a leper was cured by bathing in the tank, and this man and his wife helped zealously in building shrines around the tank, both of them becoming saints.

Srichand, son of Nanak, came out of his forest retreat to visit Rām Dās. He saw in him the same sweet humility that had marked his own father and so recognized him as true Guru of all the Sikhs. Later came the poet Bhai Gurdās, who was to write the famous and all but scriptural *vārs;* him he sent as missionary to Agra, while he bade Handal, one of his closest followers, preach at Amritsar. Everywhere the Guru, who was himself a very apostle of love, preached with great eloquence and beauty of diction, pure devotion to God as the one real Friend of all. When some criticized the Sikhs for being worldly because they lived with families he would reply that they were immersed in the Name and that 'a man may wear a yogi's garb, but without devotion in his heart God never enters it'. He also taught people to think of the meaning of the hymns as they sang them and so extract the full flavour of their sweetness as the bee draws nectar from flowers.

The Sikhs now received many favours from Akbar; but they often refused gifts of land and villages, never seeking anything from the rich but treating all men exactly alike. This increased their prestige and also brought in many converts from the upper and wealthier classes, which helped the poorer Sikhs and greatly strengthened the community. Rām Dās organized the collection of regular offerings from his scattered disciples; sad to say, many of the *masands* (teacher-collectors) became, in time, oppressive and dishonest.

The Guru's two elder sons, Prithichand (Prithia) and Mahadev, found excuses for not attending a marriage at their village home in Lahore when their father asked them; they thought their interests best served by staying where they were. But Arjan, the youngest boy, gladly obeyed and indeed was prepared to stay on in Lahore as a missionary until he should be recalled. He wrote three letters to his father pleading to see him again, but Prithia stopped two of these in transit. When the third got through, and Prithia lied to hide his deceit, the Guru at once recalled Arjan and welcomed him with great state, at once installing him as the Fifth Guru. Prithia refused to accept his younger brother, and even dared to insult his father, so he was driven from court. It was now 1 September 1581, and Guru Rām

Dās-Nanak merged into his youngest son, while 'his light was blended with the Light'.

5. Guru Nanak V (Arjan) — Self-sacrifice

1. *Early Life (1563-1581)*

Arjan was the third son of Guru Rām Dās, the first of the Gurus to be born 'at Court'. When he was a small child, Guru Amar Dās foretold his greatness; 'This grandson of mine', he said, 'shall be a boat crossing over the sea.' He was born on 15 April 1563 at Goindwāl, and his first years were passed with the Guru and his own saintly mother Bibi Mohani. When he was nearly sixteen, he was the only son who was willing to go for the Lahore marriage, Prithia being too worldly to obey, while Mahadev claimed to have renounced the world. Arjan cared very little for the luxuries around him and enjoyed only his father's presence at home; his dominant qualities were service, humility and love. When he returned from Lahore after nearly three years, Rām Dās made him his successor and almost immediately passed away.

2. *Guru of the Sikhs (1581-1606)*

Arjan spent his first seven years as Guru completing his father's city and tank at Amritsar as an act of filial piety, personally supervising and working on the great Hari Mandir which he insisted on keeping low to show that humility wins the truest respect of men. The foundation of the temple was laid in October 1588. The Guru and his wife, Bibi Ganga, the daughter of Krishanchand of Meo, used secretly every night to give personal service to the pilgrims who came there. He promised that all who bathed in the tank would be freed from their sins. On finishing the work he made great rejoicings.

In spite of Arjan's generous gift to them of all his property, Prithia and his wife Karmo still coveted the guruship, and when Arjan returned from Amritsar to Goindwāl so greatly did they trouble him that he actually had to leave and wander abroad. He was kindly welcomed at Khara, where, because of their poverty, he got the peasants exempted for a year from the payment of taxes, and this naturally made the Sikhs most popular in the district. There he had a huge tank dug, founding near the spot the city of Tarantāran, where a number of Muslim mystics and devotees came to settle.

Arjan then went to Khānpur; here the rich mocked him in his need but a poor man named Hema most lovingly invited him in and made him his guest. He moved on into Jullandhar District where he founded the city of Kartarpur in 1593, himself cutting the first sod.

After this he settled down at Wadāli, six miles from Amritsar where, with Bhai Budha's blessing, a son was born in June 1595. This infuriated the ambitious Prithia who had occupied Amritsar after a Pathān raid and had given himself out as the real Guru; three times this wicked man tried to kill the infant. In 1597 little Har Gobind nearly died of smallpox, but, to his father's great joy, recovered. Instead of entrusting his son to his second brother, the Guru sent him to Bhai Budha.

In 1599 Arjan went to Chhiharta to dig a well for the people; he then went on a preaching tour to Lahore where he built the Bauli Sahib temple at Dabbi Bazaar. (It was here that the great Akāli *satyagraha* took place in

1922-1923.) He visited the aged Baba Srichand at Barath in the Gurdāspur District. About this time (1599-1600) he wrote his wonderful *Sukhmani* which teaches how we must attain to peace through life itself, and not by running away from it. After that he returned to Amritsar where he spent the next four years. Meanwhile Prithia continued his vile plots; he went to Delhi to slander the Guru to the emperor but had little success. Akbar had visited Arjan at Amritsar and greatly admired the idea of the Hari Mandir; he had already formed his own opinion of the Guru. Nor did Arjan allow the least anger or hatred for his brother to spoil the peace and charity of his own heart. He busied himself in other ways.

First, he chose missionaries from among the most loyal of his Sikhs and sent them out to all the preaching centres and *sangats* from Kashmir to Ceylon. From the latter place he recovered Guru Nanak's *Prānsangali* which had been written there, but it was stolen on the way back and is not now in existence. He appointed new *masands* to work in all the Sikh districts and to bring their offerings to Amritsar every year on the Vaisakh day of gathering. He opened a flourishing horse-trade with Turkestan and, by the way of adventure, greatly increased the courage and skill in riding among his Sikhs besides ensuring a steady and good revenue. But though wealth gathered round him and he lived as the 'true king' in royal state, Arjan retained his personal simplicity and was indifferent to the luxury of his surroundings. The Sikhs had now become an autonomous political community—almost a state within a state—with a good deal of power and prestige such as must awaken the jealousy and suspicion in those who were ultra-loyal to the Mogul Empire.

For a time this lover of peace was left in peace. He used this interval preparing for the world one of its greatest treasures, the *Guru-Granth Sahib*. It happened in this way. Prithia, his life's evil genius, was now forging hymns in Nanak's name as if he were the real Guru Nanak, so Arjan was impelled to make an official collection of genuine hymns written in the five bodies. Most of the manuscripts were with Mohan, the eldest son of the Third Guru, who was always in meditation in a closed upstairs room. Neither Gurdās nor Bhai Budha had succeeded in getting an interview with him, so Arjan himself went and, by singing sweet songs, persuaded the recluse to give the manuscripts with his blessings for the work. Arjan then settled with Bhai Gurdās in a shady glade at Amritsar and dictated the songs to his disciple in order, arranging them first by the *rāg* to which they were to be sung, and then by the author. Meanwhile messengers had gone all over India to collect the songs by other saints which might be suitable for including in the Holy Book; many songs by Kabīr, Raidās, Nāmdev and Farīd were added.

At last the book was completed on the first day of the bright Bhadon in 1604; it was shown to the people and then kept in Bhai Budha's charge at the very centre of the Hari Mandir. The Guru also gave orders for the songs to be translated 'into Indian and foreign languages, so that they might extend over the whole world' (*Surajprakāsh* III, 41, quoted by M.) By some trick Bhai Banno made a copy for himself and added other songs which the Guru had rejected and which are not accepted by Sikhs. The *Granth Sahib* has been rightly called 'the cream of Indian thought — the essence of

Hindu philosophy'. Yet it is not Hindu in any sectarian sense but purely Sikh. Guru Arjan called it the *Guru-Granth*, saying that the very essence of the Guru was incarnated in it — which is clearly true.

Once the court musicians demanded more pay; when Arjan pointed out their unreasonableness, they went home and chanted the Guru's hymns there instead. But no one cared to listen to them; all still flocked to the Guru's presence where ordinary Sikhs had been employed to sing for love instead of for pay.

Many conversions to Sikhism now took place, and several Hill-Rājās came into the fold. But Prithia incited Chandu Shāh, vizier at Lahore, to demand a marriage for his daughter with the Guru's son. Arjan refused this marriage proposal on the advice of the Delhi Sikhs who knew Chandu's arrogance and evil heart, and the boy was married to two Sikh girls of humble birth instead. Enraged at this ignoring of his veiled threats, Chandu became the Guru's enemy; he and Prithia went together to Akbar in April 1605 as soon as he returned from the frontier, to complain that the Guru's *Granth* slandered both the Prophet and the *avatāras*. Arjan sent Bhai Budha and Gurdās to read to Akbar from the book. The Emperor found it 'a volume worthy of reverence, full of love and devotion to God', and gave gold for the book to be honoured. He went out of his way to call on the Guru and was charmed by his personality.

In July of that year the Guru moved back to Goindwāl, and Prithia died. Unhappily, at this time, Akbar also died, and was succeeded by the rather narrow-minded Jahāngir. As Akbar had left no definite orders concerning the *Granth Sahib* or the Guru

Chandu saw a chance for further mischief. When Khusro, Jahāngir's eldest son, had rebelled, the Guru had received him as he would any other guest in the *langar* while passing through Goindwāl. This was misrepresented to the emperor as sedition on the part of Arjan. Chandu took the opportunity of persuading the new emperor to order him first to expunge all the objectionable passages from the *Granth Sahib*, and then to pay a large fine. Arjan refused both these demands, replying that to him all men were friends and that he had helped Khusro for Akbar's sake, not for political reasons, and that the *Guru-Granth* was the holy Word revealed by God through the Gurus and not a letter in it should be changed. He added that fines were for worldly men, certainly not for men like himself who held themselves apart from worldliness and devoted themselves to the welfare of others. Nor would he allow the Sikhs to collect or pay this fine of two hundred thousand rupees, even when he was summoned to Lahore to answer the charges. He appointed his little son his successor and went bravely to meet what he knew would be his death.

The emperor authorized Chandu Shāh to arrest the Guru and for several days he had him most brutally tortured in prison with boiling water, burning sand, and a red-hot iron pan. But in his agony Arjan remained calm, loving, and as firm as steel, though he proved to a Muslim holy man, Mian Mīr, that he had the power to destroy his torturers and suffered only to give an example of heroic patience. Chandu still demanded the rejected marriage for his daughter and would have released the Guru had he consented.

When Arjan knew the end was near he called a passing minstrel to recite the *Japji*, in which he himself joined; then, being tortured to death, his body was thrown into the river Ravi on Friday, 30 May 1606, and so he died a martyr to the Sikh religion. In death he found an even fuller union with his Eternal Beloved.

Guru Arjan was one of the most lovable of the Ten. With sweetness he achieved in nation-building what the great warrior Umar attained for Islam. He found the Sikhs free from caste-prejudice and devoted to their leader, but a mere religious sect; he left them a nation, and entrusted them to a successor with orders to maintain an army, but in all other respects to follow the earlier Gurus. He was a great statesman, peaceful organizer, philosopher and poet. His unfailing gentleness and loving self-restraint before his spiteful elder brother would alone have shown him a true saint. His poems are a spontaneous inspired outflow and are so musical that they demand to be sung. He is unusually easy in his diction and never obscure; there is much repetition, but every line seems new and fresh, instinct as it is with the simplicity of creation. His themes are ever love, devotion and union with the Beloved after the long agony of separation; his *Barah Maha* and his *Sukhmani* rank among the best of these and perhaps recall the misery of his three lonely years in Lahore before his father called him home. His poems are the most extensive among the immortal poets whose work is enshrined in the *Guru-Granth Sahib*.

His very presence was a spiritual attraction, and none could be unmoved by it save the few who seemed to be inspired by Evil's very self. His toleration of personal wrongs, his humility and patience would have won him love among the people of any nation on the earth.

6. Guru Nanak VI (Har Gobind) — Justice

1. Early Life (1595-1606)

The new Guru was only eleven years of age but his life had already been full of exciting incidents. He was born after many prayers, to Arjan and Mātā Ganga, for his mother feared lest the guruship pass over to the line of the unworthy and hostile Prithichand. His mother went to Bhai Budha to ask him to bless her with a son, but she went as a queen with glittering equipage and Bhai Budha refused her gifts, because of the pride of her display and sent her back to the Guru. Next time she came alone and on foot, and the old saint promised that she would have a brave and famous son.

The child was born on 19 June 1595 at Waḍāli, whither his father had retired to avoid the Paṭhāns brought by the traitor Prithia to raid Amritsar. This birth greatly annoyed the Guru's elder brother. He sent poisoned medicine for the child, but he refused to drink; the courage of the nurse he had sent to carry out this vile deed failed her and she confessed the plot. Next he sent a cobra, which the child killed. Even after the child recovered from smallpox in 1597, he tried again, by bribing a servant to give poison, but the child again refused to drink it and the servant confessed and then died of colic. Guru Arjan then thought he would send his son for safety to his second brother Mahadev, but when friends warned him that this man also was not to be trusted he sent him to Bhai Budha to bring up and under that revered patriarch he learned with wonderful ease and speed. Arjan, before going to his death at Lahore, installed his little son as Guru, bidding him never to abandon the good practices of his predecessors.

2. Guru Har Gobind (1606-1644)

On the news of Arjan's passing, Bhai Budha formally enthroned the new Guru, who had the *Granth Sahib* chanted for ten days in his father's honour, then he appeared for the first time in full military insignia. He at once enrolled a small army and personal bodyguard of armed men, sending word to the *masands* that the usual gifts of money should be replaced by weapons and horses. He took to hunting and martial instead of devotional songs, which greatly pleased most of the Sikhs who were longing for revenge on the murderers of their Guru. When old Bhai Budha protested against this, the Guru replied that hereafter there should be the free kitchen for the poor and a sword for those who opposed and impoverished them. So he maintained great state, having over eight hundred horses and a splendid retinue of well-equipped soldiers. Yet though he preferred hunting and sports to poetry and meditation, the Guru was still a great teacher in his own way, and it is even said of him that 'he rained instruction like clouds in Sravan, and the Sikhs flourished under it like thirsty paddy-fields'.

Chandu Shāh was furious at this change in Sikh life, and still more so when the Guru boldly answered his threats. He complained to the emperor who summoned the Guru to court; though the Sikhs begged him not to go, Har Gobind took three hundred men with him and went to Delhi in 1612, leaving Bhai Budha and Bhai Gurdās in charge. He was welcomed with respect by Emperor Jahāngir, and joined him in hunting, having the good fortune to save his life from a tiger. The emperor took the Guru on a visit to Kashmir. On the way they visited the sons of Guru Amar Dās at Goindwāl and the temple at Amritsar. Many of the Sikhs, supported by even his own mother, had refused him money for buildings, disapproving of his present policies. They went to Lahore also, where the saint Mian Mīr showed great reverence to Gurudev. A Muslim lady, Kaulan, became a Sikh and gave up all her wealth, which was used by the Guru in digging the tank of Kaulsar. Meanwhile Prithia's son, Mihrban, and Chandu's son poisoned the mind of Prince Jahan against the Guru, in spite of the pleading of the Sikhs for them to desist. The Guru then visited the venerable son of Guru Nanak, Baba Srichand, who must by this time have been about one hundred and twenty-five years old. At Pilibhit, even though the yogis tried to drive him away from the place, the Guru miraculously restored to life the burnt pipal tree under which Guru Nanak used to sit.

Har Gobind's eldest son, Gurditta, born in the autumn of 1613, was exactly like Guru Nanak in appearance and also in his great love of humility. Later Baba Srichand adopted this lad and made him the heir to the headship over his own *Udāsīs*. On a brief visit to two devotees in Kashmir the Guru converted many to Sikhism; then he went to Baramula and by way of Gujarat to Lahore where he married a third wife; at this time most of the family alliances were with poor and obscure Sikhs. He visited Talwandi, Guru Nanak's birthplace, and when his mother died he had her body thrown into a river like Guru Arjan's.

All went well enough until one day a Sikh took the Guru for the emperor and in that belief gave him royal titles. This gave Chandu Shāh his chance, and he did not rest until Jahāngir had Har Gobind interned on false charges in Gwalior Fort; here he was so kind to the other captives that he won all their hearts. In vain did Chandu try to get him murdered, while the Sikhs outside were labouring for his release. Three long years went by, and the Guru would not go free until all the other royal prisoners were freed, himself standing surety for them.

Then the emperor handed over Chandu to be punished by the Sikhs; he was shoebeaten, covered with filth and paraded about until at last some grain parcher killed him, perhaps out of pity for his wretched state. This is the first case where we hear of the Sikhs seeking or taking revenge for their wrongs. Har Gobind became a friend of the Prince Dara Shikoh, who had a liking for saints, and visited him several times at Lahore. This greatly displeased many of the Sikhs who dared to criticise the Guru to his face for associating with Muslims[1] and neglecting hymns and devotions for the pleasures of the chase.

The long-threatened trouble with the empire began in 1628. Some Sikhs captured the emperor's hawk and killed some of his soldiers; Mukhlis Khān was sent to arrest the Guru by Shāh Jahan, who had now succeeded his father and was an enemy of Har Gobind and the Sikhs. There

---

[1] He even built a Mosque for them once.

was a fierce battle with the Mogul troops at Waḍāli; Har Gobind himself fought like a tiger, and the Moguls were driven off. With his own hands the Guru cremated the Sikhs who had fallen in his defence. Jahan was furious, but Wazir Khān, an old friend of the Sikhs, dissuaded him from taking revenge.

The Guru spent that rainy season at Ruhela on the River Beas, and there built a new city, which he called after himself, Sri Hargobindpur. His enemies brought an army of ten thousand men against him, but it was driven back with great slaughter. After the battle Bhai Budha came to the Guru, took his leave, drank water from his feet, and passed away at the age of 108, more than a century after his first coming to Guru Nanak, and Baba Srichand passed away at about the same time, shortly after he adopted the little lad, Gurditta.

The Guru's fourth son, Atal Rai, began to work miracles, raising his dead friend Mohand, and when the little boy of eight saw how displeased his father was at this he went to the temple and there died. Gurditta founded the city of Kiratpur, later to be famous in Sikh history. At this time, the Guru made several pilgrimages, meeting distant relatives and aged devotees.

For some time Shāh Jahan sought pretexts against the Guru, while Wazir Khān tried to persuade him that a man who had built a mosque could be no enemy of Islam. But at last, in 1631, a rather discreditable incident over the stealing of horses meant for the Guru and recovered for him by craft from the imperial stables, led to a punitive expedition which was defeated at Lahra or Gurusar at the cost of one thousand two hundred Sikh lives. The Guru retired to Kartarpur where a quarrel soon followed with Painda Khān, a brave but boastful officer of his.

In 1634 Painda persuaded the emperor to send fifty thousand men under Kale Khān to Jullandhar with envoys to the Guru. When an envoy insulted Guru Nanak, the Sikhs gave him a shoebeating, and a fight began which ended in a great victory for the Sikhs at the cost of heavy losses, Painda himself being slain by the Guru's own hand and Gurditta slaying his own boyhood friend. This so grieved the young man that he resolved to give up war for ever.[1] Using psychic powers in some miracle shortly afterwards he incurred his father's displeasure and at once gave up his life like his younger brother; this was in 1638.

Dhirmal, son of Gurditta and the Guru's grandson, had turned traitor before the last battle and now refused to go humbly to receive the guruship from Har Gobind's hand, feeling himself to be the natural heir and therefore entitled to the honour. So Guru Har Gobind nominated Dhirmal's younger brother, Har Rai instead. When his third wife died, whom he loved dearly, the Guru turned ascetic and became gentle and meditative, retiring to live in peace at Kiratpur. While all the fighting that he took part in during his life was in self-defence, the character of the guruship had already made that change which is so often ascribed only to Gobind Singh. It had become a military monarchy as well as a religious sect.

---

[1] This Baba Gurditta was asked in 1636 to appoint four preachers when he invested with his own strange dress, resembling that of the first Guru; their names were Almast, Fhul, Gonda and Balu Hasna, and they founded the four *dhuans*, or hearths, and proved zealous missionaries, co-operating with the other orders: *Nirmalas, Bakhshishes, etc*

Dhirmal continued to defy his grandfather, the Guru, and even, when on his mother's advice, he at last visited the Court he boasted there of his friendship with the Mogul emperor and seated himself also on a throne beside the Guru. Bhai Budha's son was called and put the *tilak* on the brow of Har Rai; the spirit of Guru Nanak changed bodies once again; Guru Har Gobind retired on 3 March 1644[1] and, bidding farewell to his Sikhs, died.

He, too, like his great father was always calm though often betrayed by those to whom he had shown much kindness. Though it is true his romantic temperament led him into ways different from those of his predecessors, it seems clear to us now that in him the One Guru Nanak willed to prepare the Sikhs to become a strong fighting nation. It was not until nearly a century later when, under Guru Gobind and the great Banda, the full shape was given to this creative idea, but it was the natural sequel to the gradually developing wealth and organization under the first five Gurus. Guru Har Gobind, whose life is given in the *Gur Bilās,* had not only to avenge his father and to teach the Muslims respect for the Sikh power, but he had to begin the work of liberating the masses so long oppressed by a cruel, corrupt and bloody tyranny. He led Sikhs who were athirst to give their lives for their religion as Guru Arjan had already given his; and he led them well.

---

[1] Others say 1645

7. Guru   Nanak   VII (Har Rai) — Mercy

1. Early Life (1630-1644)

The Seventh Guru was born to Gurditta, Guru Har Gobind's eldest son, on 16 January 1630, and even when only a tiny child he was noted for his gentle and religious disposition. As a boy he was never seen to pick flowers or even to break off a leaf, and he was also very gentle with animals; he loved to walk alone under the trees, and there he would be rapt for hours in meditation. Possibly his father's sweetness of temperament, which had so attracted the venerable Srichand, had to some extent come down to him also. Later on, when he joined his father in the chase, he delighted in bringing back the animals alive instead of killing them, and he made a little zoo in a corner of the garden. He took great joy also in being hospitable to guests, and this characteristic remained with him all through his life. He was always peace-loving and ever sought quiet places.

2. Guru Har Rai (1644-1661)

Har Rai was only fourteen when he ascended the Guru's *gaddi*, and he continued his peaceful life of strict self-discipline. He was always kind and gentle with devotees, whose needs he clairvoyantly came to know from a distance; he preferred the coarse food of the poor given him with love to the richest delicacies of the proud. He peacefully converted several important families to Sikhism, and though he has left us no hymns of his own he was fond of quoting those of the first five Gurus in apt ways. He taught his disciples to seek happiness in pondering on the Gurus' words which alone could lead them to the path of devotion, saintliness and liberation. Even those who cannot easily understand the purport of the hymns need'not be disconsolate, for, said he, 'the hymns have value even if not understood, for they bear fruit at the hour of death'. The very melody, listened to with reverence, purifies the heart from sin. With such reverence did the Guru himself treat the *Granth Sahib* that he always rose to his feet when a devotee began to recite from it.

For most of his reign he lived at Kiratpur, where he was a popular teacher of religion though with non-Sikhs he was somewhat reserved. Once he went to Kartarpur to visit his brother Dhirmal, and once he went to Mukandpur where he planted a bamboo which was still living in 1909. The Guru avoided meddling with politics, although on occasions his Sikhs were involved in fighting. He had once cured the prince Dara Shikoh of poison administered by Aurangzeb, and Shāh Jahan vowed eternal friendship with him on this account. As soon as Jahan died in 1658, Aurangzeb drove his brother Dara away, and the prince sought the Guru's help. The Guru promised him salvation but could not promise victory or the crown. When Dara Shikoh had to retreat from the River Beas, Har Rai sent a small Sikh force to cover his friend's flight, but eventually Dara was captured and executed. The cruel and tyrannous Aurangzeb then sent for Har Rai to explain why he had helped his enemy. It seemed that the story of Guru Arjan and Khusro was to be repeated.

Har Rai refused to obey the summons of a man who had openly vowed to destroy Hinduism, and as the officer who had been sent to arrest him died, Aurangzeb thought it politic to ask the Guru respectfully to visit him. This too the Guru would not do, but he sent his elder son, Rāmrai to represent him at the emperor's court. This young man worked miracles there to display his own greatness, and even dared to change a line in the *Guru-Granth Sahib* in order to flatter the Muslims and please the emperor. When Har Rai heard of this he said, 'The guruship is like tiger's milk and can only be held in a golden cup. Rāmrai is not worthy of it; let him not see my face again but stay with Aurangzeb and amass money there.'

Hearing of his banishment, Rāmrai became, like most elder sons of the Gurus, a bitter enemy. Har Rai refused to forgive him or take him back even when Dhirmal pleaded on his behalf, and in order to avoid a quarrel he left the place where he was and went back to Kiratpur. Having duly enthroned his younger son as Guru, bidding the Sikhs look on the child as his own image and put their faith in him, Guru Har Rai passed away on 6 October 1661, his 'light blending with the Light'.

8. Guru Nanak VIII (Har Krishan) — Purity

1. Early Life (1656-1661)

This young child, born on 7 July 1656, was already showing signs of a sweet and docile spirit, and of a clear insight into religious thought.

2. Guru Har Krishan (1661-1664)

At the very early age of five he was called to lead and to teach the widespread and vigorous Sikh community. He did his work well. He sent out missionaries to the farthest outposts of the religion, and himself taught with confidence those who came to him. But his elder brother Rāmrai had himself proclaimed Guru in rivalry to him; as no one paid much heed to his claims he went off to Aurangzeb to complain against his father's injustice in disinheriting the elder son. In this quarrel the emperor saw a good opportunity for creating dissension and so destroying the Sikhs, so he sent a polite message to the Guru inviting him for a visit to Delhi. His father had warned the little Guru never to let Aurangzeb meet him, but as the Delhi Sikhs longed for his *darshan* he consented to visit the capital, but not to see the emperor. Rājā Jai Singh of Amber, who had been sent to fetch him, agreed to these terms and the party set out; on the way to Delhi the very sight of the Guru healed many sick folk who went to see him as he passed. There was a Brāhman proud of his caste; the Guru taught him humility by putting divine wisdom into a passing water-carrier, thus showing how all men are equally God's children and able to be enlightened by his grace.

When Har Krishan reached Delhi he sent Aurangzeb a message that he was quite willing for Rāmrai to take over all the political and organizing sides of the guruship, but Rāmrai was furious at the suggested compromise and demanded the integral guruship for himself at once. While Har Krishan was in Delhi plague was raging in the city, and he healed many people of the dread disease merely by a few words or by the very sight of him. He again refused to meet the emperor in person but sent him a copy of one of Guru Nanak's hymns, which Aurangzeb is said to have approved.

Somehow, though, the Guru was persuaded to show

off his powers before Jai Singh by picking out the head queen; the very next day he developed smallpox which soon ravaged his fair young body. The Sikhs begged him to stay with them at least until he had appointed his successor, but he replied, 'Gurus may die, but their heart, the *Guru-Granth Sahib,* shall remain with you' (M. 4:327). He comforted his weeping mother by keeping the Holy Name always on his lips, and showing her how unafraid of death we should always be. When asked to name the next Guru, he answered only, 'Baba Bākale', by which they understood rightly that he was to be found in the village of Bākala. He forbade any to mourn for him and passed away happily on 30 March 1664 repeating the Name.

9. Guru Nanak IX (Tegh Bahadur) — Calmness

1. Early Life (1621-1664)

Tegh Bahadur, youngest son of Guru Har Gobind, was born at 2.15 a.m., on 1 April 1621 (though M. says 1622); he was so named because the Guru foresaw that he would be powerful to endure the sword (*tegh*). Even at the age of five, he used to enter into ecstatic trance (*samādhi*); and his father prophesied that he would some day come to the guruship and that his son would in turn be even more glorious and break the power of tyranny in India. When Tegh was about seven, he was married to Bibi Gūjari; he continued his quiet life of solitude with his little wife and his mother, meditating often on God and on the sorrows of the Indian people. So the years passed.

Tegh rarely showed himself to others, and it was with

difficulty that the Sikh envoys traced him to his remote village retreat when directed thither by the dying words of the boy Guru. There were twenty-one rival claimants to the *gaddi*, but none of them, except Tegh, showed any of the qualities to be looked for in the heir of Nanak. Far from pushing himself forward, Tegh protested his unworthiness for so high a place. The envoys hailed him as Guru, and most of the other claimants faded at once from the picture.

2. *Guru Tegh Bahadur (1664-1675)*

A friend of Dhirmal, the old claimant, shot Tegh, but the wound was not serious and the new Guru refused to punish the assailant, thus teaching the joy of forgiveness. When he came to Amritsar, the Sikh 'priests' shut the doors of the temple against him, but the crowd of worshippers singing the Guru's hymns, came out to where he quietly sat āt Walla. When he returned home, he made the Sikhs restore the original *Granth Sahib* to Dhirmal's custody.

Personally, Tegh Bahadur was a simple, kindly and humble man, and though he kept up a magnificent royal state so as to uphold the dignity of the Guru and the Panth, he was never so happy as when he could slip away into retirement and remain absorbed in God. He was always conscious of the unreality of this worldly show, and the sufferings of the poor — indeed, the pains of all created things — filled his heart with pity; but he combined that pity with a lion heart of courage which made great self-sacrifice possible for him. The keynote of his hymns is renunciation of the world's illusory delights, and regret that so few care to look beyond the veil to the Reality behind them; but he combined this 'pessimism' with passionate devotion to God and the knowledge that one must be ceaselessly aware of the world and its needs. Typical of his attitude is the verse given us by M. : 'Shed your tears for the sorrows of the world, but make them into a rosary for the repetition of God's Name!'

In 1665 he founded his new capital a little way from Kiratpur at a place called Anandpur, but he did not spend much time there himself. Rāmrai again claimed the guruship, and Tegh moved to Mulawala in Patiala, where he turned bitter water sweet, to Handiaya, where he ended an epidemic fever, and so on into south Punjab being everywhere welcomed with reverence and working various kinds of miracles here and there, so the historians tell us. He dug several wells and preached against the newly introduced and growing use of tobacco. Then he went to Kurukshetra, where he was honourably received, and visited Prayāg and Banaras; at Sahasrawan he occupied a palace a devotee had built long before for his use. At Gaya, like the first Guru, he refused to offer *piṇḍa*, and he left his mother and wife at Patna so that the coming child of promise might be born there.

Meanwhile Rāmrai had persuaded Aurangzeb to call the Guru to Delhi so as to break his 'ambitious plans'; there he was lodged with Rājā Rām Singh of Amber, who satisfied the emperor about his loyalty. So he accompanied the rājā on his eastern campaign, preaching to and organizing the Sikhs in every place he visited. When he came to Dhakka he was welcomed with loving enthusiasm, and in Assam he made such a complete conquest of the Kamrup king's heart that he submitted to the empire and war was avoided.

At this point came news that a son was born to him, so he hastened back to Patna to see the baby Gobind Rai. Here he lived quietly for some time with his family, encouraging the child in all manly sports and skills. Then, in spite of his mother's pleading to remain at Patna, he left to see his Sikhs in the Punjab where little Gobind soon joined him. After a while he again visited Banaras, Ayodhya, Lakhnau and the Ambala District, and then returned to Kiratpur and Anandpur. Everywhere he and his young son were equally admired and loved.

Aurangzeb now began to work out a scheme for converting the Hindus to Islam by means of bribes and cruel tyranny. He started in Kashmir with brutal massacres and forced conversions. The Kashmir pundits went to Anandpur to appeal for help from Tegh Bahadur. The Guru replied that no one could free the land from such tyranny unless he were ready to die; the boy Gobind heard this and at once broke in: 'You are the most worthy for that!' The Guru agreed, so he told the Kashmiris to tell Aurangzeb that if he first converted the Sikh Guru they would all embrace Islam. This message filled Aurangzeb's heart with joy for he thought it was a condition easy to fulfil. He sent at once for Tegh Bahadur to come to his court.

Tegh girded his sword on young Gobind Rai and proclaimed him the next Guru, bidding him destroy tyranny in revenge for his father's imminent death (cf. *GGS* 1:1 and 53:1-2). Then he left Anandpur in order to pass the rainy season with a Muslim friend at Saifabad.

The emperor's envoys could not find him at home, nor was he at Amritsar, so they reported that he had fled; Aurangzeb at once ordered his arrest. Taking with him five Sikhs,[1] the Guru journeyed towards Delhi, everywhere prophesying the fall of the Mogul Empire. At Agra he waited quietly to be arrested.

Aurangzeb demanded that he embrace either Islam or death, but Tegh Bahadur replied: 'The Prophet of Mecca who founded your religion could not impose one religion on the world, so how can you? It is not God's will.' He then showed that all three, Hindus, Sikhs and Muslims, would survive together. He was imprisoned until he should change his mind; time and again they tortured him, but again and again he refused to apostatize. Matidās, one of his 'five' followers, was martyred for urging that Islam should be destroyed; they sawed his body in two while he was repeating the *Japji*. Three others were released and they fled; only Gurditta, of Bhai Budha's family, stayed with the Guru, who sent a consoling message to his own family that they should not grieve on his account. His son replied with a copy of the fifty-fourth śloka: *balu hoa bandhana chute sabha Kichu hota upāi, Nānaka sabha kichu tumarai bātha mai tuma hī hota sahā*i. In return, Tegh Bahadur sent orders for the immediate installation of his son as Guru with the usual rites and offerings.

Once more his captors urged him to submit and once more the Guru refused; they sentenced him to be beheaded in the Chandni Chauk. While he recited the

---

[1] It is interesting how often the earlier Gurus thus foreshadowed the actions of their successors; here we have the prototype of Guru Gobind Singh's *panch-piāre* and his promise in *GGS* 54:7.

Japji, the execution took place on Thursday afternoon 11 November 1675. The wind blew sand into the eyes of the Moguls present under the banyan tree, which is still there; the Guru's head flew into the lap of the Sikh messenger who hurried with it back to Anandpur for cremation. Some faithful low-caste Sikhs hid the body for some time in their own humble village, and there it was burned. Over where the ashes were buried the shrine of Rakabgunj was built.

This brutal murder affected even Aurangzeb and he soon repented of what he had done, but never really regained peace of mind. It turned the Sikhs of the Punjab into a fiery nation thirsting for revenge and inflamed with hatred for the Muslims. In his death the Guru became the brand which was to set North India alight.

10. Guru Nanak X (Gobind Singh) — Royal Courage

1. Early Life (1666-1675)

Guru Gobind Singh was the fifth Guru who acceded before the age of twenty, and in some ways he may be regarded as almost as original as the first Guru Nanak himself. Yet it is possible to exaggerate the novelty in his innovations, for almost all of them were at least fore-shadowed or led up to by his predecessors. He led the Sikhs further along the path to nationhood than did Guru Nanak I, Guru Arjan or Guru Har Gobind; so much it is correct to say, but we should not say much more than that. Circumstances in the country had changed greatly; India was under the ruthless and bigoted control of Aurangzeb, and there was no constitution to protect her people from his brutalities. Under him Hindus had no legal rights, their temples were burned, and they themselves subject at any moment to forcible conversion, massacre or, at the least, to heavy poll-tax and fines. There was nothing else to do but to submit like cowards or resist like men; the Guru was forced into resistance by the incessant attacks of jealous Hill Rājās, who could not tolerate the rise of Sikhism beside them; he used violence and the sword, as the surgeon, when all other means have failed, takes up the knife. The evil of the day could be combated only in that way.

Gobind Rai was born at Patna on 19 December 1668 according to the usual Sikh reckoning (M. would put it in 1666). He was a playful and lovable child, brave and active, and very early showed a love of fighting, complete fearlessness, and eagerness to use the catapult. The strong sense of humour, which was a marked feature of Nanak himself, showed also in the Tenth Guru; in later years he could sport with his disciples, even in the greatest crises of his life.

In 1673 his mother took him to join Guru Tegh Bahadur in the Punjab, and he travelled with him to many places in what is now Uttar Pradesh. All who saw him admired his beauty and his noble bearing; they recognized him as a child of destiny as they watched him arranging sham fights among his boy playmates. Crowds came out from every town to see and admire him. It was he who suggested to his father the noble act of self-sacrifice by which he won respite for the Kashmiri Brāhmans at the price of his own life; and when the Guru was in jail and about to be beheaded he sent him a verse which encouraged him in his martyrdom.

When the Sikh messenger brought Tegh Bhahadur's head secretly to Anandpur, it was the young Gobind Singh who himself lit the pyre and consoled the Sikhs while he performed the customary rites. Early next year, 1676, the son of Gurditta of Bhai Budha's line, formally enthroned him as Guru.

2. Guru Gobind Singh (1676-1708)

At first the Guru remained more or less in retirement; he was only eight years old and he knew that he must prepare for the work God had given him to do. He lived quietly for some years at Anandpur, practising archery and riding, so as to fit his body for the strenuous fighting for which it was destined. His mind too became suited to a soldier; he became arrogant and boastful, and when his mother Gūjari and her brother Kripāl scolded him for this, saying it was for the Guru to be humble and pious rather than forceful and quarrelsome, he replied quietly but with decided firmness that he would never use his sword save in self-defence and, in effect, that he knew his own business best. In 1677 he married Jito, the daughter of Bhikhia, a Sikh from Lahore; she was later known as Sundari because of her beauty.

He perfected his knowledge of Samskrit and Persian and called fifty-two poets to his court, employing them on translating the Purānas and Epics into Brajbhāshā verse, so that the stories of heroism in them might inspire his own people for the coming war. His own writing of Hindi poetry became so skilled that he is rightly regarded as one of the masters of Hindi literature. It was during these days (perhaps 1683-1685) that he wrote his greatest poems, the *Jāpu Sahib*, the *Akāl Ustat*, and the *Sawwaiyas*. Meanwhile, his army grew, many Muslims and Hindus joining him and he waited for the hour to strike. He was now convinced that he had been sent into the world to free the Hindus from tyranny as Krishna fought the Rākshasas in his day.

In 1684 he went to the State of Nahan to stay with his friend Rājā Medni Parkāsh, and he hunted much in the hill forests acquiring great skill in riding and strength of body. We are told that he killed a tiger with one stroke of his sword. Another of his good friends at this time was Rājā Fateh Shāh of Srinagar.

One day Rāmrai, his second cousin, visited him to complain about being harassed by the *masands*; this former claimant to the guruship was still the leader of a small and decaying group of adherents at Dehra Dun. One day he lay in a trance and the *masands* took this as an excuse for having him cremated alive (1685); perhaps they fancied that the Guru would approve, but he punished them for it and consoled the widow, Panjāb Kaur.

At this time the Guru founded a fortress on the Jamna bank; it was called Paunta Sāhib. Rājā Fateh Shāh invited Gobind Singh to the marriage of his daughter with Rājā Bhimchand's son; now this Rājā of Kahlur, the strongest of the Hill Chiefs, was very jealous of the Guru's growing power and popularity, and when the Guru refused to lend the white elephant presented him by the rājā of Assam, Bhimchand became his avowed enemy. As Gobind Singh felt that his presence might spoil the marriage festivities, he sent Divan Nand Chand with costly wedding gifts for the princess.

Rājā Bhimchand sent the Guru a message demanding that he vacate the fortress and get out of the way of his son's army and marriage procession, lest the two armies clash. Gobind Singh allowed the marriage procession to pass, but forced the army to go by another route. This further enraged the rājā, who began to seek excuse for fighting the Guru. On his way back from the marriage he enlisted the support of twenty-one other rājās who had attended it. The procession went to Bilaspur by a different route, but the Hill Rājās collected their forces and on 5 May 1687 marched upon Paunta Sahib.

As advised by his friend and admirer, Sayyid Budhu Shāh, Gobind Singh had employed five hundred Paṭhān soldiers whom Aurangzeb had dismissed and whom no one else would engage for fear of incurring the emperor's anger. As soon as the Hill Rājās attacked the Sikhs at Bhāngani, these mercenary Paṭhāns deserted, but Pīr Budhu Shāh of Sadaura, a Muslim leader, arrived with seven hundred men just in time.

After a fierce fight Gobind Singh won a decisive victory, and in October Bhimchand made peace. The Guru, his happy relations with the hillmen having been broken, returned to live in Anandpur.

3. At Anandpur: Days of Peace (1687-1700)

It was not all peace even there. In 1689 Alaf Khān, the Nawāb of Jammu, demanded tribute from the Hill Rājās; Bhimchand refused to give anything, and asked the Guru's help. Gobind Rai was unable to refuse aid to anyone who asked him, so he sent his forces to help Bhimchand win a victory at Nadauna. But next year, 1690, the same Bhimchand united with Dilawar Khān in a treacherous attack on the Guru; this was defeated and the Guru was then left for some time in peace.

He made Anandpur a centre of literary movement; his pundits laboured at translation work, and as Raghunath Pandit refused to teach Samskrit to the Sikhs, who were of all castes, the Guru sent five young men to Banaras to learn it there. When they returned they taught Samskrit to all who cared to learn; these were the first 'Nirmalas', who lived pure ascetic lives devoted to study and teaching the Sikh religion in a somewhat Hinduized form.

Once the *masands* tried to cheat the Guru and were angry when he discovered their deceitfulness; he decided to abolish the order. He punished many of them for extortion and dishonesty and they threatened to join Dhirmal, the Guru's enemy, elder brother of Guru Har Rai. Bhai Pheru, who showed great humility to the Guru, was forgiven and honoured, and entrusted with teaching the district between the Beas and the Ravi.

In 1695 Gobind Singh set himself to the swift building of a nation; the Hindus were too mild and modest, too desireless, too resigned to fate or the results of their own 'karma', and had to be stung and encouraged into a braver and more vigorous attitude to life. This the Guru achieved by means of his daily teachings and the special methods we shall read about shortly. In such ways he replaced devotion and piety by manly valour and pugnacity, implanting in every Sikh the heart of a lion and a self-respect which soon earned them the respect of others.

When Baba Nandchand stole a beautiful copy of the *Guru-Granth Sahib* from the *Udāsīs*, the Guru ordered him to restore it at once; he defied the order and fled to Kartarpur, where Dhirmal killed him. The Guru did many strange things in those days so that those who could not understand began to doubt if he were wholly sane. Thus, to teach simplicity and hardihood, he once burned all the costly cloths he could find in Anandpur and threw much treasure into the river Sutlej. He introduced the wearing of long hair among his warriors and taught all Sikhs to carry arms at all times. He organized a great arms factory at Anandpur, making swords and daggers in plenty. Then to make fun of the Hindu sacrifices he once sacrificed an ass instead of a cow at Thāneśwar. The Brāhmans were unwilling to join his armies, saying they could win victories only if the goddess Durga were first appeased. He playfully agreed to this, and for nine months kept up the farce of elaborate sacrifices to Durga, just to show how futile such things are. When the goddess did not respond, the priest suggested that perhaps a human sacrifice was necessary. The Guru at once proposed the priest himself as purest and most welcome sacrifice whereupon the poor Brāhman hastily took to his heels. The Guru then threw the remains of the offerings into the fire; in the terrific blaze he showed himself with drawn sword, crying, 'Here is the Durga who shall win us the victory!'

It was in the following year, 1699, that Gobind Singh invited all the Sikhs to come for the great annual Vaisakh Fair. On 29 March he carpeted and screened off a mound; the crowds camped there that night. Very early in the morning the Guru rose, and after his usual ablutions and devotions, he put on his martial uniform and weapons. The crowds were seated before the mound. Suddenly the Guru drew his sword, looked very fierce, and shouted, 'If there be any true Sikh of mine here, let him give me his head as a proof!' Three times he repeated the terrible invitation: then Dayarām of Lahore stood up and offered his life for his Guru. Gobind Rai led him inside the enclosure and shortly afterwards came out, his sword blood-stained. He again called for a sacrifice, his eyes and face getting redder and fiercer; and one by one the bravest of the Sikhs stepped forward to die, and he led each of them inside the enclosure, later coming out alone with his dripping sword. Meanwhile some of the Sikhs ran in terror to Gūjari, the Guru's mother, crying that her son had gone mad and was murdering all his disciples. Others simply ran away from the place in blind panic.

Then he robed the first five volunteers, Dayarām, Dharmdās, Muhkamchand, Sāhibchand and Himmat and brought them out before the crowds. He called them his 'Five Beloveds' (*panch piāre*), saying, 'Brothers, you are now in my form and I am in yours; there is no difference at all between us now.' Then he spoke to the crowds, 'These five Sikhs who are totally devoted to the Guru shall refound Sikhism and spread its fame over the whole world.' The disciples cheered and envied the favoured five.

The Guru next replaced the old custom of drinking water poured on the Guru's feet (*charaṇāmṛta*) with a new kind of nectar. Putting water in an iron bowl, he stirred it with a two-edged sword while repeating *Japji, Chaupai* and some of his own *Sawwaiyas*. At that moment Sahib Kaur, his spiritual spouse[1] whom he declared to be the mother of all Sikhs, passed by with some sweets; he told her to throw the sweets into the bowl, that the Sikhs who drank of it might be united in sweet comradeship; he was begetting his disciples, and she would be their mother through this offering. Then as he bade them, the Five, drank five handfuls of the sweetened water; five times he sprinkled the 'nectar' on the hair and eyes of each, and he taught them to repeat with each handful his new mantra: *Vāhigurūjī kā Khālsā, Vāhigurūjī kī fāteh!* He then named them Singhs (lions). He also gave them the 'Five K's' (long hair and beard, comb, short drawers, a ring on the right arm, and sword in hand), and taught them to be courageous and chivalrous, never to turn their back to a foe, never to leave the poor and helpless unaided. Hereafter their former caste was washed away, they were all brothers, sons of the one Guru, and they should look on all brother Sikhs as their own family, having no contact with renegades or apostates, with idols or Hindu shrines.

Then Gobind Singh folded his hands, stood suppliant before his disciples and prayed them to baptize him also in the same way. When they demurred he said, 'I have acted on God's order in thus making you five of the new *Khālsā* as Guru of the Sikhs; it is proper for you now to

---

[1] Professor Jodh Singh explains it thus: 'She was presented to him as his wife by her parents, but by that time in preparation for his wars he had taken the vow of *Brahmacharya* (chastity). But as the parents insisted, and the girl prayed that she did not want anything else but to be allowed to remain with him to serve him, he permitted her to do so and declared *Khalsa* to be her son.'

let me join you as one among you.' So he received baptism at their hands.

After this, he said to all the Sikhs present, 'The Lord can be seen by the eyes of faith in the general body of the *Khālsā*; taking your motto as Unity and Courage, you too may join the *Khālsā*.' The next batch of five were Rāmsingh, Devasingh, Tahilsingh, Īsharsingh and Fatehsingh, whom he called the 'Five Liberated Ones' (*panch mukte*). Thousands followed, coming up in batches of five, and the *Khālsā* grew mightily, to the great anger of orthodox Hindus who were furious at the ending of caste-slavery among so many and the uplifting of outcastes to the level of Brāhman converts. The Guru invited the Hill Rājās to join his new *Khālsā Order* but they refused and consulted together on how to deal with this new menace to their established order.

It was about this time that the Guru ordered that every Sikh household with four adult male members should give two to the *Khālsā*; thus he raised an army of 80,000 men. He gave almost daily speeches instilling brotherhood, equality, the highest bravery and ethics among the Sikhs. He also practised what he preached. He used at times to visit the Guru's kitchen in disguise, and so he learned with what contempt the cooks often treated the poor and destitute. He gave strict rules that the free kitchen should be open to *all* comers, and not only to Sikhs. He was always apt and able to teach or warn through the verses of the earlier Gurus and his own (thus he gave detailed prophecies of history up to the war of 1857-8) and approved of all songs, religious or otherwise, which did not actually lead the mind away from God. He continued with his hunting to keep his body fit, and with his recruitment of soldiers ready for the war which he knew well was imminent.

4. Last Days in Anandpur (1700-1704)

In 1700 it began. The Hill Rājās planned to destroy the Sikh power before it grew too strong; and the Emperor Aurangzeb sent armies to help them under Din Beg and Painda Khān. Gobind Singh put his Five *Piāras* in charge of his own forces. There was a fierce fight in which Painda Khān was killed. Then the rājās demanded that the Guru should pay a rent for the site of Anandpur, which he of course refused. They made two vain attempts to storm the city and then besieged it for two months. Disliking this violence in the Guru, Dunichand left him with his men, but was killed by a cobra at Amritsar. After one more sharp fight, the rājās withdrew from Anandpur for a time.

In 1701 they again got help from Aurangzeb, urged to activity by the increasing number of Sikh recruits and converts and the failure of an attempt to murder the Guru. The forces of the emperor drove the Guru across the Sutlej at Kirtipur where he rested and hunted for some time until he could quietly reoccupy Anandpur. In spite of the unwillingness of Rājā Ajmerchand, son of Bhimchand, the other rājās made peace with the Guru, but his breach with orthodox Hinduism and his continued teaching of courage against all foes, together with unity and fellowship among the Sikhs, made his enemies feel that peace would be brief.

Indeed, next year Ajmerchand renewed the war with the help of Alif Khān of Jammu; they furiously attacked Anandpur, but the attack failed when first

Saiyad Beg and then Alif Khān himself joined the Sikhs. Another attack by Ajmerchand alone also failed, and when he retreated the Guru made a total separation from all Hindu and Muslim customs alike, condemning free association with non-Sikhs.

In 1703 the emperor sent Saiyad Khān's army to help the Hill Rājās. The Guru fought with great heroism against heavy odds so that the enemy-general actually prostrated to him in admiration, but he had to evacuate the city. Yet the Sikhs soon recaptured all the booty they had lost and re-entered Anandpur. When Aurangzeb proposed peace, the Guru scolded him roundly for oppressing the Hindus and unjustly warring against the peaceful Sikhs.

In 1704 the jealous Hill Rājās again complained to the emperor that the Sikhs were disturbing the peace of the Punjab, and Wazir Khān was sent to uproot them. He besieged Anandpur with vast numbers but met with stiff resistance there, the Sikhs fighting with great valour, making many sallies and repulsing every storming-party. But a four months siege reduced them to great want and famine; the Moguls offered a safe conduct away from the city, and mother Gūjari urged the Guru to accept it. Gobind Singh knew the offer was a trap, and showed this by sending out sacks of rubbish, elaborately packed to look like treasure; they were promptly carried off. Still Gūjari harped on the idea of escaping, and the Sikhs wanted to surrender, saying that it was mad to resist such odds. When the Moguls demanded that they should all embrace Islam, the young Ajit Singh boldly and indignantly defied them.

But the food and courage of the Sikhs had given

out; the Guru asked them to wait for five days, but they refused; then he told them to go and die, since they insisted on it. Eventually, on the besiegers giving assurance on oath that the Guru would not be molested, Guru Gobind Singh left Anandpur. But the Mogul and Hill Rājās' forces treacherously fell upon the Sikhs as soon as they came out, although the Guru, with forty-five of his followers, was able to escape. In the general confusion Mātā Gūjari and two of the Guru's children were separated from the others. Still pursued by the enemy, the Guru's party entered the fort at Chamkaur, near Ropar.

Here, on the 22 December 1704, the Guru put up a gallant fight and his heroes, including his little sons Ajit Singh and Jujhar Singh, went out one by one to die. With three faithful Sikhs the Guru left this mud fortress while the two other survivors stayed behind to cover his retreat, and died there.

Gobind Singh was helped to safety by two old Muslim devotees from Macchiwāra (Malwa) in Patiala, who disguised him in the blue clothes of a Pīr. Thus he escaped to Jattapur, and while he was there he heard of his sons' fate. The little children, Fateh Singh and Zorawar Singh, were sheltered with their grandmother, Gūjari, in the house of a Brāhman at Sarhind, fifty miles off. This man not only robbed the party but betrayed their presence to Wazir Khān who arrested them all. Khān ordered the two children to embrace Islam, but they boldly refused, and then he had them most brutally buried alive under the foundations of a wall, but when the wall fell down they were taken out unconscious and butchered on the third day by the professional executioners. This was on 27 December. Their grandmother died of grief and remorse because her obstinate resistance to the Guru's word had had such terrible results. When this news came to the Guru at Jaṭṭapur, he dug up a shrub with his dagger and said, 'So shall the Turks be extirpated!'

He retired to Dina, where a faithful Sikh, Shamira, hid him and when his presence was known refused to surrender him. Here he gathered together a few soldiers and wrote his *Znfarnāmā*, a terrible denunciation of the emperor's irreligion and treachery, explaining why he himself had to resist and how he was defeated only by overwhelming odds. This letter in Persian he sent to Aurangzeb, and it makes most moving reading even today.

He was now a fugitive; moving from place to place, often refused even shelter and pursued everywhere by his foes. Near to Kapura he gave up the blue disguise which had served him so well and which was the uniform of Jhujhar Singh's troops.

5. The Closing Years (1705-1708)

With him now there were only a few companions, one being Bhai Daya Singh, yet he still refused to give up hostilities and submit to the emperor. Some of the Sikhs had even repudiated him as Guru, but now his fortunes began to mend. The forty men who had fled from Anandpur were so reproached by their women-folk that they had consented to return to their Guru under the leadership of Māi Bhāgo; near Firozpur, Wazir Khān met this tiny company at Khidrana and was repulsed. Then at Muktsar in the desert they stood up against Wazir's army and died to the last man; one of them was found by the

Guru dying on the field and begged for his forgiveness now that they had washed away their treason with their blood. The Guru tore up the list of their names, forgave all the forty and honoured them with the title the 'Forty Saved Ones', remembered in prayer by all Sikhs ever since.

Gobind Singh gathered a few more men and moved about in East Punjab for some time, until at Damdama he was sheltered by Bhai Dalla, who twice refused to betray him. At Damdama, after a short visit to Bhatinda and back, he resumed his literary work. He asked Dhirmal for the copy of the *Granth Sahib,* which had been so long in his custody, but this man rudely replied, 'You are so clever that you may as well have a *Granth* of your own!' The Guru then sat down and, from memory or by clairvoyance, dictated the whole of the *Guru-Granth Sahib* to Bhai Singh, adding his father's verses in the appropriate places. His own *Dasama Granth Sahib,* containing his own poems and the translations of the Purānas by the pundits — though many believe he really wrote the whole himself — was compiled or edited by Mani Singh at Amritsar in 1734.

The Guru wrote another protest, the *Fatehnāmā,* to the emperor against being continually harassed; his envoys were allowed to leave court safely.

With a few men, he travelled southwards, and in October 1706 he traversed Bikaner and Pushkar, hearing, while in Rajputana, that Aurangzeb had died in the Deccan in February 1707. At that time Bahadur Shāh was away in Afghanistan, and his younger brother Muhammed 'Azim usurped the throne and seized the treasury and army. As Bahadur Shāh was less well equipped, he sought help where he could. Hearing of the Guru's victories over the Hill Rājās and the imperial forces, even though at the moment his power had apparently been broken, it was clear that a word from the Guru could bring loyal and brave soldiers into the field at any moment.

So Bahadur Shāh sent his secretary, Bhai Nand Lal, who had long dwelt with the Guru and had once obtained his blessings for the prince, and asked Gobind Singh to help him obtain the throne. This cause seemed worthy to the Guru, the prince being a better man than his brother, the usurper, and he sent Bhai Dharam Singh and other Sikhs to give Bahadur Shāh all possible help.

In course of time Bahadur Shāh defeated and killed his brother and ascended the throne in Delhi. He then sent Dharam Singh to inform his ally, the Guru, of the victory and to thank him for his aid, asking him to postpone his journey to the south and visit him. Graciously the Guru moved northwards and met the new emperor at Agra, being received with all the honour due to an ally who was also a holy man.

From August till November 1707 the Guru remained with Bahadur Shāh, who was milder and more tolerant than Aurangzeb had been, and who greatly enjoyed the company of the Guru and religious discussions with him. Gobind Singh at this time hoped that by using his influence with the emperor he might initiate an era of peace and understanding between Muslims and non-Muslims, often stressing the folly of the bigotry and hatred with which they regarded one another, and pointing out several instances of cruelty shown by the Muslim rulers.

Then Bahadur Shāh had to march south, and invited

the Guru to accompany him. They travelled through Rajputana together, and on the way several Rajput rājās came to pay homage to the Guru. After passing through Jaipur, Jodhpur, and Chitor they reached Nander on the Godavari, now in Andhra State.

On reaching Nander the Guru parted from the emperor for it was here lived the man he wanted to visit. In a beautiful spot near the river was the *āshram* of a *bairāgi* named Lachhman Dev, who was known to have great occult powers and to be fond of playing practical jokes on the simple *sādhus* and fakirs who came to see him. When the Guru arrived the *bairāgi* was out and so the Guru sat on his couch to wait. One of Lachhman Dev's disciples ran to tell his Master of this sacrilege, and he came and vainly tried by magic to overturn the couch. He then fell at the Guru's feet and owned himself as *banda*, or slave, of the Guru. After he had been taught the tenets of Sikhism, he was baptized as a member of the *Khālsā*, and at his own wish his name was changed to Banda Singh, by which name he is known to history. The Guru settled down at this little town on the Godavari, sending Banda to the Punjab to kill Wazir Khān and the Hill Rājās, and to punish the Punjab Muslims who had so opposed him at every stage.

Three young Paṭhāns were deputed by the Nawāb of Sarhind to murder the Guru; one of them is said to have been Gul Khān, the grandson of that Painda Khān whom Guru Har Gobind had slain in battle. The young men went to the Guru's durbār at Nander but they found the Guru too well protected and had to go away disappointed. However, they returned day after day, no suspicion being aroused because the Guru had many

Muslim disciples. Meanwhile they were studying the situation and decided that evening was the best time to carry out their plan.

Most of the Sikhs had already retired for the night and the only man near the Guru had gone to sleep; Gobind Singh himself was sitting on his bed, and lay down to rest for a few minutes after the Paṭhāns came as usual. One of them seized his chance, sprang to his feet, drew his sword and plunged it twice into the Guru's belly; but Gobind Singh rose and with one sweep of his sword cut off the Paṭhān's head. The man's two confederates tried to escape but were cut down by the Sikhs who ran up at their Guru's call.

Bahadur Shāh was camping nearby, and at once sent his surgeon to attend to the Guru's wounds. After three or four days on his bed, the Guru tried to draw a powerful bow to its full stretch and reopened his wound. Knowing that the end of his earthly days was near, he took a little food and retired for the night. About 1.30 a.m., he rose and began to recite the Divine Word. Then he called his people and gave them calm and beautiful farewell instructions. He opened the *Granth Sahib*, laid on its pages the customary coconut and five pice, bowed before it as Guru, entrusted the *Khālsā* to God (cf. *GGS* 54: 7-9), lay down on the bier and quietly passed away to the eternal Home. He was the last personal Guru for the Sikhs.

The Sikhs were overawed at the unexpected event and were greatly distressed that they had had no chance to talk fully to the Master before he departed from their midst. They decided to cremate the Guru's body before daybreak; this was done on the fifth day of the bright half of Kārttik, Sambat 1765.

It was on Thursday, 7 October 1708 that Guru Nanak, as it was thought, ended his long incarnations in separate human bodies, which had begun in 1469, nearly two hundred and forty years before. His religion was founded, consolidated and confirmed by the blood of many martyrs, strengthened by the fierce and cruel opposition of its neighbours, organized into a brave and manly 'nation', and sent forth into the modern world to interpret the Guru's words in the changing circumstances of life from generation to generation through all time to come.

4. SIKHISM THROUGH THE GENERATIONS

1. The Dream of Revenge

Banda Singh began well the work of avenging the wrongs done to his people on which the Guru had sent him to the Punjab. Gathering an army, he soon spread the terror of the Sikh name over a wide area of the Mogul Empire.

Banda, a man of great courage and personal magnetism, was born at Rajauri in Poonch in 1670. The story goes that remorse at killing a pregnant doe led him to renounce the world and he became an accomplished yogi. At Nander he met Guru Gobind Singh who made him a Sikh but had too little time to make the conversion very deep. He gave Banda orders to maintain celibacy and truth, give obedient service to the *Khālsā,* and not start a new sect or display kingly pride. The Guru sent a letter to all the Punjab Sikhs ordering them to help him, and thousands did so, eager to fight and die in the Guru's cause. Mercenaries and outlaws also joined him, and he soon gathered a formidable army.

After killing at Banur Wazir Khān, the murderer of the Guru's two little children, Banda marched on Sarhind with 40,000 men. He entered the guilty town on 30 May 1710 and for three days there were fearful scenes of looting, forced conversions, and massacre. Banda Singh Bahadur was now the Hindus' recognized protector, at all time ready to help them against the Punjab Muslims. He also punished the treacherous Hill Rājās, and ravaged the whole province with fire and sword, destroyed towns, put whole populations to death from Lahore to Panipat. Delhi was in a panic and would have fallen had he attacked it immediately and the whole empire would have been at his feet.

Then, on 10 November, came his first defeat at Amingarh. He took refuge in the Lohgarh fort and when that fell he fled disguised as a *sannyāsi*. The Moguls took revenge for his depredations by killing thousands of Sikhs in batches during 1712-1713. When Bahadur died there was confusion in Delhi, and Banda again took to raiding and burning towns in 1714. But, defeated at Kota Mīrzajān, he had to retreat to the incomplete fort at Gurdaspur. Here he held out bravely in a siege but had to surrender in 1715. He was taken fighting in a sally from the fort; 8,000 of his 10,000 men fell in battle and the others were martyred in daily batches of a hundred, competing eagerly for the honour of giving their lives for their religion. The scene, graphically described by British envoys, was perhaps the first glimpse of Sikhism given to the West. They record that not one man bought his safety at the price of his faith. Banda Singh himself was chained in an iron cage, forced to cut the throat of his little son, and was then torn to pieces with red-hot pincers.

He had done his work, though in it we can find little of the real spirit of the Gurus, nor can we help deploring his quarrel with the *Khālsā*, which led so many of the Sikhs to make a treaty with the Muslims in return for the safety of Hindu temples and the cessation of forced conversions to Islam.

2. The Glories of Martyrdom and Resistance (1716-1750)

In 1714, Ala Singh, one of the great Sikh warriors of this age, became ruler of the Phulkia *misal*,[1] which belonged to Phul's family; in 1716 Chajjia Singh, a convert of Banda's, turned freebooter and founded the Bhangi *misal* I, and in 1718 Jassa Singh Kalal, who founded the Ahluwalia *misal*, was born in a brewer's family. We shall hear more of these later.

With the fall of Banda began a most savage persecution of the Sikhs. All were outlawed; it was death for any Hindu to wear long hair or a beard; twenty-five rupees was the reward for the head of a Sikh, and five to ten rupees were given for information leading to an arrest. Flying columns up to 10,000 strong scoured the country to hunt them out; many reverted to Hinduism; many fled to the hills and forests, and while they wandered, eating roots, wild berries and fried grain, their families were tortured to death. Hundreds were killed daily, no mercy was shown, and until 1724 the surviving Sikhs lay in hiding. Then they began to form

---

[1] A sort of democratic military state

bands for guerrilla war and plunder, to punish traitors and persecutors.

In 1725, the two parties of Banda'is and *Tatwa Khālsā*, almost came to waging civil war at Amritsar. But as both honoured Mātā Sundari, she sent Bhai Mani Singh to reconcile them. It was decided by lot that the *Khālsā* should control the temple and so the Banda'is were driven out.

In 1726 a flying column was chasing the Sikhs here and there, but in time they grew stronger; it was that year when Ala Singh defeated a Rajput army and took its weapons, and in 1730 the Sikhs captured the whole imperial treasury on the road to Delhi and fled with it to the hills. Next year they raided the country up to the very gates of Lahore; there they suffered two repulses and gained one success. Ala Singh defeated Nawāb Asad Ali's forces and was joined by many Sikhs eager to plunder and punish their persecutors. In 1733 the Muslims tried to divide them by concessions and bribes; they offered an estate worth a hundred thousand rupees, more or less in jest, to Kapur Singh, a fan-puller; so he became a Nawāb, founding the Singhpuria *misal*; he converted many low-caste people, killed many Muslims with his own hand, and died with the reputation of sanctity in 1753.

The courage of the Sikhs inspired the timid Hindus to greater boldness. In 1734 Hakikat Rai of Waḍāla, a boy of fifteen, was angry when his classmates ridiculed a goddess and in return abused Fatima, the Prophet's daughter. He was arrested and ordered to embrace Islam, but bravely refused. The Lahore court sentenced him to death in spite of the pleading of great crowds, and the Nazim confirmed the sentence, offering life and wealth if he would recant. Even his mother tried to persuade him, but he was firm, and died like a hero, beheaded in the centre of the city.

That was the year Bhai Mani Singh, who lived quietly at Amritsar, revised the *Granth Sahib*, rearranging its songs according to the Guru-authorship; but the *Khālsā* rejected this innovation and imposed a penalty on the saintly man. The Sikhs were now divided into older and younger groups, the latter again into five sections, all settled near Amritsar and entrusted with the defence of the religion. In 1735 the Muslim governor cancelled Kapur Singh's estate and he took to the usual guerrilla warfare; the *Khālsā* resumed its raids but was driven across the Sutlej. In 1736 they suffered a defeat at Basarke, but two other bands won another fight, and desultory war went on. The Rajputs were now freed from the Mogul rule, and the Mahrattas under Bāji Rao menaced Delhi in 1737; the empire was breaking up under a series of weak rulers on account of its exotic character and the quarrels among its officials.

In 1738 Bhai Mani Singh asked for leave to hold the Diwali Fair, agreeing to pay five thousand rupees afterwards. Thousands of Sikhs responded to his call and came, but when the Lahore ruler sent large bodies of troops they feared treachery and withdrew, so there was no fair. Mani Singh was nevertheless ordered to pay the money or embrace Islam; he refused to give up the Sikh faith, and his friends brought the money too late; he was cut into pieces. Soon after this the Lahore authorities desecrated the Amritsar temple with parties of dancing girls; this was in 1740.

There was another great martyrdom in 1745; Shahbaz Singh, a Sikh boy, refused to accept Islam at his Muslim teachers' order. They tried to make his father use pressure on him, but he refused to help, and both father and son were broken on the wheel and died bravely for their religion.

The Sikhs had a great raiding centre at Derah Bābā Nānak on the Ravi, whence they attacked Nādir Shāh's army laden with Delhi spoils. Two thousand of them from Emīnābād began to raise funds from the villages and looted Divan Jaspat Rai's sheep, killing the Diwan himself. Lakhpat Rai sought revenge and defeated them near Jammu, slaying all his prisoners near the Delhi Gate in Lahore. Another terrible persecution followed. Muinuddin (Mīr Mannu), governor of the Punjab, destroyed the Sikh fort at Ramrauni, martyred hundreds of Sikhs daily at Shahidganj in Lahore as they were betrayed to him by the Hill Rājās, and forcibly shaved hundreds more, so that surviving Sikhs fled to the Basohli Hills and the deserts of Malwa. There was a time of confusion, when Mannu, Lakhpat Rai and the Afghan Durrani were up and down in turns, but all were enemies of the Sikhs and did what they could to destroy them. But the Sikhs hit back hard; when Durrani fled back to Kābul from his defeat at Sarhind, Jassa Singh Kalal fiercely harassed his rear and built a fort near Amritsar with the loot; so also Ala Singh built the new fort at Bhawanipur. Once the Sikhs raided Lahore itself and burnt the outer city, but this success was followed by a more brutal persecution than ever so that all the Sikhs there were slain or driven into exile.

Thus during these thirty-four years we see the Sikhs

on the one side enduring terrific persecution, and on the other side fiercely hitting back at their foes. Their growing power is ascribed by Narang to the Iranian invasion by Nādir Shāh, the weakness of the Delhi emperors and the rulers of Lahore, many of whom incited the Sikhs against one another, the rise of the Mahratta power, and the inspiration given to the whole community by the courage of its martyrs.

3. The Sikhs Take Power (1751-1799)

Muinūddin (Mannu, 1748-1752,) defeated the Multan governor and now became practically independent; he defied Ahmed Shāh Durrani, but was defeated in six months' fighting near Lahore; yet the Afghans left him in power there even after they took the city, and on his death his wife succeeded him in office. Adeena Beg had routed the Sikhs at Makhowal, but they soon resumed their depredations; in 1752 Ala Singh captured Patiala and made it his capital, building there a strong fort. Next year died Kapur Singh, the 'Nawāb' who had formed the *Khālsā Dal*, the first regular Sikh army since Banda's days, and shown the way for other Sikh leaders to follow and carve out kingdoms for themselves. His successor, Khushal Singh, added much territory and converted many to Sikhism.

The next Afghan invasion in 1755 stormed Lahore, Delhi, Agra and Mathura, but the Sikhs harried Ahmed Shah's army as it retired homewards, the Durrani leaving his son Taimur in charge of the Punjab. Taimur promptly destroyed the Ramgarh fort at Amritsar, and in 1757 the great temple of Amritsar itself, filling the holy tank with its ruins. Adeena Beg and his friend Jassa

Singh of Ramgarh conquered Jullandhar from the Afghans, defeated Taimur and then retired. Joined by thousands of eager Sikhs, Jassa Singh Kalal of the Ahluwalia *misal* marched on Lahore and collected the taxes of its suburbs for himself. That same year Ala Singh defeated a Mogul army; the Sikhs were poised for victory and empire.

Next year, 1758, the Sikhs entered Lahore; Jassa Singh became king there and issued Sikh coinage for the first time. Adeena Beg called some Mahrattas to help him, but the Sikhs were able to plunder Sarhind before Raghoba's Mahrattas arrived; these took Lahore, Multan and Attock almost without resistance. The Sikhs were now raiding in all directions; with the forced help of Muslims they repaired the shrines of Amritsar. For a short while Adeena Beg troubled them, but on his death they immediately rose again, and in 1759 the Mahrattas fled before the returning Afghans of Ahmed Shah.

Meeting at Amritsar in 1760, the Sikh armies again attacked Lahore, burning its walls, looting the city, and taking a tribute of thirty thousand rupees from its people; they also overran the districts of Amritsar, Gurdaspur, Ambala and Ferozpur. When Ahmed Shāh totally broke the Mahratta power at Panipat in 1761, the Sikhs built forts at Lahore, Gujranwala and all over the Punjab as soon as Ahmed Shāh withdrew as usual every year. In 1762 they obtained their first cannon.

There followed a confused period of about six years, Sikhs, Afghans and Punjab Muslims alternating in power, with a kaleidoscopic series of changes in the boundaries of the Sikh *misals* or states. In 1762 the Sikhs held their first *gurmatā*, or religious council, at the rebuilt Amritsar; after the Ludhiana slaughter in 1763, the Afghans again swept down upon Amritsar, blowing up the temple and desecrating the tank and shrines, slaying many Sikhs and washing the walls with their blood. But the Sikhs rose again as soon as they passed on, sacked Kasur and Malerkotla, totally destroyed Sarhind again, and brought under their control all between the Jumna and the Sutlej, together with Saharanpur. They now began to feel themselves to be one nation and entitled to rule in the Punjab. The defeat at Kalanaur in 1764 was at once wiped out by the recapture of Lahore, city and fort, and they once again restored the temple at Amritsar. In 1765 the Sikh religion was declared to be paramount in all the Punjab, coins being struck in Lahore by Rājās Lehnā Singh and Gūjar Singh of the Bhangi *misal II*; that same year Ala Singh died. During the usual Pathān invasion in 1767 the Sikhs had to withdraw once again from Lahore, but they at once returned, and in 1768 stormed Rohtas and advanced their boundaries to the River Indus. The Punjab was now a confederacy of twelve Sikh states (*misals*) or military kingdoms.

These *misals* were ruled by chiefs with the good will of their followers who formally elected them. National affairs were settled by *gurmatās* at Amritsar, meeting before the two *Granth Sahibs* after prayer, each group sitting behind its leader and speaking through him; resolutions were always discussed until unanimity was reached, usually on the views of the most respected leaders. Such meetings could take place only when all the Sikhs present were 'one in the Guru', willing to agree in the interest of the common Sikh causes. The soldiers were like feudal retainers and could change their masters at will; they used sword, spear and musket; they wore turban, shorts and tight slippers, while their chiefs had chain-armour, steel helmet, and breastplate. Their flag was of saffron colour and their war-cry *Sat Sri Akāl* ! They fought by skirmishing, breaking off for their meal of chapatti or parched grain; they followed as far as possible the Gurus' chivalrous rule of giving water indiscriminately to all the wounded and burying or burning the dead according to their own rites. Booty was equally divided, and the chiefs imposed light taxes upon all trade. They treated the peasants fairly, dividing produce with the cultivators on a fifty-fifty basis; a panchayat in each village settled all civil disputes, while criminal cases were judged by the chief who took his own reward from each side Fines were the usual penalty, being graded by the wealth of the convicted and largely replacing capital punishment, though mutilations were not unknown. There was no poor law; guests were a common charge on the whole village, and the indigent were given food and clothes from the funds of the local temples.

In 1772 Hira Singh of the Nakai *misal* took Pākapattan, while Jhanda Singh of Bhangi *misal I* at last stormed Multan with the help of traitors; and in the following year Jai Singh of Kanhia *misal* took the Kangra Valley. The Sikh kingdoms were extending their area, but at this time began another period of internal war, the states competing with one another for pre-eminence. In such times it was natural that little attention was paid to Sikh theology, and most of the converts thought of little beyond baptism and taking up the sword to war upon the enemy and thus gather wealth.

Education also sank to a low level and many Sikhs were really hardly in any way different from the Hindu masses around them, following the same degraded practices and holding the same superstitious ideas. In 1778 Jassa Singh Kalal annexed Kapurthala and took the title of King; he was a very brave and generous man, once rescuing girls abducted by the Afghans and sending escorts with them to see them safely home. He was the first to issue his own coins, and it is from him that the recently ruling house of Kapurthala is derived.

In 1780 at Gujranwala was born one destined to be the first Sikh emperor, Ranjit Singh of the Sukarchakria *misal*. There was a quarrel in that same year over the booty of Jammu, and in 1785 Jai Singh of Kanhia *misal* conquered the province for himself.

By this time, the Sikhs had altogether a total of from two to three hundred thousand cavalry; had they united, they could easily have swept over all north India, but they were still too parochial for that and quarrelled among themselves instead. So when Ranjit Singh, the 'Constantine of Sikhism', who came to his throne in 1792, really turned his attention to his neighbours, their thrones came toppling to the ground at his feet. Jai Singh of Kanhia was succeeded in 1789 by his daughter-in-law Sada Kaur, who ruled the state wisely until 1820; in 1790 Gīan Singh of Nakai *misal* prudently married his sister to Ranjit Singh and so became a friend of the rising star. Other states continued their fratricidal struggles to the end.

4. The Sikh Empire (1799-1849)

The beginning of that end came in 1799 when Ranjit

Singh captured Lahore, expelling Chet Singh of Bhangi *misal II*, and was recognized by the Afghans as king. Up to 1800 we learn that all the Sikh states together had only forty cannon; they still fought mostly on horseback, and when George Thomas, the Irish adventurer, was at the court of Sahib Singh of Patiala, he reckoned they had altogether about 60,000 cavalry, lightly armed and quite without military discipline. In 1802 Ranjit Singh took Amritsar, and Gurdit Singh fled from there to Tarantaran. Jassa Singh of Rāmgarhia *misal* died in peace in 1803, and five years later his successor Jodh Singh quietly became a vassal of Ranjit Singh. After the battle of Ludhiana in 1806, Sahib Singh of Patiala came under his control, and on the death of Kharak Singh in 1807 Nakai *misal* was also absorbed and Faridkot taken. Next year Nishanwalia was added, and at this time almost the whole of the Punjab, with areas also beyond its boundaries, formed a single state under Ranjit Singh's imperial rule. It was his idea, in fact, to replace the Mogul Empire with one under Sikh control, and so to complete the liberation begun by the Gurus.

It was the crossing of the Sutlej to Ludhiana in 1806 which led to his first rebuff. The Sikhs of Jind soon regretted calling him in and appealed to the British who, in 1809, forced a treaty on Ranjit Singh declaring the Sutlej to be his frontier and letting him keep only police forces to the south of it. That was the year when Ranjit Singh employed French officers lent by Napoleon to complete his fort of Gobindgarh at Amritsar and to introduce military discipline in his army, though not with very great success. It was the important year also when he abolished the practice of holding political *gurmatās;*

he also began to consult non-Sikhs about his political measures. Teja Singh has pointed out that this was in order to make all his subjects feel they had a place in his kingdom, and that they all—Sikhs, Hindus and Muslims —formed one nation of the Punjab and owed a common loyalty to a common throne.

The year 1812 is noted for the issue of J. Malcolm's book, *Sketch of the Sikhs,* wherein he tried to be fair and pointed out the weakness of disunion which underlay the outer show of Ranjit Singh's power. In 1818 his general stormed Multan after a siege, taking it from Muzaffar Khān of the Afghan Kingdom, who fell there with his five sons. In 1819 Misr Chand defeated the Pathān governor of Kashmir, Jabbar Khān, and Ranjit Singh annexed Kashmir to his empire. By 1823 he also exercised rule over Bannu, Peshāwar and beyond Srinagar, though his actual sway often did not extend far beyond the forts. That year, 1823, was also important for the issue of Bhai Santokh Singh's *Nanak Prakāsh,* dealing with the life of the Founder in Gurumukhī verse.

In 1829 Sawanmal was made the governor of Multan, and the empire enjoyed some years of comparative peace, though we are told that the Muslims did not enjoy much prosperity under its rule. In 1834 Ranjit Singh had a paralytic stroke, due in part to his excessive drinking of alcohol; in 1835 Ferozpur lapsed to the British, and in January 1837 Hari Singh Nalwa was killed in the most gallant defence of the Jamrud fort against the Afghan army of Dost Mohammed. In December 1838 the Maharājā gave permission to the British to advance upon Kābul through his territory and in the next year, 1839, Ranjit Singh died at the age of fifty-nine.

Certainly he was a great man, of great ideas, but he lived in an age when the growing power of the British made those ideas impracticable. He made Sikhism kingly, giving costly jewels, gold, estates and precious canopies to endow and adorn the temples, yet we are told he was always, even in his proudest days, proud to serve the poorest Sikh in the *sangat*, or the religious meeting. But, like Constantine, he was poorly instructed in the religion he professed; at his death Hindu ceremonies were performed along with the Sikh rites, and he even caused queens and concubines to be burned with his dead body in the cruel rite of *satī*.

His empire did not stand after him. Kharak Singh, who followed him, was a man of poor understanding, and he died in the next year, 1840; his son Nāunihal Singh was returning from his father's funeral when a gateway fell on him and killed him (November 1840). After that Sher Singh took the throne and ruled until he was murdered in September 1843 by the Sindhanwalia Sirdars, being succeeded by the infant son of Ranjit Singh, Dulip Singh, in whose reign the real power lay with Rājā Gulāb Singh of Jammu.

That tragic year was marked, more happily, by the issue of Bhai Santokh Singh's second and greater book, the *Gurpratap Surya*, usually known as *Suraj Prakāsh*. This is a sort of epic, giving the lives and teachings of all the Ten Gurus, in beautiful Gurmukhi verse, which is said to excel the beauty even of the *Rāmāyana* and *Mahābhārata*. It is quoted by orthodox Sikhs as having almost canonical authority and is the source for much of our knowledge. It is probably based largely on oral tradition among the *giānis*.

In 1844 Sawanmal was shot, and his son Mulrāj succeeded him as the governor of Multan. The Rānī was always inciting the Sikhs to war with the British, having no idea of their resources, and in December 1844 the Sikhs crossed the Sutlej in force at the Harike Ford. The British at once declared war and annexed everything to the south of the Sutlej; the first battle at Mudki on 18 December was defensive, but four days later the Sikhs, after a fierce battle, were driven from their trenches at Phirushahar. In the middle of January 1846 the Sikhs won a slight success at Badowal, but on 26 January they were defeated at Aliwal by Sir Harry Smith, who had only half their strength; Ranjodh Singh was outgeneralled and, bravely as they fought, the Sikhs had poorer discipline and could not stand before the British fire. They were driven over the river, lost ten thousand men and all their guns. On 10 February they were again routed at Sobrāon; there was a terrible slaughter on the collapsed bridge, few escaping and none surrendering. The war ended, the British annexed the Jullandhar Doab, and gave Kashmir to Rājā Gulāb Singh when he paid a war indemnity of seven thousand five hundred rupees; he had to resist both a Hindu and a Muslim claimant to the province before it fell to his dynasty. For the rest of the Punjab a Council of Regency was set up, advised by the Resident in Lahore, Sir Henry Lawrence.

Trouble began again on 20 April 1848 when some European officers were murdered in Multan and the Sikh soldiers and people rose under Mulrāj to throw the foreigners out. After skirmishes at Rāmnagar (22 November) and Sadulpur (3 December), Multan was stormed by the British on 2 January 1849. On 13 January Gough fought a drawn battle at Chiliānwāla on the Jhelum, where the Sikhs had the advantage and won back some of their lost guns. But Gough took command and, reinforced by troops from Multān, on 21 February totally routed the Sikhs at Gujarāt on the Chenab, after no more than one hour's severe conflict. They were chased to Rawalpindi, where the whole Sikh army surrendered. Then Dalhousie deposed the nine-year-old Rājā Dulip Singh and annexed the Punjab. The short-lived Sikh empire came to an end with little glory beyond the praise given by an Englishman that they were 'the bravest and steadiest enemy ever encountered in India by a British army'.

5. Under the British (1849-1947)

The Lawrence brothers, and later Sir John alone, took over the rule of the Punjab; they reduced land taxes, introduced the usual neutrality towards religions other than Christian mission work, built a chain of forts along the frontier, disarmed the people, improved communications, opened many village schools and courts, and succeeded in winning the general satisfaction of the people whose condition certainly improved greatly above what they had known in the days of incessant war, rapine and massacre.

This wise policy bore fruit in 1857 when almost the whole of North India was in revolt against the British in support of what began as a mutiny of Indian soldiers. Though there was a certain amount of unrest even in the Punjab, so that small risings took place at Peshawar, Multan and other places, Nicholson's flying column was easily able to disarm the men there, to secure the arsenals at Ferozpur and Phillaur, and to pacify the country, so that his forces could soon be moved to Delhi and help to take the city on 20 September 1858. This was made possible largely by the attitude of loyal support to the British yielded with open heart by the vast mass of Sikhs in the Punjab—a loyalty for which they were noted to the last days of British rule in India.

In 1849, soon after the annexation of the Province, J.D. Cunningham brought out his *History of the Sikhs*, a praiseworthy attempt to display the truth about those who had so lately been the fierce enemies of the writer's own people. The country was at the time in a strange position. Under Ranjit Singh, whose idea was purely autocratic, democratic functions had little place and the Sikhs gradually lost their instinct for them. This, as Teja Singh says, really hurt the community more than the persecution of earlier days; political *gurmatās* had been abolished early in his reign, and the religious *gurmatās* began to degenerate because those who issued them were mostly illiterate fanatics. Many of the temples were still in the charge of *Sahijdhāris*—Sikhs who had not accepted baptism or the outward emblems of the cult lest they bring on themselves a martyrdom for which they were unprepared; these men gradually lost what little they had known of Sikh doctrine and in effect lapsed into Hinduism. The maharājā regularly consulted Hindu astrologers in fixing auspicious times, and in many other ways conformed to Hindu practice; Sikhism was becoming, even among the *Khālsā* members, largely a matter of fashion in turban and beard. Under Ranjit Singh no central association like the *Sarbat Khālsā* was possible; as the numbers of Sikhs increased their zeal was diluted. When they lost even what political power they had held, and their lands came under foreign rule, they were for the time so depressed that they all but abandoned interest in their religion altogether.

Now from the time of the Tenth Guru, as Teja Singh says, 'there was no room left for any wavering on the borderline. All who would want to serve humanity through Sikhism must join it seriously as regular members and receive its baptism as the initial step....Changes for the worse have always synchronized with the lack of insistence on the baptismal vows. This was in the days of the Sikh rule, when luxury and power tempted our people to consider the vows too hard for them. They lost their identity as Sikhs and became as superstitious about God and his worship as they had been before the time of the Gurus. With the modern revival the Sikhs have found themselves again.'

At first both Hindus and Muslims were being converted almost equally, but as Mogul resistance and tyranny increased it became more and more difficult for the Sikhs to recruit any save Hindus; their constant fight for existence prevented them from giving proper teaching to the converts and these gradually corrupted the whole with their old Hindu ideas. But under Ranjit Singh many Muslims were converted, partly for social and economic reasons, and many *Khālsā Sikhs* did hold to their own Sikh customs and beliefs. The British so admired the courage of the Sikhs that they showed definite sympathy with them after the conquest; devoted Sikhs found that in the British army they could maintain the *Khālsā* vows intact, so many Sikhs enlisted, and their regimental panchayats kept up the tradition among them. In this way the swing towards absorption into Hinduism was checked.

Baba Rām Singh started the *Nāmadhāri* movement, largely as a protest against the luxurious materialism of the Ranjit era. This stressed great simplicity, with an inner life based on hymns and meditation, and discouraged lectures and philosophy thus checking the drift towards Vedanta.

At about the same time was founded the *Nirmalākhārā*, with its motto *ride giān, mukh bhagati, vartan vairāg*—'wisdom in the heart, devotional love in the mouth, unattached behaviour'. These Nirmalas traced back their spiritual ancestry to the first five whom Guru Gobind Singh sent to Banaras: Rām Singh, Karam Singh, Ganda Singh, Vir Singh and Sobha Singh. They had their own central office and several branches in different parts.

It was in 1872 that the Sikh revival may be said to have begun. The spread of English education and knowledge of western ideas of scholarship and democracy led the Sikhs to start many small *divāns*, where they could meet together for discussion. They came to realize that Sikhism would perish altogether if it were allowed to merge into the Hinduism around it, and although they could not yet form one authoritative body which would govern all the affairs of the community, they started in Amritsar in this year the Singh Sabhā which proved the source of many things.

In 1875, Swami Dayānand Saraswati founded the Ārya Samāj, and two years later toured Punjab with his lectures, founding branches there. Giāni Dit Singh stood up as the champion of Sikhism against this Hindu propagandist; in debates and lectures and by his book, *Dambha Nivāran*, he urged that Hindu elements be cast out of Sikhism and the pure doctrine of the Gurus be taught everywhere.

That year, 1877, also saw the first attempt of a European scholar to give the world the teachings of the Gurus. Dr Trumpp, a German missionary, had studied the *Granth Sahib* under Atmā Singh, a Nirmala *sādhu* of Amritsar, for seven years, and now produced a translation of about one-third of the book. But his work has been universally disapproved because of his hostile bias; he took every opportunity to misrepresent and to belittle the Guru and the Sikh religion. However, this proved an encouragement to those who dreamed of raising Sikhism to be a worldwide religion; in 1879 the Singh Sabhā was reorganized on stronger lines in Lahore. Also about this time Rājā Bikram Singh of Farīdkot got scholars to print the whole *Guru-Granth Sahib* with voluminous comment-aries according to the orthodox tradition of the *giānis;* this made it far more possible for scholars to study the Book all over the world.

Meanwhile the British rulers were planning great things to increase the wealth and prosperity of the Punjab, wherein the Sikhs had a full share of the benefits and so acquired the means of establishing schools and colleges of their own. In 1882 the British opened the Great Sarhind Canal, drawing the waters of the Sutlej at Rupar through Ludhiana and the Phulkia States to irrigate the southern half of Ferozpur District.

In 1887 Tara Singh, who was inspired by his patron Rājā Narindra Singh, published his important book on

Sikh doctrines, the *Gurmat Nimāi Sāgar*, the first effort in Punjabi to produce a solid work on Sikh theology. In 1889 the Singh Sabhā was renamed the *Khālsā Divān*; this later gave off a branch, the *Chief Khālsā Divān of Amritsar*, which has done very much to educate Sikhs on western lines, to awaken in them pride and keenness for their own religion, and to break them off from Hinduism.

Another great forward move was taken in 1894 when Dr Charan Singh of Amritsar, Sādhu Singh, and other scholars joined to form the Khālsā Tract Society, long ruled by the saintly Dr Bhai Vir Singh; this society has flooded the Punjab with cheap reprints of parts of the *Guru-Granth Sahib*, many of them with translations and commentaries, together with other historical and literary treasures of the early days of their religion. Each is on sale very cheaply, many being issued in serial form. Books also have been published, such as Rūp Singh's *Sikhi Mārga*, in 1916. The Sikh Tract Society, formed by a few graduate Sikh scholars, tries with missionary zeal to do the same in English; it has published many pamphlets by Dr Teja Singh and by Sardar Sardul Singh Caveeshar on historical and exegetical topics.

But Swami Rāma Tīrtha (born near Gujranwala in 1873) became a *sannyāsi* in 1899 and almost at once filled Punjab with his ecstatic poems, recalling many Sikh hymns from the *Granth Sahib*; this drew people towards Hindu Vedanta and its influence continued till the swami's accidental death by drowning in 1906.

In 1900, the British opened the Lower Chenab Canal, irrigating more than 2,500,000 acres of dry land and greatly increasing the wealth of West Punjab. Next year the Frontier Province was separated from the Punjab, bringing many Sikhs there under a different government. During these years Kahan Singh's books were appearing, increasing the gulf between the Sikhs and Hindus and insisting on the total independence of Sikhism from all other religions.

The year 1909 is one which Sikhs and Europeans alike will have cause to bless. An officer of government had resigned his work some years earlier to give his whole time to a sympathetic study of Sikhism and Sikh history. In 1909 Mr M.A. Macauliffe, taught by orthodox *giānis,* published his six large volumes, which will always be remembered as the real foundation for all later study of Sikhism in western languages. Though he did not translate the book entire, he gave a fair and favourable view of its contents under the heads of the various authors, in many cases showing how the hymns arose in different circumstances of their life. The book received a sort of imprimatur as substantially correct from some of the leading *giānis* of the day, though his pessimistic view of the future of Sikhism has now little likelihood of coming true; knowledge of the religion is no longer dying out. Indeed, some such *giānis* still wander about the countryside with their disciples, teaching people as they go.

More or less on Nirmala lines, Khazan Singh in 1914 published his two volumes on the history and philosophy of the Sikhs. But many of the Singh Sabhā members devoted themselves to the special work of Gurdwārā reform, aiming that those in charge of the temples be men able not only to teach the religion but also to live it; even up to this time most of the Gurdwārās were still in the control of *Udāsīs* and *Sahijdhāri Sikhs.* These reformists started a great agitation through the press and on many platforms that all such Hinduized guardians of temples be removed and that orthodox *Khālsā Sikhs* be put in charge, that the Punjabi language be taught everywhere to enable a wider knowledge of the Guru's words, and that the Sikhs organize themselves as a nation. They formed themselves into what was called the Akāli Movement, which soon put Nirmala books and all semi-Hindu customs and doctrines out of vogue.

During the four years of the 1914-1918 world war, the Sikhs won further admiration all over the world through their heroism in battle, their loyalty and discipline, their faithfulness to their own customs; indeed they and the Gurkhas almost seemed to aim at a monopoly of Victoria Crosses at one time. It was with pleasure to the British, then, that in 1917 the Triple Canal Project was opened; this carried the surplus water of the Jhelum to the lower Bari Doab, irrigated more than 2,000,000 acres, and reclaimed a huge extent of waste land.

After the war came the non-co-operation movement, with the horrible shooting atrocity at Amritsar in 1919; the Sikhs played a heroic part in the national upheaval then led by Gandhiji. At the same time they were waging a great fight of their own; they tried, at times by force, to get possession of the temples and to drive out the unworthy *mahants* who held them. In 1921 Lachhman Singh, Dalip Singh and 130 other Sikhs were killed at Nankana Sahib (Talwandi) by a Mahant Narain Dās, and in 1922 many Akālis were brutally beaten in the Guru-ka-Bagh. The Akāl Takht passed a *gurmatā* that there should be no meeting with the government until all

Sikh prisoners were released, so the Sikhs could not discuss the proposed Gurdwārās Bill openly and were forced to negotiate indirectly and in secret. Teja Singh held that *gurmatās* must be only religious, not social or political, in a country where non-Sikhs also live; for example, the adoption of the Punjabi language for East Punjab was not a purely Sikh affair. At last in 1925 the Gurdwārās Bill became law, the Akālis gained most of the shrines, and obtained a central body for communal government; peace was restored.

In 1926, about ten miles east of Pākapattan, were opened the head-works of the important Sutlej Valley Project, and next year the Bikaner Gang Canal irrigated 1100 square miles from Ferozpur to Shivpur; Punjab had never known such irrigation, and swiftly increased in prosperity and in population; by 1930 there were 19,555 miles of canals in the province.

The Khālsā Tract Society issued in 1927 the important *Sri Guru-Granth Kośa*, which for the first time enabled outsiders to make effective study of the scriptures; not less important some years later was Dr Sahib Singh's *Gurbāṇi Viākaran; Gurmat Nirṇai* came from Bhai Jodh Singh in 1932, showing the general teachings of the Guru by arranging hymns under certain heads. Since that time there has been a constant flow of books in Punjabi, Hindi, Urdu and English, many scholars enriching the literature with their studies in various parts of the *Guru-Granth*; Dr Sher Singh's *Philosophy of Sikhism* in 1944 also marked an era.

In the second great national struggle of the century launched by Gandhiji in 1930 the Sikhs again played some part; perhaps one who captured the imagination and inspired the masses of the whole of India was young S. Bhagat Singh, leader of the revolutionaries, who was hanged with two Hindu comrades at Lahore in 1931 under disgraceful circumstances. So, too, while thousands of Sikhs fought in Africa and elsewhere along with other soldiers of the Commonwealth, winning fresh laurels of glory by their heroism during the war of 1939-1945, others, such as General Mohan Singh and many Sikh soldiers, stood by Babu Subhaschandra Bose in his Independence Government abroad, and fought for freedom round Imphal in the Manipur Hills. After the first two days of savage massacre in Calcutta, launched by fanatics on 16 August 1946 in the vain hope of driving all non-Muslims from the city, the Sikhs stood side by side with the Hindus in repelling these assailants who had the open sympathy and help of the then Bengal Government. Yet they rescued 5000 Muslims and 20000 Hindus from dangerous positions and fed them side by side in their local Gurudwārā Jagat-Sudhar. So, too, when on the partition of the Punjab a mass slaughter of non-Muslims began in the western half of the province, the Sikhs were the first to rally in defence of their own women folk and of Hindus, and indeed took a bloody revenge which would have satisfied the soul of Banda Singh Bahadur himself, could he have seen it. Happily, peace then supervened.

In 1953 the Sikhs in Calcutta formed the Sikh Cultural Centre which through its English monthly, *The Sikh Review*, and in other ways, is doing much for the spread and maintenance of the religion in many lands.

And now what is their future? Their holy land is cut asunder, half of its shrines lost to the community in hostile territory where Sikhs hardly dare go as pilgrims;

Talwandi, Lahore, Punja Sahib are among the holy places lost to them. Most of them lost their valuable lands and had to flee as refugees to Delhi, Bombay, Calcutta — wherever they could find a living. The most heartening thing we can say about them is that nowhere have they shown the least inclination to despair or beggary; they energetically started tiny and growing businesses where their resources were small, and opened bigger affairs where they had greater funds; the streets of Delhi were filled with their stalls where everything could be bought. The army, navy and air force of India are full of them; almost every driver in Calcutta is a Sikh; we can hardly go anywhere in India today without the eye falling on a member of the *Khālsā*. As a Sikh friend said to me in 1950, perhaps unconsciously remembering Guru Nanak's remark about the friendly village (p. 24), 'God has scattered them over India so that they may carry the manly spirit of the Guru everywhere and plant it in every Indian heart'.

He may be rich or poor, clever or of little mental brilliance, the true member of the *Khālsā* can always face life with confidence and courage, for he feels himself equal to 'a lakh and a quarter' (*savā lākh*) so long as he is united to the Guru as a faithful son of Guru Gobind Singh.

5. SRI ADI GURU-GRANTH SAHIB

1. Reverence to the Granth as to the Guru

The *Guru-Granth* is the Guru's own book, through which he speaks to his disciples from age to age. Thus it is also called *Gurbāṇi* the 'Guru's voice'; he who attentively reads, sings, or listens to its hymns is brought into direct personal contact with the Guru, who is in a very real sense 'incarnate' in those hymns. Guru Arjan bade the Sikhs regard it with the same reverence that they regarded the Guru's own person, and on his passing from their visible midst the Tenth Guru declared that he could be found in its hymns if diligently sought.

Thus it must always be natural and proper for the Sikhs to show outer reverence to the Holy Book wherein they find by their own experience the living Guru in their midst. A like reverence is shown by the Jew who stands when the scrolls of the Law are brought in and bows when they are opened by the reader, and by the Christian who stands to hear the Gospel read. An even greater reverence is shown by the Vaishnavas when the *Jnāneśwari* and the *Bhāgavata* are taken in procession, and even the Muslim takes care that the Holy *Korān* is kept covered from dust and no other book is allowed to lie upon it. As Dr Sher Singh says: 'The *Granth* contains the word of the Guru, and its worship by the faithful Sikh should not have much of an unhealthy influence of an idol. He always expects some good counsel from the book,' just as the disciple finds the most profound and inspiring teachings in his Guru's lightest words.

It is a habit, therefore, with many – a habit shared by men all over the world with their own scriptures – to open the book haphazard and to take the first verse seen by the eye as the Guru's counsel at that time. It may be 'superstitious', or it may not be, but experience shows how very helpful such consultation often is in pointing out the better way. Before the *Guru-Granth Sahib* is read, a short prayer is offered, and the reading usually commences from the beginning of the stanza at the top left corner of any page where the book opens. So also names are chosen for new Sikhs by taking one beginning with the initial of the first word on the page whereat the Book first opens.

The *Granth Sahib* is to be regarded, and therefore treated, as the very body of the Guru himself. Thus it is always kept in a clean silken cloth on a raised 'throne', is opened under a canopy, and a fly-whisk is constantly waved over it while it is being read. Those who enter the special room, or the Gurdwārā, where it is kept, should have just bathed, put on clean clothes, and covered their heads; before taking their seat in its presence they bow to it as to the Guru. But no lights or incense are to be waved before it, no flowers offered as to an idol, nor are bells to be rung in worship; worship in the true sense, is due to God alone in his own proper person, and no Sikh can be a bibliolater.

Yet it may be true here and there that, as Dr Sher Singh says: 'The *Granth* is taking the place of an idol among the illiterate Sikhs.... A Sikh finds a great artistic satisfaction in beautifully clothing the *Granth*, making a luxurious bed for it in a well decorated room, offering flowers to it and washing the floor of the room in which it is kept. But a faithful mind goes further and expects that in doing so he is performing a deed which is inherently good and which will help him in attaining the salvation in the Vaishnava sense.' Of course, such practices, understandable as they are, constitute a part of that relapse into Hinduism against which the whole modern trend of Sikhism, like the original mission of the Gurus, is an open protest.

I have called it 'understandable', for where there is

love in the heart it must crave to express itself in outer actions; where love becomes intense, emotional, those outer expressions may easily run to excess. The true Sikh sees in his *Granth* not merely a *book* written by his Guru, but he was taught by that very Guru to see himself in it, and in its words to find the life-giving teaching of his utterance. The Book is full of the beloved name of the Guru, almost every stanza ends with a verse containing it; it is not strange then that Puran Singh writes: 'There is a fragrance of roses as we name Nanak. While writing about him I have felt the shower of rose petals on these pages and the perfume of the Golden Temple all about me. When I was sitting in my room, miles away from the country of roses, and when the season of flowers was passed, their fragrance was still there. Name *Nanak* and the Mystic Rose returns.' He also says: 'Many of my Sikh sisters...have told me that they have found more than all the world could give them in Nanak's songs.' How can the disciple fail in his love and reverence for a book containing such a treasure?

It is customary for pious Sikhs to sing or read the *Japji*, the *Jāpu Sahib*, and Guru Gobind Singh's ten *Sawwaiyas* first in the morning, though many prefer to start the day with the *Sukhmani*. In the evening the *Rahiras* is taken, with a *Chaupai* of the Tenth Guru, and part of the *Anand*; at night, before sleep, the *Kirtana Sohila*. Friends and relations read the *Sukhmani* for the dying, and during cremation the *Sohila*, reminding all that what we call death is but the night, and that day follows on its darkest hours. The *Anand* is recited at deaths, marriages and all such ceremonies.

2. *The Nature of the Guru-Granth*

The *Granth Sahib* is a collection of devotional hymns and prayers. In it there is little of explicit philosophy or ethics; both can be deduced from countless scattered references. It is hardly an exaggeration to say that the Guru assumes these in his Sikhs, although he does not hesitate to insist on them from time to time. The philosophy, so carefully and skilfully described by Dr Sher Singh, differs little from that of Vaishnavas, save in its total rejection of incarnations, idols and caste, nor does the Guru teach the mechanical repetition of any word or phrase on the grounds of it being God's Name or full of magical power. As Dr Sher Singh says, it may indeed be regarded as a merging of Advaita Bhakti (more or less as found in the *Jnāneśwari*) with Sūfīsm. The ethics of the Guru differs in no real sense from that of every other true religion, stressing as its fundamental sanctions the law of karma and the pleasing of God as the better motive; it teaches that no happiness can be found save in that blissful Lord of Love.

In literary form and content the hymns closely resemble those of the Hindu devotional saints, many of whose songs the compiler included in the Holy Book. They recall much in Tukārām's *Abhangas*, in the Hebrew Psalms, in the Manichean Psalms found in Coptic, and in the Protestant hymnaries of Christianity. We may note several resemblances to the Song of Solomon, Jayadeva's *Gīta Govindam*, and to other mystical works. There is of course much repetition, but this does not weary the reader because of the fiery sincerity and devotion which blaze out from every line of the hymns.

We are told that in the *Granth* there are 3,384 hymns,

consisting of 15,575 stanzas, two-fifths of which were written by the Fifth Guru and one-fifth by the First; my copy covers 1,430 pages and is a volume $10\frac{1}{2}$ by 9 inches size. All the ten Gurus contributed to it save the sixth, seventh, eighth, and tenth; Guru Gobind Singh wrote the *Dasama Granth*, which we shall glance at presently. Guru Arjan also included hymns by a number of Muslim and Hindu saints, whose chronological order is thus given by Sher Singh: Jayadeva, Nāmdev, Trilochana, Paramānand, Sadhna, Beni (?), Rāmānanda, Dhannā, Pipa, Sain, Kabīr, Ravidās, Farīd, Bhikkan and Sūrdās. We have passages from almost all of these in our 'Gospel'. A hymn of Mīrābai was first included and then later struck out by the Guru; it remains in Bhai Banno's edition, together with a few other 'apocryphal' hymns from the first Guru Nanak. These devotee-poets cover the period from about 1150 to four hundred years later. Then there are various *Sawwaiyas* in honour of the first five Gurus, written by various bards, of whom Sher Singh counts seventeen: Mathra, Jalap, Bal, Harbans, Talya, Salya, Jalya, Bhal, Kalh Sahar, Kal, Jal, Nal, Kirat, Dās, Gayand, Sandrang and Bhikha. One Sundar wrote the *Sadd* in Rāmkali, and in the same *rāg* the bards Satta and Balwand wrote the *Coronation Ode;* there are also hymns by Mardana. Thus forty-two authors in all are represented in this Holy Book of the Sikhs.

3. Arrangement of, and Reference to, the Granth

Dr Sher Singh gives us the reason for the hymns being arranged according to *rāg* instead of by author, date or subject. It is in order to stress the essentially aesthetic element in the Guru's 'Word' — music for the first time perhaps playing the dominant part in religion, though the Prophet Mānī certainly made it important in his. He tells us that the special note of Guru Nanak's religion is wonder; he calls it a *viśmāda-mārga* (path of wonder), a way to God through admiring delight in his greatness, in the wisdom and beauty of his universe, and in his dealings with men. It is more akin to the rapture of the nature poets of the West, to the awe and reverential love which sweeps the heart of the astronomer as he gazes through some great telescope into the unfathomed vastness of space, to the ecstasy of the mystic who finds God in a shining dewdrop and holds the universe in a flower.

For convenience in picking out quickly the hymns suited to certain moods, they were grouped in the thirty-one *rāgs,* or musical modes most of which are represented in our own selection. Under each *rāg* they are thus arranged; *chaupadas* (hymns in four-line stanzas), *ashtapadis* (hymns in eight-line stanzas), *chhaṇts* (six-line stanza hymns), special short poems, *vārs* or odes (consisting of one or more *ślokas* and one *paulai*), and before the *chhaṅts* came special long poems, like *Sukh-mani;* at the end of each *rāg* the hymns of non-Sikh devotees are arranged in the same order. In addition, the musical clef *(ghar)* in which each hymn is to be sung is often given.

In this book for convenience, all references to the *Granth Sahib* are given in brackets after the passage, thus: First comes the initial of the author's name, in capitals; **N** (Nanak, Mohala I); **A** (Angad, Mohala II, etc.); **AD** (Amar Dās); **R** (Rām Dās); **Ar** (Arjan); **T** (Tegh Bahadur); **G** (Gobind Singh); **K** (Kabīr); **F** (Sheikh

Farīd); **Nd** (Nāmdev); **Rd** (Ravidās); **D** (Dhannā); **B** (Beni); **J** (Jayadeva); **S** (Sadhna); **P** (Pipa); **Ra** (Rāmānanda); and **SB** (Satta and Balwand).

Next comes the name of the *rāg* and its subdivision, as *Āsa Chhaṇt* or *Gaurī ki Vār*, printed in italics; or the names of special hymns, which will be found in the following *rāgs*: N. *Sidh Goshti* and *Dakhni Oamkār*, which will be found in Rāmkali; N. *Barah Maha* in Tukhari Chhaṇt; and N. *Alāhaniā* in Vadhaṅś; AD. *Anand* in Rāmkali; Ar. *Barah Maha* in Mājh; Ar. *Sukhmani* and *Bawan Akhari* in Gaurī; Ar. *Ruti Śloka* in Rāmkali; and Ar. *Phunahe* at the end of the Book; K. *Bawan Akhari* in Gaurī. The clef (*ghar*) is given in Roman numerals where it is stated: e.g. (R. *Āsa* II, 2:1).

Last comes the reference to hymn number and verse number. The *Sawwaiyas* are quoted under the name of the Guru to whom they refer, and the verses are given consecutive numbering; it should not be hard to trace these few references.

Little use has been made for this 'Gospel' of the *Sri Dasama Guru-Granth Sahib* of the Tenth Guru, outside the *Akāl Ustat* and the *Vichitra Nātak*, the former a sublime hymn to God, the One worshipped by all true religions but unknown to sectaries, and the latter an autobiography of Guru Gobind Singh. References are given by the name of the author and the hymn, with the number of the stanza; e.g. (G. *Akāl Ustat* 86) and (G. *Twaprasādi Sawwaiya* 2).

Passages from elsewhere derived only from Macauliffe's *The Sikh Religion* are thus quoted, e.g., (1:34 N), (1: xli AD), (5: 243 G), which will be found respectively on page 34 of his first volume under Nanak, on page xli of the introduction to that volume, and on page 243 of his fifth volume under Gobind Singh. These passages, not being traced to canonical scriptures, are printed in italics also.

With respectful diffidence I would beg my Sikh friends to adopt some such clear way of referring to passages in the *Granth Sahib* in the future. It is not enough merely to refer to the *rāg* and *Mahala*, as 'Guru Amardās in *Vār Gaurī*', nor even to the page number of some particular edition of the book in their personal possession. All scriptures need some such easy mode of reference which enables a text to be quickly traced in the original even by one who is not a profound scholar of its contents.

6. THE KHĀLSĀ PANTH

1. Admission

One is not born a Sikh, even if born into a family of Sikhs. After a child is born a friend recites the *mūla-mantra* (*GGS* 2:3) and touches its tongue with sweetened water on the point of a dagger (*kirpān*); the mother later gives thanks in the Gurdwārā, and the *Guru-Granth* is read, the name of the child, boy or girl, being chosen as we have seen (p. 119). 'Singh' is added to the name of a boy, and 'Kaur' to a girl's. Part of the *Anand* is recited, *karah prasād* (made from flour, sugar and ghee) is made by stirring with a ladle and then given to all present after prayer has been offered, and it has been consecrated with a dagger.

Later comes the ceremony that is almost parallel to Christian Confirmation, when the Sikh fully enters the

Panth and assumes all its privileges and duties. This is called the *pahul* or the 'Amrit-rite', and it closely resembles Guru Gobind Singh's original initiation of the *Panch Piāre* at the birth of the *Khālsā* in 1699. Five Sikhs in good standing represent the first five members of the Panth, while the candidates, including new converts, come forward after bathing and putting on the 'five K's' (*panch keśa*) These are keśa (uncut hair: symbol of the saintly devotee), *kanghā* (comb: symbol of discipline and order), *kacchā* (shorts or drawers: symbol of activity in service), *karā* or *kangan* (iron ring on right arm: symbol of self-control in action) and *kirpān* (sword or dagger: symbol of courage and self-respect). Their heads must be covered with a turban or shawl, and they should wear no ornaments or signs of other religions—for Awat Singh Mahtab Singh thus defines a Sikh: 'Anyone who solemnly declares that he believes in the Ten Gurus and their teachings, and that besides the Gurus and *Granth Sahib* he does not recognize any other binding authority in religion, should be called a Sikh.' The candidates stand meekly with folded hands.

One of the five sponsors then recapitulates the essential doctrines of Sikhism, emphasizing that it is primarily, as Awat Singh says, 'a discipline of life and not a philosophy'. It is a way to the One God through loving memory of him while busy in the selfless service of his world. When the candidates declare their faith, the *amrit* is prepared as it was by the Tenth Guru; sweetened water is stirred with a dagger in an iron vessel, portions of the scriptures are read, and one by one the candidates receive five handfuls of *amrit*, in their mouths, hair and eyes, while the *Khālsā mantra* is being repeated; the remnant of the *amrit* is drunk straight from the vessel by all the candidates in turn, symbolizing their brotherhood. Then all repeat the *mūlamantra* five times and one of the *piāras* administers the vows of discipline (*rahat*) to the neophytes, who have now become full disciples of the One Guru, true 'Sikhs', members of the Khālsā Panth (sect of the purified), and heirs of its splendid traditions.

2. *Responsibilities*

Membership of any human society requires the keeping of certain rules arising from the nature of that society. At his initiation (*pahul*) the Sikh undertakes certain vows and obligations which mark him out from all non-members of the Panth. Let us consider some of these for a moment:

(1) He promises never to be at any time without the *panch kaka,* which the Guru chose as the uniform of the Khālsā.

(2) All ideas of caste, of polytheistic deities and non-Sikh customs and rites are repudiated.

(3) He will abstain from the four *kurahāts* (misconducts): the shaving or cutting of hair or beard, eating meat killed in the slow way used by Muslims, adultery, and the use of tobacco or intoxicants in any form.

(4) Nor will he commit any *tankhāh* (penal offence), such as associating with apostates, dyeing or pulling out white hairs, giving or taking cash dowries, using drugs or liquors, revering non-Sikh shrines or tombs,[1] raising monuments over the dead. A Sikh who does any of these

---

[1] Guru Gobind Singh was himself once fined Rs. 125 for saluting a shrine with his arrow, which he did as a test of his Sikhs.

things must confess in public before five *piāras* of the nearest local *sangat* (assembly) and faithfully do the penance they impose. Those who indulge in a *kurahāt* become apostates (*patit*) and have to receive initiation afresh after their penance has been performed.

(5) He will obey all regular *gurmatās* (decrees) and *hukamnāmās* (religious edicts) issued by an authorized meeting of the collective Panth at one of the four *Takhts* (thrones): Akāl Takht at Amritsar, Patnā Sāhib, Keshgarh at Anandpur, and Hazūr Sāhib at Nander in the Deccan. Appeals against the voice of any *sangat* lie in the Akāl Takht, whose decision is binding on all Sikhs.

(6) He is expected to train his own spiritual life by frequently reading and meditating on the *Granth Sahib* and the *Dasama Granth*, by regular personal prayer, and taking an active part with other Sikhs in the religious and social life of the local *sangat*. He will also serve all in need, irrespective of caste or creed, beginning with cheerful menial work in the Gurdwārā and the Guru's Kitchen, to the expenses of which he is expected to give what he can.

(7) He is to observe the *anand-form* of marriage after full maturity is attained, and at death his body is to be cremated or thrown into flowing water with the usual Sikh rites.

Above all, he is never to forget that he is a member of the body founded by the Guru himself, to behave at all times with an eye to its honour and reputation, to look on all fellow-members as his brothers and sisters, and to strive ceaselessly to become worthy of the great honour conferred upon him by becoming a member of the *Khālsā*.

3. Privileges

It is hard in a few words to sketch the privileges of a man or woman who enters upon the *Khālsā Panth*; they are so numerous and some so subtle that only a deep spiritual insight reveals them. A few stand out as obvious:

(1) He becomes a member, a part, of the Guru's own Body in the world, through whom the Guru works upon mankind, leading it to God. The Guru himself said: '*Khālsā mere rūp hai khās*' (The *Khālsā* is my very form); what strength, what courage, what inspiration, to know that this is true!

(2) He becomes an integral member of the noblest and bravest of religious groups in the world, sharing their great wealth of heroic and saintly tradition.

(3) He finds in every other Sikh a real brother or sister, ready and willing to serve him even to the sacrifice of life.

(4) Through the Guru's spirit imbued in every sentence of the Holy Book he is guided to the highest knowledge and love of God wherein alone is true peace and enrichment of the soul. This fullness of intuitive understanding cannot be gained from it by any non-Sikh, however sympathetic he may be.

4. On the Use of Outer Symbols

The Guru, in his first form as Nanak, inveighed against the external show delighted in by yogis and *sannyāsis* and even by caste-proud Hindus, displaying *namam* and sacred thread corresponding to no inner reality, with their ceremonial 'eating-squares', their offerings to the dead, their ritual pilgrimages, and filthy *prāyaśchitta*—some have wondered therefore why the Tenth Guru established the rite of *pahul* (initiation) and imposed the 'Five K's' on all who would henceforth be accepted as real Sikhs.

It is true that one may be—in a certain restricted sense like the *sahijdjāris* and many 'Sikhs' who form a part of Hindu or Muslim society as Vedantins or Sufis —a disciple of the Guru by meditating on the *Granth Sahib* and on God's omnipresence, serving him by the humble service of mankind. But as Lakshman R. Pāngārkar says in his valuable Hindi life of Tukārām, if one would truly enter into the spirit of any *sampradāya* (community) one must gladly embrace all the elements of its life, all its disciplines and modes of training; for the system of each *sampradāya* is a reasoned and scientific whole, whereof one picks and chooses by his own taste to his own loss and impoverishment.

The Guru imposed these outer signs of a Sikh: (1) as a test of the disciple's courage and firmness; it cost something to proclaim oneself thus visibly a Sikh when Sikhs were hunted down to torture and death. Thus the wearing of long hair trained men in courage, in being ready at all times to be martyrs for the faith, and thus greatly increased their love and faithfulness for Sikhism. When laxity in such things creeps into any community, their faith grows cold; (2) so that Sikhs might know one another at once in any place and be sure of meeting brothers wherever they might go. The Freemason's signs have the same purpose today; and (3) the wearing of a common uniform strengthens *esprit de corps*, binds each individual to be morally worthy of the whole, creates a pride and a sense of participation in the work of his brothers of the same society.

It may be that, as Dr Sher Singh tells us: 'As time rolls on the shift of emphasis is becoming more and more on the external appearance of a Sikh than on his inner purity. Intolerance and a narrow outlook on life are the natural consequences.' Lakshman Singh adds: 'Baptism was (at first) wholly voluntary and never meant for all Sikhs, but now it is imposed on all converts and real belief in Sikh ideals is not asked for—so false conversions are common. Yet on the whole Sikhs do lead in social reform, and Punjab Hindus gain much from contact with them and the *Granth*. Sikhism should once again be widely taught and spread on all sides to uplift the whole nation.'

That is, of course the remedy for any such pharisaical lapse to which all human rites are liable as time passes on. More education, the printing and distribution of portions of the *Granth Sahib* for a few coppers each, with translations into modern Punjabi and Hindi, and an explanation from the standpoint of daily life, the adoption of the Punjabi language in Gurmukhī script as the official language of at least East Punjab, for which Master Tārā Singh and the Akalis agitated, the organizing of regular missions among the Sikhs to popularize the beauties of the Guru's hymns and to recruit men and women to spread the knowledge and love of them far and wide are necessary. Such activities will, under the blessing of the Guru in the *Granth* and *Khālsā*, be a sure defence against the growth of any such superstitious reverence for outer signs while forgetting the inner reality, and will lead the Sikhs to that high place in Indian thought and life which they so fully merit, so that in a purified and revitalized Panth it may soon come true that '*Rāj karega*

Khālsā' (the Khālsā will rule), and then we shall live in a real '*Rāma-rājyā*'.

7. A FEW BRIEF NOTES

1. The Name of God

Dr Sher Singh made a thorough study of the Names of God in the *Granth Sahib*. He classifies these Names under various heads; those which we shall meet in this book are noted here.

Historical Names

Hindu: Bhagavān, Bishan, Brahm, Gobind, Gopāl, Gosain, Hari, Isara, Mādho, Murāri, Pārabrahm, Prabhu, Raghurai, Rām — of which the favourite are: Hari, Rām and Prabhu.

Muslim: Allāh, Karīm, Rabb, Rahīm, Razāq, Sāhib.

Sikh: Mitu, Piāra, Pritam, Vāhigurū.

Attributive Names

Ek Oamkār, Anek, Kartār, Khāliq, Karan-Kāraṇ, Hukami, Mūl, Tek, Adhar, Jagajivan, Prāṇādātā, Prāṇa-pati, Nirguṇa, Sarguṇa Mālik, Paramjot; Ātma, Sarabjot, Sarabnivasi, Nere hi te Nera, Bhogi, Khalaq, Ape-āp, Sohang; Tat; Bhugta, Nirlep, Niranjana, Abhogi; Agama, Agādha; Sat, Sachu; Purakh, Akāla-purakh; Kamalanain; Mīr, Shahanshāh; Nirankār, Anīl, Akāla-mūrat, Ajūni, Abināsi, Achala; Abhed, Bharpur, Ached, Nirākar, Sai-bham, Amolak; Sāgar, Dariāo; Ādi, Anādi, Beanta, Eko-veśa, Akāl; Adeśa, Sarba-biāpi, Haduri, Dana, Antarjāmi; Sukh-sagar, Shahj, Guṇatās, Guṇinidhān, Anand, Binodi, Amrit; Dīna-dayāl, Anatha-nāth, Dayāl, Datar, Dukha-bhanjan; Patita-pāvan, Bhāgatavatsal; Bābā, Pitā, Mātā,

Kānt Khasam, Bhai, Mitar, Satiara, Sakha; Piru, Piāra; Nirbhau, Nirvair, Abhul, Adol, Achal; Pavitra, Punita; Deva, Guru, Sat-Guru; Sundar, Manamohan, Sohna; Rājā, Patshāh, Sachā-patshāh; Asipan, Sarba-Loha; Thākur; Alekh, Akarama.

The multiplicity of His names is well summed up by the supreme name of Anām, 'the Nameless'.

2. *Nāma-Mārga or Nāma-Simran*

Dr Sher Singh points out how false is the idea held by most European and Sikh scholars hitherto that the 'repetition' of the Name meant for the Guru the mere utterance of one or more of these or other 'names' of God with the lips. That would have been the teaching of mere magic, of gross superstition, and Guru Nanak called such use of the 'beads' a hypocritical show (cf. AD. *Gūjari*, 4:1); this 'remembering' of the Name is not a muttering with the tongue as so many think, but a communion in the heart (cf. N. *Mālār* 6:2 and R. *Mālār* 7:3).

What, first of all, is the 'Name'? Professor Teja Singh calls it 'the manifestation of God or his attributes, his bounties, his mercies, from which we know him'; Dr Sher Singh says: 'In short, *nām* is the sympathetic and aesthetic communion of man with man and with environments.' It is 'as much of God's real Being as he sees fit to reveal from time to time to his devotee'. 'A body is dead without life and a life is dead without *nām*', says Sher Singh it is 'the link of the finite soul with its parent Infinite God', so that even 'an animal is much better than a man without *nam*'. This self-realization of God 'does not come from without, rather it goes out from within' the heart; and it is when the heart of man loves, comes into an affectional relationship with the outer world, that is with God in his creation, that *nām* manifests in him, and then a feeling of ecstatic unity with the whole universe of which he is a part leads to the man realizing God both in his own body and in the universe as a whole.

This realization requires no book-knowledge in the practitioner, it calls for no meditation or special training in yoga, but yet it affects his entire life and raises it to a new and higher octave of experience. It can be spoken of only in part as the aesthetic enjoyment of beauty and reverential awe or wonder (*vismād*), in a state wherein God, universe and self merge, as it were, in one sense of delighted admiration. All three become that wonder and all three enjoy that wonder (cf. N. *Āsa dī Vār* 1 Sl.3). Now this practice or *sādhana* requires one outstanding qualification — a sensitiveness to beauty akin to that of the great poets. It expresses itself in an involuntary cry of 'How lovely that is!' or simply, 'Wonderful Lord!' (*vāhigurū*!) To such an ecstatic all the universe is pure and good and full of beauty and wonder. Others may divide things into ugly and beautiful, and select from them for their own purposes, but the *vismādi* makes no such dissection of the world; to him a toad, a fungus, the workings of the excretory organs are as wonderful as divine, as the loveliest flower or sunset. The true scientist also comes near to this concept; he, too, takes all he finds, dispassionately, as the material out of which nature has been built, and finds all of equal interest and beauty.

At first such moments of ecstatic realization of God in the all are necessarily rare; the devotee has to practise them — to practise the repetition of them — thus 'remembering' God's 'Name'. As Teja Singh tells us: 'To practise *nam* means to practise the presence of God by keeping him ever in our minds by singing his praises, or dwelling on his excellences.' This, however, does not limit us to spoken words of praise; the aspiring love of admiration for God is itself enough. Sher Singh says: 'Such an attitude is to be made permanent. This is what is called the continuous remembrance or repetition of the name of God.'

The soul in such a state will be found ever active in his own proper work for livelihood (*kirt*) and in service of others (*sevā*). He will not flee from one form of God (the domestic life) to another (the forest), knowing that God is everywhere where he would have us be, and that he places us just there! When this becomes a permanent, unbreakable feeling of delighted union with His will, His beauty, His providence, His sovereignty, we have what the hymns call *liv* — an ecstatic oneness. It is by being busy in the world about God's work, without forgetting him but working in his Name and memory, that man becomes a *brahmgiāni*, a *jivanmukt* or *panch*, and so attains the object of his earthly life.

Then the egoism which has been a screen between him and the beauty and glory of God's world falls away; 'I' changes to 'Thou', and God is seen in all; selfishness becomes impossible and sin disappears, so that even the subconscious mind is purified and the dream-life is suffused with God. This is not an easy, quick path to tread, for it involves a total change of personality even down into the unseen strata. Love for God becomes more and more direct, simple, instinctive, like that of the child for its mother's milk, of the fish for water, of the flower for sunlight and rain. And it is the gift of God's grace, not earned by human merits; so we have to pray humbly to him for success in our search of him.

3. The Living Guru

Most great religions and reforms backslide from the high ideal given by their Founder almost as soon as he is dead. Different interpretations of his meaning arise in various groups of the disciples; there is no one universal authority to resolve them and so they harden with time into sects and heresies, while the masses lapse back to some extent into the marsh from which they had been rescued, renaming their countless old gods as angels, and rationalizing their superstitions by the names of sciences.

As Teja Singh points out, this could not happen in the case of Sikhism, because (1) the Founder arranged that he in person should teach, direct and train the young church or nation for 239 years after his birth in 1469, and (2) he contrived to continue the same control and guidance even after 1708, though personally invisible, through the *Granth Sahib* as inspiring the properly organized *Khālsā* itself. This continuity of Guru Nanak's life, passing from one body to another of the Ten, 'as one lamp is lighted from another' (Guru X), has been the certain faith of Sikhs from the beginning (cf. AD. *Sorathi ki Vār* and SB. *Rāmkali ki Vār*). It was clearly declared also by Bhai Gurdās in 1610 in his *Vārs* (24:1:X *Stanzas*), by Mohsin Fani in his *Dabistan-i-Mazahib* (ii, p.253) in 1645, by Bhai Nandlal in his *Jot Bikāsa* in about 1692, while about the same time Bhai Kesar Singh wrote in his *Bansāvali-nāmā*: 'Consider all the Ten Gurus as Baba Nanak.' The testimony of the

Tenth Guru himself in his *Bachitra Nātak* (cf. *GGS* 52) puts the matter beyond dispute for all Sikhs. When the Guru realized that the Sikhs had become able to lead themselves with his guidance veiled, he passed on the 'light' received from Guru Nanak to the *Khālsā*, which then became the mystical body whereof the Guru's 'Word' in the *Granth* is the living spirit.

At first sight this idea may seem strange to European readers, but Dr Sher Singh has pointed out how closely it resembles the doctrine of the continuity of life among certain high Tibetan lamas. Much is told us of this by Alexandra David-Neel in her remarkable book *With Mystics and Magicians in Tibet*; it is a striking fact that ever since the death in 1470 (the year after Guru Nanak was born) of Gedundub, disciple of the great reformer of Tibet, Tsong-khapa, his successors ruling the Gelugspa (yellow-cap) sect were recognized as his 'reincarnations' from the time of their accession. Nearly two centuries later, the fifth of these, Lobzang Gyatso, declared that he himself was actually an incarnation of Chenrezigs (Avalokiteśwara), while his teacher the Tsang-panchhen-rim-poche (Tashi or Panchhen Lama), was similarly a reincarnation of Odpagmed (Amitabha Buddha); from that time the continuity of life in the Dalai Lama and Tashi Lama is a matter of history. This is a case of the soul of a saint or great man passing at will from body to body (*paradehapraveśam*). Nanak may well have acquired the power to do this from the *siddhas* with whom he stayed in Tibet. The idea is also not entirely unknown, we are told, among the Sūfīs and even in certain *maths* of Hindu schools. It is a curious fact that the Guru was much in contact with the disciples of Gorakhnāth, pupil of

Matsyendranāth, who has often been identified with the same Avalokiteśwara.

Teja Singh points out how valuable is such adaptability of the interpreter and ruler of a community to changing circumstances which the doctrine we are considering confers. Of course, it is a sort of parallel to the Catholic doctrine of the Church as Christ's Mystical Body, perpetually guided by the Holy Spirit, when gathered in regular Church Councils, through the universal sense of the faithful or teaching bishops, or by the Pontiff when proclaiming a doctrine of faith and morals for universal acceptance. When a religious body has no such provision for continuity, it is laid open to constant splintering into new sects which form with every generation. No such sects can exist in Sikhism, for those who differ from the *Granth* or the *Panth* cease to be Sikhs at all. At the same time with this capacity to adjust to the new needs of changing society, there is in the *Guru-Granth* the unchanging Word to hold Sikhs for all time to the fundamental truths first given by the Guru.[1]

4. On the Originality of Sikhism

Orthodox, modernists, and foreigners have differed

---

[1] It is a rather curious fact that 239 years after his birth in 1469, the *Khālsā* took charge as Guru, and 239 years after the beginning of this second era, in 1947 it was called to take its place in a free India, its holy land was rent asunder, its members were scattered all over the country as perhaps they never were before. This happened soon after the great revival of Sikh studies, Sikh national pride, and the popularizing of Sikh scriptures at a higher level, as during the 30's and 40's of this century, than ever before.

on this point, the most absurd claims being put forward by some to the effect that the Guru was a crypto-Muslim, a disguised Christian convert, a clever compiler of eclectic ideas, and the like.

But we have simply to ask ourselves whether the Guru was sincere or false when he claimed to be saying just what God taught him (cf. *GGS* 3, 4, 53; also N. *Tilang* 2-3-5, Ar. *Suhi Chhant* 3, and *Bachitra Nātak*, etc., etc.). Accepting the sincerity of these and countless other similar statements scattered throughout the Sikh scriptures, we are left with no. alternative to admitting the essential originality of the Guru's teaching as received direct from God through that intuitive realization of truth which he himself called the Name. History shows that, however clever it may be, no eclectic philosophy has survived much beyond the generation of its invention, yet the personal influence of Guru Nanak on his disciples is certainly no less today than it was two hundred years ago and may even be growing warmer and more devotional. Professor H.G. Kumar has also shown evidences from the *Japji* that Guru Nanak had direct vision and experience of the realities of the inner planes, that he had clairvoyant powers, and the same is told of most of the later Gurus by contemporary historians. Such men do not build up their doctrines from the collated accounts by others for they have no need for such tortuous methods. The early lives of Guru Nanak agree in describing his commission as received direct from God, much as was the case with Isaiah, Zarathushtra, Muhammed, and most other prophets in human history. This, too, has always been the view of the orthodox Sikh.

Dr Sher Singh has made a thorough study of this question and, on the whole, considers that a middle position may be tenable. Of course, the Guru spoke to Hindus and Muslims of his own day; had he been born in Western Europe, he would have used the phrases and ideas current there, but that would certainly not prove that he was indebted to Christianity. Even today the Sūfī and Vedantic preachers in the West have had to clothe their doctrines in terminology familiar to their hearers, as above all others perhaps the Manichean missionaries did in their days—assuming Parsi, Buddhist, Chinese, Jewish, Gnostic, or Christian guises according to the environment in which they worked. Yet they did not preach Buddhism or Christianity, but the teachings of the Prophet Mānī.

It is the same with all. Sikhism arose in India out of the sea of concepts known vaguely as 'Hinduism' whipped to a storm, as it was, by the violence of the Muslim impact. The Guru spoke to both Hindu and Muslim audiences; to some he spoke in Persianized Punjabi, with words redolent of the Korān, to some he spoke in Samskritized Punjabi, with words recalling the Purānas, the *Gītā* and the Upanishads. He arose as the climax of a great religious and social reform among Hindus, led by the Vaishnava saints and poets—a reform of liberalization, of personalization of God, of a great simplification of religious life and thought, discarding many of the absurd exaggerations of caste and ritual, and concentrating on the loving service of a God of love. Side by side with this was the timeless group of forest anchorites, yogis, *siddhas*, with whom the Guru came in close contact and engaged in controversy, pointing out the extravagance in some of their ways and practices, insisting on the omnipresence of God at home as much as in the forest. He clashed also with the narrow bigotry of the Muslim leaders of the time, the sheikhs and mullās; he shared in delightful spiritual comradeship with at least one great Sūfī of the Chishti line, Sheikh Ibrahīm.

Among all these influences he kept to the truth received, as he held, from God direct; he wandered in many lands, not to learn but to teach that truth. If he met Christians in Travancore or Buddhists in Ceylon, this does not show that his doctrine owes anything to either even where it coincides with theirs on certain points. It is as absurd to say the *Granth Sahib* reveals the Christian Redeemer as to say the *Gītā* is the effect of Christian missionary influence. The Guru may have picked up words and phrases here and there from those with whom he spoke; he may have woven these into the pattern of his revelation; but the teaching he gave the world was won 'from his own undisturbed communing with nature, his own soul and with his Creator' during those days of solitary brooding in his childhood and early youth. Sikhism is not a reproduction of earlier religions, but a profound modification of them, so profound that it cannot critically be regarded otherwise than as a new revelation altogether.

Hinduism: It is correct to say that this is a culture rather than a single religion; it is the culture of the whole Indian people. Sikhism is of course Hindu in so far as it is Indian in origin, yet even in the time of the Third Guru the Hindus recognized it as quite separate from their own creed, and a little later Fani, of Muslim origin, declared it to be separated equally from Islam. Guru Nanak, though often referring to the Purānas, does not show any clear proof of having read any Hindu scripture for himself, but seems rather to rely on hearsay such as he would have acquired from the Hindus with whom he talked. It is really absurd to suggest that Guru Gobind Singh's Purānic stories, told to awaken courage in his Sikhs, imply in any way a relapse into Hinduism, nor does his elaborate play at the sacrifice to Durga show any such thing either. His teachings may be said to have a certain relationship to those of 'Hinduism', much as the teachings of Christianity arose out of a Jewish environment and to some extent reflect its higher ideals.

Islam: Mirza Ghulām Ahmed, in his *Sat Bachan*, (1911) is quoted as putting forward the extraordinary claim that the *Granth Sahib* is simply a sort of commentary on the *Kurān esh-Sharif* and that Nanak was simply a Muslim preaching Islam to the Hindus. Those of the Guru's own day evidently had other ideas when they so ruthlessly persecuted him and his disciples for many years! Indeed the *Granth* shows little sign of the Guru having direct personal knowledge of the contents of the *Korān*, or indeed anything beyond what he could well pick up through casual conversations with Muslim divines (*udāsīs*) during his preaching tours. To say that he owed his knowledge of monotheism to Islam is impossible to anyone acquainted with the teachings of the Vaishnava devotees of his age. His hatred of idolatry and the outer show made by so many Hindu caste-men was only such as is shared by spiritually minded men everywhere in many ages, and was by no means unknown among the Hindus themselves; Ekanāth got into serious trouble for so totally ignoring caste rules as to treat untouchables and Brahmins the same — which is indeed implied by the basic teaching of Vedanta.

That Guru Nanak may have personally contacted the Sūfī Ibrahim and even the Vaishnava Kabīr, whose teachings are so close to his own that many of his hymns hold an honoured place in the *Guru-Granth*, does not mean that he became in any sense a disciple of either of them; it is far more likely and in harmony with the records that he met them as an equal friend or devotee. Indeed, there is no evidence that he met Kabīr at all, and as Sher Singh says, his humility was such that he would surely have referred to such a meeting had it taken place. The date of Kabīr is under dispute; most scholars favour 1440 to 1495, while Sher Singh and a few others put it earlier, from 1398 to 1443; it certainly cannot be claimed as long anterior to the age of Guru Nanak himself. But even the later date would make a meeting unlikely; Kabīr was wandering through the plains of north India at the same time as the Guru was travelling in the same area, but that in no way suggests that a meeting was inevitable — the area is large. The differences between the two men are also not to be ignored in considering the possibility of either having been a disciple of the other.

So, we come to this. The Guru taught in a certain environment and had to clothe his teaching in words which that environment could understand; he had himself indeed arisen from out of that environment, and his own earliest visions of the truth had been received within it. But he taught what he had received from 'God' through direct experience of the truth. Without a careful study of the nature of inspiration, which is so different yet none the less real in the Hebrew Prophets, the visions of the greater Gnostics, the hymnists of the Rig-Veda and the nature poets of the West, it is impossible to analyse the real sources of Sikhism as it comes down to us from the Guru in his *Granth Sahib*. It is enough for us to take it as it is to hear the lovely music in the truths he sang, to try to live the life of inspired service and practical devotion which he taught. For these things the world will always be in debt to Guru Nanak and to those through whom he spoke in the succeeding generations.

A Brief Sikh Catechism

1. *How did this universe come into existence?*
There was nothing but God; he willed, and out of the Word which expresses that will the universe is being ceaselessly made.

2. *What is God?*
The One Eternal and Infinite Unmanifest, who has manifested himself to us through his works. He is King, Father, Lover of all, abiding in all and also the Ocean of pure Being wherein all abide.

3. *Where is God?*
He is in all that he has made, as their inmost Self.

4. *Is there then no special temple for Him?*
The whole universe, the heart of each living being, the place where the Word is loved and sung — these are God's temples.

5. *Why does God create the universe?*
So that he, being good and by nature the giver of all, may give out himself through its countless forms, and that they may all share his life of infinite blissfulness.

6. *Does he desire to gain anything through this work?*
Being perfect, he can gain nothing for himself, but he desires recipients of his love.

7. *Is matter eternal?*

No. Through the action of God's creative power (*māyā*) it comes into being, and at his will it ceases to exist. But its duration is of inconceivably vast extent.

8. *Are Hell and the Heavens eternal?*

No. Nothing is eternal save God and the soul which merges into him. All states and planes exist only until he brings the 'play' to an end.

9. *Has this universe any real existence?*

Being created by the one supreme Reality, it is a real expression of his eternal truth (*sat*); but as it arises and vanishes at his will it has no real or independent existence of its own. Compared with the Creator it is like 'the shadow of a cloud', a 'flying dream of the night'.

10. *Is the universe good or bad?*

In itself it is good because it is the visible expression of the will of the one absolute Good; it may become relatively bad for the soul which chooses it in preference to him.

11. *What is sin, or evil?*

The deliberate turning from the service of God to the service of the petty 'self', and the seeking of worldly pleasures for their own sake. That is, it is the wilful disobedience of what is known to be God's will.

12. *How did evil come into existence?*

God gave man free will so that he might choose Him above all, but a free choice involves the possibility of wrong choice; man chose 'ego' instead of his real Self, the Life of his life, that is, God.

13. *Why does God let evil exist?*

So that many may learn through effort how to reject all things save the love of Himself, and thus acquire those virtues which bring about union with him.

14. *What does God do if evil seems about to conquer the world?*

He sends a messenger with His own power to teach and inspire the people to righteous life, drawing them to Him through his own saintly example.

15. *Is there a devil in the Sikh religion?*

Sinners by rebelling against God's will are like 'devils', but there is no great opponent of God who can challenge his omnipotence.

16. *What is man?*

The creature or child of God, mortal while he identifies himself with the perishable world and body, but with the power of becoming truly immortal through union with Him; until then, doomed to wander in the outer darkness of the world, unable to see and really love Him.

17. *Why did God create man?*

So that a living creature might choose to love him above all things and so at last unite with him and share his glorious eternal work.

18. *What is the origin of the individual soul?*

Like that of a spark from the One Fire, a wave arising in the One Sea. The soul comes forth from God, is always really in him as a partial expression of his Will, and at the last manifests it perfectly in union with his perfect Self.

19. *How was man imprisoned in flesh?*

He found himself in a body of whose sensations he was conscious; thus, in confusion, he thought himself to be that body whereas in reality he is as free as the air around.

20. *What is man's duty on earth: to God, to other men, to himself?*

To love and worship God, holding his Presence always in mind, and doing all actions in his Name and to his glory; to serve and help mankind in all humility, gentleness and courage, fulfilling the duties of his state with perfect honesty; to aspire continually to become a perfect devotee of God, and to do His work on earth faithfully so that he may gain those qualities which enable His grace to unite him with God.

21. *How can man become free?*

In contact with saintly persons, a continuous dwelling on the thought of God, and faithful discharge of duty, egoism perishes and man realizes that his real Self is the One ever-free formless God.

22. *Can he do this unaided?*

No. In order to break his bonds God's grace is absolutely necessary.

23. *How does God help him?*

When he is ready to be helped, God sends him the intimacy of a saint, whose contact, teachings and example awaken true spiritual vision in his heart and so set him free from bondage to the 'ego'.

24. *Why does not God give this help to all?*

His will it is that all should long for such aid, and prepare themselves by effort for it; the moment any soul is thus made ready, His grace at once descends, and the saint, the Guru, gives enlightenment.

25. *What is the result of righteous conduct?*

In this life virtues attract grace, and so they swiftly bring the soul to surrender and to union with the One supreme Good; in the other, God draws the righteous soul near to himself so that it never falls again into the shadows of earthly life.

26. *What happens to wicked men?*

In this life, they suffer by deprivation of grace and the enlightening bliss of saintly contacts; in the next, they suffer miserably in Hell, the results of their own bad deeds, until they fall back into incarnation and resume their wanderings until the lesson is well learned.

27. *Is the soul born again in a physical body?*

It must be, until it deliberately turns away from purely worldly delights in order to seek God with a full heart and sincere longing.

28. *What should a sinner do to escape this evil lot?*

Repent of his sins and wash them away by ceaseless dwelling upon the thought of God; he can do this when by serving some saint with faithful devotion he has won his grace.

29. *How can man find God?*

With the saint's grace, he does all his actions and meets all the events of his life in the mood of conscious adoration of God; then his heart is so purified that God himself comes to dwell in it and takes him to himself in loving embrace.

30. *Can the true knowledge of God be given by another?*

Not fully; the Guru's touch of grace opens the soul's eyes to God's light, which is always there, and enables him to see the Lord. In reality it is God who gives the knowledge of himself, but to that end he takes the form of the Guru.

31. *Who really is the Guru?*

God, who dwells in the heart of every living being, who teaches all through the gentle voice of conscience, and appears 'outside' in human form to those who crave such visible aid. Really the 'Enlightener' is the inner Self who recognizes truth and embraces it when found in a human form or voice, a book, or the universe itself.

32. *Was Guru Nanak a man or a divine incarnation?*

All the 'Incarnations' (*avatāras*) were men sent by God to do His work of saving the world age after age. Guru Nanak, too, was such a messenger of God. But as Guru, his was and is to each Sikh the voice of God arousing the soul to true spiritual effort.

33. *What is the relationship between the Ten Gurus?*

One divinely taught Soul, in full spiritual union with God, was teacher of men for several generations through these chosen bodies, so that the Sikh community might be formed and trained. Personally distinct, the ten were spiritually one, Nanak being the inspiring soul in all.

34. *How does the Guru manifest to Sikhs today?*

By the will of the last of the Ten, through the hymns of the *Guru-Granth Sahib*, and the *Khālsā* or community of faithful Sikhs, expressed by 'Guru's decrees'; also he is still to be found by search in the heart of each individual Sikh, and in the universe which is pervaded by his grace.

35. *How does one become a Sikh?*

By declaring one's total faith in the Guru, surrendering to the Lord, and accepting the 'baptism'of nectar and the sword, adopting and faithfully adhering to the *Panch Kakas*: the five K's[1], and the *Rahatnāmas*[2] (codes of conduct).

36. *Why did Guru Gobind change the form of Sikhism?*

In reality he made no essential change, but in days of persecution more stress had to be laid on manly courage, so he introduced external signs and insignia, which led to the martyrdom of many, and thus preserved the precious treasure of the religion from reabsorption into Hinduism or Islam.

37. *What do you mean by God's 'Name'?*

The name is the expression of a person; God's Name is the expression of God, the Eternal Omnipresent Person. His 'Name' is all that he has made — this whole universe, and the conscious soul itself.

38. *How does a man repeat God's Name?*

By holding himself always conscious of God's presence in his own heart and in all around; this may be

---

[1] see page 126.   [2] see Responsibilities, page 127.

greatly aided by the chanting of his glories or the Guru's hymns, by the company of a saint, by the repetition of one of his names — such as Hari, Rāma, Vāhigurū.

39. *What is the final goal of life?*

The total loving union of the soul with God, in his active work of creation and uplift, and in the blissful contemplation of his perfection.

40. *Can you sum up this religion in a few words?*

It is a life of active effort towards the upliftment of the world under the Guru's guidance, so that all souls may attain the final Goal. It insists on human equality, and rejects caste, race prejudice, the use of images for God, and all external show of piety; it insists on absolute sincerity and persevering action for the love of God.

———————

Synopsis

PART ONE – SIKHISM

Chapter One: THE PERFECT TEACHER. 1. When evil prevails the Divine Teacher comes forth with a message of peace and justice; a few blessed souls drink in the outpouring of God's grace. 2. In such a dark age God called Guru Nanak and, though he protested his own unworthiness, bade him teach men His infinite glory revealed in His Holy Name and creation. 3. Nanak knows that he, a frail creature, is nothing of himself but in God's power he can serve mankind. 4. Others may mock and slander him but as the messenger of God he is proof against their ill will. 5. He is miserable save in the company of this one Friend, absence from whom is a painful disease cured only when a saint restores the broken intimacy. 6. In union with this Beloved alone lies the highest bliss, wherein He is found always and everywhere. Having reached that ecstasy, Nanak is now mad with love for God. 7. From whom he can never part again, because He lives in his very heart and makes it all divine. 8. Because he relies wholly on God and finds all life's sweetness in him, God helps him always.

Chapter Two: THE GLORY OF GOD. 9. Adoration of the One God who out of his own will created all things and, pervading all, blissfully maintains them throughout eternity. 10. All are like sparks from him, the One Fire, and return to the fullness of his life when illuminated by the Perfect Teacher. 11. Formless, infinite, omnipresent, and yet eternally free is He, who wears the whole as a radiant garment. His glories are endless, numberless are his names and uncountable his forms—yet he is ever *one*. 12. Many try to describe this Ineffable, but have no power; those only know him to whom he reveals himself as the Secondless, and they are the world's elect. 13. Being at the centre of all hearts, he knows all that is in them, and yet, in spite of man's wickedness, gives him all he needs. 14. Joy and sorrow alike; and whatever he gives is good, the source of spiritual fruit and blessedness, because he loves us all. 15. He is the Life of our life, the Light in everything; within and without, all is God, in loving whom the universe is loved and all dissolves in ecstasy. 16. He alone IS, and all events and actions are really expressions of his will; our happiness lies in a glad surrender to that will. 17. At his order prophets come and go; he alone is real and eternal, the unchanging cause of all this play of ceaseless change we call the world. 18. By obeying his laws the whole universe worships him, for he is in all. No human rites are worthy of him before whom the sun and moon are but lights waved in adoration.

Chapter Three: MORTAL MAN. 19. As the body and all wordly things must perish, it is useless to be attached to them and thus draw ourselves back into recurring birth and death. 20. Affections for worldly things fill us with sins and trap us in the body; by true devotion to God we are cleansed from sin and freed from the unreal. 21. Rebirth comes from identifying ourselves with the physical body, its pleasures, desires and passions; thus arise egoism, enmities and misery, which can be ended only by dissolving the separateness of the self and humbly serving God and all his children. And this is union with the Beloved, true liberation. 22. Death is inevitable for all; in that hour man must face his destiny alone, stripped of all but his faith in God and the virtues rooted therein. To the devotee who wants only the Lord death is very delightful. 23. After death comes a strict enquiry into all the acts and hidden thoughts of the soul, and there is exact recompense for the good and evil done in life. 24. No rites can save from the just results of action; it is only sincere love for God that can deliver from hell and the miseries of a rebirth separated from the one real Friend of souls. 25. Taught by the perfect Teacher and immersed in thoughts of God, the devotee finds in death no terrors but rests blissfully in the Beloved's arms.

Chapter Four: THE TRUE GURU. 26. Only with the help of a saint who himself loves God and has become one with him can the soul find and attain to that Divine Friend. 27. The saint is one who is uniformly kind to all and intensely devoted to God's eternal presence; such a one alone can teach the soul. 28. This is the only real Muslim, Brāhman, Yogi—one wholly surrendered to God and doing always his will. Outward professions matter little, for true renunciation is in the heart. 29. God is not found by learned talk but by silent contemplation on him and on the words of his saints; in this 'meditation' egoism is burned away and virtues flower under the soft showers of His grace. 30. Union with God is interior, spiritual, and needs no external show or special garb; the essence of true religion is to live selfless in the world.

Chapter Five: THE DIVINE NAME. 31. The Unmanifest can be reached only by adoring and serving the Manifest Deity. This devotion to God's 'Name' washes away the stains of sin and blossoms into spiritual beauty; it is the richest gift of God's grace. 32. God is our very life; how can we live save in continual communion with him? To turn from him is real death, and not the mere dropping of a body. 33. This holy Name is the source of all true happiness, for how can sorrow enter where God, the Ocean of Bliss, pervades? By treasuring that sweet Presence in his heart man becomes like, indeed, merged in, God himself.

Chapter Six: THE WAY TO GOD. 34. Nothing can lead man to God but the teaching and service of a saint, and that holy contact is His special gift to the few [35] who surrender unreservedly to Him with heartfelt devotion. 36. God is in all; he is to be loved and served in all with kindness and humility. We should come to him with a child's simple trust and ask for his grace which liberates and fills with joy. 37. As God is in all, none are to be hated or despised; the heart must be pure, and for that no ritual cleanness suffices. Holiness depends not on diet but on true devotion and the patient cultivation of virtues. 38. We can safely rely on God our Strength, who gives all delight to those who serve him with full surrender and total trust. 39. All worldly things are perishable, unreal; God is the sole Reality and, joined by love to him, the soul finds eternal life and joy, its only worthy aim. 40. True bliss lies in the ceaseless practice of God's presence in the heart and in all around. Such a devotee shares his infinite beauty and, recognizing and gazing on the Beloved everywhere, lives in a trance of love's delight, doing all his work for him. 41. Those who thus live in God are his saints; they are ever blissful, and blessed are those who meet and serve them, for they reveal God's beauty and grace even in their own persons. 42. Saintliness is God's gift to those who sincerely seek and long for him, finding in him alone all their delight. 43. But this love for him comes to those only who with the saint's help have driven 'self' out of the heart's inmost shrine; He can be found there by one whom He calls to the meeting within. 44. That call comes only when our love for him is so intense a fire we cannot live without him; when we weep and grow mad with longing, then he gives grace and takes us in his arms.

Chapter Seven: UNION WITH THE BELOVED. 45. Though in our blindness we think God far away, he is always with us. 46. The devotee longs to meet her Beloved and is in misery while she feels herself alone; she is ready to die for sight of him, without whom life is to her like death. 47. She knows that he must first deck her with his own graces and beauties, and only then will he appear to her and let her find happiness; she herself unaided can do nothing to win his love. 48. Yet she must try to prepare herself for him by washing in his purity and faithfully obeying his will; seeing her thus adorned with his own jewels, he will come to her. 49. Tenderly he takes her to his embrace as his own pure bride, filling her with overflowing joy in the knowledge that she is eternally lost in him. 50. He graciously accepts her little services and greatly honours her, his poor little spouse, taking away all her sorrows and blending her life with his own. 51. Eternally freed from the egoism that so long kept her separate from God, the human bride is for evermore ecstatic in his embrace and calls the whole universe to share her joy.

Chapter Eight: THE GURU'S DESCENT. 52. Nobly did Guru Nanak do God's work through the bodies of the first nine Gurus of the Sikhs and firmly established the religion. 53. Then God called Guru Gobind Singh to protect it from the violence of unbelievers and the craft of compromisers; he, too, nobly performed the task. 54. In its hour of need God sends the true Teacher who loves fallen humanity; he brings the message of truth and love which is real freedom. Essentially all religions are the same, for they all worship the same God under various names. The Sikh religion is one among the world's religions, yet it recognizes God's Word and his saints in others also. Hereafter the Teacher will be seen in the scripture and in the community; the true Sikh will cling to the worship of God and the Guru's teachings, and so will come at last to life's eternal goal.

PART TWO — THE GURU'S HYMN
Chapter Nine: JAPJI, THE GURU'S HYMN. 55. The One Infinite and Eternal God cannot be reached through the deepest meditation or speculative thought, but only through obedience to his will. 56. He creates and

governs all beings, ordering every event, and each according to his own abilities tries to express His action and mighty power. 57. The only real worship we can offer him is a ceaseless loving memory of his goodness; no act of ours can earn his grace which is his noblest gift that glorifies our souls. 58. This constant remembrance of him destroys all our defects and sorrows; it exalts us to the highest knowledge, wisdom and goodness — to the very threshold of divinity. 59. Steady adherence to his known will, whatever form it may assume, saves us from all evils, keeps us in the straight path, and guides us to the highest goal. 60. All created things in the endless universe obey God's will and thus contribute to his glory — even sinners, by reaping the fruits of their wicked deeds. His will rules all, for he is present and reigns in all. 61. The love of God purifies the heart from sin, though each soul has still to receive the harvest of its own deeds; before this omnipotent love religious acts and external virtues have little value. 62. Only God knows the secrets of His own work in the countless worlds and in his own infinite generosity, and none else can fathom them. Nothing is equal to the ceaseless loving thought of God. 63. God and his righteousness are the most precious of all things; though every creature tries to utter the truth he fails utterly, for it is inexpressible. 64. In his glory God sits in the highest heaven, ruling the universe and receiving the adoration of every creature in each of the worlds; they come and go, but he remains, the eternal changeless One. 65. Adorning ourselves with all virtues and the jewel of self-surrender, let us truly adore him, the infinite and all-pervading Lord of all. 66. Yet we can do nothing of ourselves; all comes only from his grace. He gives us grace and then watches how we use it, well or ill. 67. After transcending this physical plane of strife between right and wrong, the soul ascends through the higher planes of variety, beauty and power, to the fifth, the very dwelling of God himself. 68. He sends his grace to those who work at self-purification through obedience to the scriptures; down here we have to choose between God and the false petty 'self', and according to our choice so is our future state — a sad wandering in the outer darkness, or blissful residence with God.

EK ONKĀR SATIGURPRASĀDI

PART ONE

Sikhism

PRAYER

[O Lord, grant] to the Sikhs the gift of [true] teaching, the gift of loyalty,[1] the gift of faith, the gift of heroic sacrifice,[2] the gift of the Name—bathing in the holy tank of nectar,[3] ... the power to read, to contemplate and understand the Guru's Holy Book:[4] [all of you] say: Glorious is the Guru[5] (*Ardās*)!

---

[1] G: *rehitā*; lit: the quality of being able to do without; i.e., the readiness to give up all other things for the ideal

[2] lit: giving the head

[3] i.e., Amritsar, where Guru Rām Dās prepared the holy tank for Sikhs to bathe in

[4] lit: *Śri Guru-Granth Sāhib*.

[5] The literal meaning of the Name of God as specially honoured by Sikhs—*Vāhigurū*. The Name is a response after each part of the prayer.

CHAPTER ONE

The Perfect Teacher

The hour of deepest darkness precedes the dawn; it is when human hopes are at their lowest that God is at hand to save his children. When wild men from across India's western borders swept like locusts over Punjab's fair fields, carrying slaughter and famine, he sent among the sorely stricken people his chosen messenger to tell of his eternal love for them, and to teach them how to find in him a perfect Friend and Consolation. Guru Nanak showed the humility of all true saints, but he showed also the quiet firmness of God's elect; unmoved by the world's criticisms, he pressed on to secure the victory of God's cause by his own perfect faith and his passionate love for God and man. Thus he attained the perfection of his own life, and at the same time saved millions who through the centuries enrolled themselves as his disciples (*Sikh*) and therefore pupils also of the Eternal Guru who is over all.

1. THE COMING OF A TEACHER

1. When the world is in trouble it prays sincerely, the True One listens with attention, and in the kindness of his nature grants consolation;[1] he gives orders to the Cloud[2] (l:xli AD), and nectar rains down in torrents[3] (Ar. *Sri III*, 2:14). But the thirst of very few is quenched (Ar. *Gauri*, 154:1); to few is the Word (of God) taught by the Guru (N. *Maru Solhe*, 15:15). Among millions (of souls) very few are [God's] servants; all the rest are worldly [folk][4] (Ar. *Gūjari*, 2:1). It is the one who thirsts for a sight of God who uplifts the world (Ar. *Gauri*, 131:2); [and now] he himself has stood up and remains to do the work of the saints, [saying]: (Ar. *Suhi Chhant*, 10:1): 'To punish the wicked, to slay demons, to destroy the guilty have I come;[5] I have arisen mightily to crush the oppressor, to uplift the fallen, to drive back hell !' (G. *Akāl Ustat*, 211)

2. Thrice blessed is the man who has come [to us], by whose grace the whole world is saved! This is the

---

[1] The theme recurs in all religions which teach a divine saviour (cf. GZ 52:1, *Gītā* 4:7).

[2] The 'Cloud' is the Prophet who brings to men God's refreshing help, just as the dark rainclouds of the monsoon bring life and greenness to the fields parched by India's summer heat.

[3] i.e., the sweet waters of eternal life

[4] This is the experience of all religious teachers (cf. EH 49 :2, *Gītā* 7:3).

[5] A close parallel to *Gītā* 4:8.

object of his coming, that by contact with a man [of God] the Name might enter the minds [of men] (Ar. *Sukhmani*, 28:8). And now has the decree of the Merciful come into force, that none should give pain to another, that all should dwell in happiness, and that this should be a benign regime (Ar. *Sri III*, 2:13). He who preaches to others but himself does not practise comes and goes in births and deaths;[1] the world is saved by the teaching of one in whose heart the Formless dwells (Ar. *Sukhmani*, 5:7).

God always answers the appeal for aid, but his help benefits only those who avail themselves of it. The student learns nothing from his teacher unless he attends his class and makes his own efforts to comprehend and follow the advice freely given him. Alas, few indeed in every age are those who really seek God—most of us prefer the worthless toys of worldly life! But those who turn to him, who sit at the feet of his messenger, find the immortal bliss which he has brought to men. An age enriched by many such would be indeed the 'Kingdom of God'—a true *Rāmarājya*.

2. THE CALL OF NANAK

1. *[One morning after his bath Nanak saw God,[2] who gave him a cup of nectar with the blessing:] 'I am with you; I have made happy both you and those who*

---

[1] Rebirth is here the effect of insincerity; those who belie the truth they know cannot dwell in the inner realms of truth.

[2] So too Jesus sees God at his baptism in water as did Zarathushtra on emerging from the waters of the Daitya (GMC 21:3, GZ 27:2-4).

take your name. Go and repeat my [Name] and cause others to do so too.[1] *Practise repeating my Name, charities and bathings, worship and contemplation. I have given you this cup of nectar as a proof of my regard [for you]'* (1:34N).

2. [*Nanak arose and prostrated before God, and then he sang: 'What am I before Thee, my God?*] Were my life [to last] for millions of years, were my food drinking the air;[2] were I [to dwell] in a cave and saw neither moon nor sun, nor slept even in a dream, still I could not grasp thy glory! How can I describe the greatness of the Name?[3] O true and formless one in thine own place, … if it please thee show mercy! Were I cut down and chopped up again and again [into tiny pieces], ground [to powder] in a mill, burned in the fire and mingled with the ashes, still I could not grasp thy glory! How can I describe the Name? Were I to become a bird and fly away into the skies, were I to pass beyond the sight of everyone[4] and neither to drink nor eat anything, still I could not grasp thy glory! How can I describe the greatness of the Name? Nanak

---

[1] On the significance of 'repeating the Name' see the Introduction.

[2] A renowned saint met by Sri Rāmakrishna was known as Pavahari Baba, whose name means 'the air-drinker'; the idea connotes the extreme of harmlessness and asceticism.

[3] lit: How great do I call the Name? i.e., How can *I* call the Name great?

[4] lit: were I not to come into the sight of anyone.

says: Had I thousands of tons of paper and the will [to use it all] after deepest study, were my ink never to come to an end, and were I to move the pen like the wind,[1] still I could not grasp thy glory! How can I describe the Name?' (N. *Sri*, 2:1-4)

3. *[God said:] 'You have seen my sovereignty, O Nanak!' [and Nanak answered him:] 'O Sire, what is there that any mortal can say [of that]? What can be spoken or heard after what I have seen? Even the lower animals sing thy praises [in silence]!' [And then Nanak sang this hymn:]*[2] (1:35 N). 'One Supreme Being, the true and eternal Name, the Creative Person fearless and unopposed, the timeless Form unborn and self-existing, [known] through the enlightener's grace; true in the beginning, true in the night of ages, he is true even now, and will be true [eternally], says Nanak!' (N. *Japji*)

4. *[Then said God:] 'O Nanak, be kind to the one on whom my look of grace may fall, and then I too shall be gracious [to him]. My Name is indeed the divine First Creator, and you are the divine Guru.' [And Nanak sang this hymn]* (1:35 N). 'Thou art an ocean of

---

[1] The same thought is found in Islam and in several Hindu scriptures.

[2] These important verses read thus: *Ek Oamkāru sati nāmu kartā purakhu nirabhu niravairu akāla mūrati ajūni saibham gura prasādi. Adi sachu jugādi sachu hai bhī sachu Nānaka hosī bhī sachu.* The first sentence plays almost the same part in Sikh prayer as the Ahunavairya in Parsi, the Paternoster in Christian, the Fatha in Muslim, and the Gāyatri in Hindu.

generosity and wisdom; how can I a mere fish grasp the whole? Wherever I look, there art thou; separated from thee I should fall to pieces and die! I know not the Fisherman, I know not the Net; but when I fall into trouble, then I remember thee! Thou art omnipresent while I believed thee far;[1] whatever I do is present to thee—thou seest even when I try to hide. [I have not acted] in thy work, nor in thy Name, yet I eat just what thou givest.[2] There is no other door [to ask at], to whose door then shall I go? Nanak utters this one prayer: soul and body are all with thee; thou art near and thou art also far, thou art in the midst; thou seest and thou also hearest, by thy creative power[3] thou didst make the world! Nanak, whatever pleases him, that is a command to be accepted' (N. *Sri*, 31:1-4).

This reconstruction of the scene when God called Nanak out of his simple village home to carry light and joy from one end of India to the other, is built up from the sources used by Macauliffe in his valuable life of the Guru. It is apparently based on an almost contemporary account, the *Janamsakhi*, or biography, by Sevadās.

When God assures Nanak of his approval and promises his help, the saintly lad protests his total unworthiness to praise God's infinite glory; how much less fit must he be to

------

[1] St Augustine says the same in his immortal *Confessions*.

[2] i.e., I receive whatever thou hast destined for me even without meriting it.

[3] G. *kudarati*, almost the Hindu *māyā-sakti*

teach others so to do! But God reminds him of his own direct vision of that glory, thus suggesting that he can at least tell as much as he himself has seen. Nanak replies that only silence can describe the ineffable, continuing with the *mūlamantra* of the Sikhs, which proclaims the eternal unknown God whom the true teacher's grace reveals. Again God asks Nanak to dispense that grace to all with the same generous love that God has given it to him; Nanak finally yields and agrees to do as much as God enables him to do, without whom he is but nothing and on whom alone he totally relies.

3. THE HUMILITY OF NANAK

1. From age to age I tenderly serve God (Ar. *Sri III*, 2:21); he has made Nanak the servant of his feet, turning [his] mind to affection for the Lord (Ar. *Ruti Śloka*, 4:2), [so that] he continually contemplates[1] the beloved God (Ar. *Sri III*, 2:7) and abides in him who is seated in every heart,[2] acting so as to please the true Guru (N. *Sidh Goshti*, 3). From myself nothing can come, O God! (Ar. *Gauri*, 14:1) It is God who appointed [me] for the one work, and I carry it out as he desires (Ar. *Sri III*, 2:3). Gladly have I come and gone at his command; Nanak is always obedient to him (N. *Sidh Goshti*, 3).

---

[1] *Dhyāidā*, the word commonly translated as 'meditate'; but strictly 'meditation' is a mental process of logical thought while *dhyāna* is more correctly 'contemplation', the wholly delightful process of peacefully holding the heart and mind on the chosen Object—God.

[2] Note that such immanence does not mean pantheism or identity; God is *in* all, but not *limited* to all, infinitely transcending all that He has made.

2. I confess fully all that I have done; utterly defiled, I wash [myself] thoroughly (N. *Mājh ki Vār*, 6 Sl. 2); I am not good (N. *Maru Kafi*, 2:8), I know not, alas! how to adore God (Ar. *Sorathi*, 13:2). Among the lowly of humble birth I am the lowest of the low; how can Nanak rival the great in their very presence? (N. *Sri*, 3:4) I am a fallen sinner and a great deceiver[1] (N. *Sorathi*, 5:1); I am always straying into offence, but thou art the forgiver (Ar. *Bilawal*, 34:1), thou, the pure and formless one! (N. *Sorathi*, 5:1). There is none so kind as thou, [while there is no] sinner like me. Save, O save, my God, the man who seeks thy protection! (N. *Bilawal*, 3:4, 1). I know nothing and my understanding is but little; yet in my heart I adore the Name of the Lord! (Ar. *Āsa*, 69:3-4)

3. To be firmly established in God the Seat[2]—such is the Guru's teaching I received, [and that] if the disciple understand and realize, the self, then being true he will merge into the True One (N. *Sidh Goshti*, 3). Naturally attractive is the fruit of humility, the fruit my true Guru has given me (Ar. *Gauri Ashtapadi*, 1:1). Where thou observest the lowly, there thy gracious look [is his] reward (N. *Sri*, 3:4). I have built a real

---

[1] In such expressions of humility the *Guru-Granth* resembles in places the Hebrew Psalms; it is the foundation of spirituality to realize that one is nothing, and God is all.

[2] God is the 'Ground' of the whole universe, its 'warp and woof' whereon the vast web is spun; to abide in him is to be still while all else moves.

temple[1] and to it led the Guru's pupils; [and now] I wash [the Guru's] feet, and wave the fan, and ever and ever fall before him prostrate (Ar. *Sri III*, 2:10). [In this way] Nāmdev, Trilochana and Kabīr, thy servants, and the tanner [Ravidās] became liberated souls! (Ar. *Gūjari*, 10:2)

4. I see no friend but thee (N. *Gaurī Ashtapadi*, 1:5); thine is my soul, all the body thine! (R. *Gaurī*, 20:1) I am thy slave, the dust of thy servants' feet! (N. *Tilang*, 1:4) At thy lotus feet is the home of my heart; ... with the rope of love is thy servant bound, ... what is the use of escape? (Rd. *Āsa*, 4:1, 3) I am nothing at all; he alone IS, he is the One in the beginning and the end![2] (Ar. *Āsa*, 83:4)

Nanak insists that he himself can do nothing for God, but in his perfect faith that God has chosen him for this work he will go on with it. His loyalty to God, his deep affection for him, his ready obedience to his lightest word—all promise his ultimate success. He knows that it is only by thus clinging to God as his infinite strength that he can do anything at all; by faithfulness to the teaching of his own (inner) teacher, by truly serving and guiding the disciples, he can give real homage and love to his Beloved Lord.

In himself he is very small and weak, ever ready to stray

---

[1] G. *Dharamsālā*; lit: hall of charity, or inn. The idea may well be the old one that this world is an inn where we can stay only a short while, or that it is the place where we are to show good deeds.

[2] G. *kama kichu nāhī ekai ohi iāgai pachkai eko soī.*

from the right path; but God is always at his side to lead him, to raise him from the mud of failure. God seems specially tender to the weak and helpless; as a shepherd carries the lamb on his shoulder, so God goes after the lost soul with unfailing patience till he brings it home. This is why he often chooses saints from the lowest families and makes them stars of inspiration and guidance to millions: Nāmdev the converted dacoit, Trilochana the shopkeeper, Kabīr the foundling weaver, Ravidās the cobbler—God was not ashamed of their company, but raised them to the heights of spiritual perfection.

How can Nanak help loving so good a God as this? He knows that God has tied his heart with love's unbreakable bonds, ('I have loved thee with an everlasting love'—Jer. 31:3) and now he is wholly God's, dependent for everything on God's sweet will, finding in him the only friend.

4. THE SAINT IS CRITICIZED

1. If one acts honestly[1] and then loses by it, if there is no [real] penance in the house of penance, if one on taking the Name [meets] obloquy—these are the signs of the dark age[2] (N. *Rāmkali Ashtapadi*, 1:3). [*So is it today:*] *When I remain silent they say I have no understanding in my heart, when I speak they say I chatter too much; when I sit they say I have spread my bedding,*[3] *when I go away they say I*

---

[1] lit: true; *G. satu kare*

[2] cf. the signs given in GH 34, GZ 48:4, GMC 47-48, and in the *Vishnu Purāna*, etc.

[3] i.e., I impose myself as an unwanted guest.

have thrown dust on my head,[1] *when I prostrate they say I am performing devotions through fear. I can do nothing by which I may pass my time in peace!*[2] (1:80N)

2. [But if I] be slandered I shall go to heaven and make the precious Name dwell in my heart; the heart becomes pure when there is slander, for the slanderer washes my clothes! (K. *Gauri Purbi*, 71:1) The more he slanders the saints, the happier the saints feel (Ar. *Āsa*, 41:3); all the words saintly people hear...and whatever happens [to them] they feel that to be happiness! (Ar. *Sukhmani*, 23:4) [As for me], as much as the Lord has taught me, so much does my tongue pronounce (Ar. *Āsa Chhant*, 5:4); I speak those words which the Master gives [to me], (Ar. *Sri III*, 2:14), as the word of the Master comes to me so exactly do I make it known! (N. *Tilang*, 5:1)

The age of darkness (*kaliyuga*), into which God sends his light by some messenger, can easily be known by certain signs: the righteous are made to suffer, honesty pays no worldly dividend, those who profess to be spiritual make only an empty show while there is no religious spirit in their heart, and the saints who love God in various revealed forms are slandered and abused. This is what Nanak himself finds; men criticize whatever he does. With

---

[1] i.e., I insult my host by signs of mourning etc. (cf.Mt.10:14).

[2] The passage in italics is not in the *Guru-Granth Sahib* and so must be regarded as unauthentic. Yet it well expresses the truth of how the world receives the saint, (cf.Mt.11:16-19 and many places in the *Korān*).

the same unreasonableness in earlier days they afflicted Muhammed [*GI* 34-36] and Jesus [*GJ* 63 and *GMC* 35], they complained of all his actions. But the idle chatter of fools cannot shake the God-inspired; like his predecessors, Nanak knows well that such slanders, bravely borne, only serve to purify his heart. The saint rejoices at trouble, for it, too, is the gift of the all-loving Providence and sure to work out for good if he is faithful to his God-given task. In mocking him, the foolish critics really mock at the infinitely wise—children throwing stones towards the sun and being struck by them as they fall to earth.

5. NANAK LONGS FOR GOD

1. O God, what is my condition in thy creation? Without God I cannot live for a moment[1]! (N. *Barah Maha*, 1) Without God my soul burns away [as] a sacrifice! (N. *Sri* 1:1) Seeking and seeking I have become a wandering beggar[2] and roam athirst for a vision of the Lord (Ar. *Gauri*, 118:3) miserable without the Beloved, I have no friend; I drank nectar from the devotee[3](N. *Barah Maha*, 1) and a saint has told me the way to the Lord (Ar. *Gauri*, 127:4). On asking my guru I have seen there is no other refuge

---

[1] *Gharri*, lit: about twenty-four minutes, but often used for a very short time

[2] *Bairāgini*, lit: one who has given up all desires of the world

[3] *Gurumukhī*, lit: one who sits before the guru and listens carefully to whatever comes from his mouth, so: disciple, devotee, saintly person. Nectar is the knowledge of God.

[but God]; if I had **all other luxuries**, might I not on seeing them foolishly forget thee so that thy Name might never come into mind? (N. *Sri*, 1 : 2) Why should I forget the Beloved, my life's support? (N. *Gūjari*, 2:1) God[1] is the only love! (N. *Āsa*, 37:4) Without him I cannot live a moment in the world, such is the thirst of my yearning! (N. *Mālār Ashtapadi*, 1:1)

2. [Once] I forgot the Master and took to the enjoyment of pleasure; then disease arose in the body—a pain of separation and a certain pang of hunger (N. *Mālār*, 7:2,1). A doctor was called for a remedy; he took [my] hand and felt the pulse; the stupid doctor did not know that the trouble was in the mind! (N. *Mālār ki Vār*, 3 Sl. 1) O doctor, he is a real doctor who first identifies the disease and then administers such a remedy as will radically cure diseases (A. *Mālār ki Vār*, 3 Sl. 2). Without the true guru [my] disease will never go (Ar. *Bhairo*, 20:3).

3. When God shows kindness to anyone, he takes his hand and leads him out of all disease. Fetters burst [when man] has won the company of a good man; Nanak says that disease is expelled by the Guru (Ar. *Bhairo*, 20:4); from the Guru a pure nectar is obtained, **and** on drinking that nectar he is always satisfied with grace and his thirst is quenched (AD. *Mājh Ashtapadi*, 20:2, 17:1).

---

[1] *Parabrahm*, the Absolute.

4. I have become a mad *sannyāsi*,[1] famishing for a sight [of thee]; day after day I beg at thy door so that I crave for a sight [of thee]; I beg at the door to receive alms[2] (N. *Tilang*, 2:1). Give [me] a sight [of thee], O Lord of kindness, and grant me understanding that I may attain the goal! (N. *Barah Maha*, 14) I am a sacrifice, ready to cut myself in pieces [for one look]; look graciously for one moment![3] (N. *Maru Ashtapadi*, 9:1) Thou art my Comrade, thou alone my Friend;…thou art my Husband, thou art my only Ornament; without thee it is impossible to remain for an instant! …Whom have I but thee, my Beloved and life's support? The state of my heart thou alone knowest, thou alone art the beloved Friend, and from thee have I obtained all joys (Ar. *Gaurī*, 18:1, 128:1). Nanak's burning [pain] was taken away on meeting the dear Beloved (Ar. *Āsa*, 143:3).

Even now he enjoys that love for God he owes to his mysterious Guru; yes, but the lover is never satisfied and always craves a closer union—'Nearer, still nearer, close to thy heart!' is his constant cry. Every moment without the rapture of that full union he has known in rare ecstasies is an intense agony; he can no longer live without feeling God at his side and in his heart. Driven by the burning thirst for love's full satisfaction, Nanak has wandered for ages

---

[1] *G. atitu*, lit: one who is without possessions, defects, etc.

[2] Rabindranath Tagore was also fond of this figure, so also was Thākor Haranāth.

[3] *Hika bhori*, the short time of sunrise

through life's wildernesses, seeking, seeking the infinite bliss of union. Guided one day by a true saint of God, he found the way to His beloved feet. And after that one vision of perfect loveliness he cares no more for earth's treasures; he drives them from his heart lest they form a mist around him and hide God from his longing eyes.

He tells us how intense was the fever of that longing, until God at last gave himself to him. People thought him mad because he could not play like other boys, or take his food at the right time, or work at any business, but always wandered here and there seeking the unseen Beloved of his soul. Such a fever can be cured only with one medicine; no other remedies avail. The heart must be filled with the sweetness of its Love, the poor mortal seeker must be folded in God's 'everlasting arms'; He who shot love's arrow in the heart must himself pour balm into the wound or it can never heal. And God sends his saint to draw the stricken lover, distracted by the hot fever of *viraha*,[1] to the cool unfailing fountain of perfect Love where for evermore he can quench his spiritual thirst with the nectar of his Divine Beloved.

Recalling those dreadful days of agony, perhaps passed in earlier lives on earth, Nanak becomes once more in memory the roaming beggar, asking at every door for one who can show him the Immortal God. Only when he no longer held anything to be of value, when he was ready to cast away his very life for the love of God, when he realized that God alone could give it meaning and that without him life must be intolerable agony—only then did he find the priceless Pearl, embrace the eternal Lover, and for evermore enter into the still peace of the Bridegroom's Arbour.

---

[1] The agony of separation

6. NANAK HAS FOUND HIM

1. The very memory of birth and death, of pain and fate[1] passes away; Nanak's happiness is that which pleases the Lord (Ar. *Āsa*, 113:4); bliss arose in the heart after meeting the beloved God (AD. *Sarang ki Vār*, 32:2). Easily[2] I met the Friend and, acquiring virtue, became like him in nature (N. *Barah Maha*, 15). When I came to know myself, my light merged in the Light; **Nanak**[3] says: Now my heart has known and honoured God (K. *Bilawal*, 11:3); my mind and body are drenched with the love of God[4] (R. *Gaurī*, 27:2). God and **Nanak**[3] have become one, no one can distinguish them (K. *Rāmkali*, 3:6).

2. By repeating 'Thou, Thou' I have become Thou; in me no 'I' remains.[5] When the difference of selfhood was once removed, wherever I looked there wast Thou! (K. *Śloka* 204-205) When I saw thee then I sang [thy Name], and then I a man took courage (Nd. *Sorathi*, 1:1). In every heart God speaks (Nd. *Mali Gaura*, 3:1); after seeking and

---

1 The word *kāla* means time, death, and so fate.

[2] *Sahaji*, i.e., naturally, without resistance, habitually, intimately

[3] In the original, of course, the name of Kabir stood here, but for the sake of uniformity I have replaced all such authors' names by 'Nanak'.

[4] *Merā manu tanu Hari rangi bhinnā:* the meaning of *rang* is rather *colour* and so *dye*; as the lover takes on the same hue as the beloved, it obtains a secondary meaning of *love*. We may read 'are steeped in the dye of God'.

[5] *Tūm tūm kartā tū hūa, mujh mahi rahā na hūm.*

seeking, the Self is found. And now I have become mad [by his] secretly stealing away the mind, I have been easily merged [in God] (K. *Bhairo*, 7:4, 4:4). Bliss, intense bliss! I have seen that Lord! I have tasted, I have tasted God's sweet essence, God's sweet essence has welled up in my heart; I have become intimate[1] [with him] through pleasing the true Guru! (Ar. *Āsa Chhant*, 1:1) People say that Nanak is insane; Nanak's secret only God has perceived (K. *Bhairo*, 6:4). [It is this:] Wherever I look, there is God! (Nd. *Gond I*, 2:4)

3. [My God], all is thine, and thou art my Beloved; night and day I thrill with love [for thee]! (N. *Barah Maha*, 2) When [I have] thee, then have I all; Lord, thou art my capital![2] In thee I dwell in happiness, in thee lies my triumph!...Thou art ever unattainable, immovable, and I must ever fall back exhausted while uttering [my love]. What can I ask? What say or hear? I hunger and thirst for a sight [of thee]! (N. *Suhi Suchaji*, 2:1-8) The *chatrik-bird*[3] cries 'Prio, Prio!' and sweet is the koel's[4] note (N. *Barah Maha*, 2); by the Guru's word I have obtained the Lord, the prayer of Nanak is fulfilled! (N. *Suhi Suchaji*, 2:10)

---

[1] *Sahaji*, i.e., naturally, without resistance, habitually, intimately

[2] i.e., I have invested my all in thee; thou art my only wealth.

[3] *Papihā;* this bird's cry resembles the word for 'beloved'; it is said to await the first drops of rain from the monsoon cloud; so too the devotee accepts no substitute for God's grace.

[4] Often miscalled the 'Indian cuckoo'.

And now that long agony has passed into his memories; the long ages of separation from his Lord have ended; Nanak finds perfect bliss in the sweet company and delightful service of his Beloved. The intimacy of their contacts has transformed him into a living likeness of his God, nor can anything now come between them to disturb that perfect union. The petty candle flame of his self has faded in the glory of the risen Sun, and he rejoices in that eternal mergence into God—lost as the little wave in the endless sea.

It was indeed only that petty self, with all its vanities, which so long held him apart from God; when its walls fell, when he let the sunlight pour like a cataract into the dim corners of his heart's chamber, all darkness fled away and he knew himself irradiate with eternal Light. Then came jubilation; seeing God everywhere around him, he knew no more pain and loneliness; now he rejoices in the visible presence of the infinite Beloved. To the eyes of a purblind world he is indeed mad, for its foolish little ambitions and griefs have for ever dropped from his view; but to the eyes of the wise, who see, he alone is sane, for he knows nothing but the One who is all in all.

Nanak knows Him, and therefore he is full of love for him—for who could know the infinitely Lovable without dissolving in a surging tide of love for him? In him who is all good, Nanak finds peace and happiness; it is true that he can never attain to the utmost depths of the Infinite, but he is ceaselessly thrilled by plunging deeper and deeper into his unending glories, and finds anew in each a boundless bliss. What can he say of God beyond the cry 'Beloved, Beloved!'? His human birth is thus fulfilled; taught by the real Guru in the heart, Nanak has found the Beloved of all the ages and in his embrace has entered on eternal bliss.

7. HE DWELLS IN NANAK'S HEART

1. Thou pervadest every place[1] (Ar. *Sri III*, 2:16); so I know [thou art] not afar and admit [thou art] within [me too], recognizing [myself as] God's mansion (N. *Barah Maha*; 6) for in my heart I hold him who is immanent in every place (N. *Āsa Ashtapadi*, 1:1). I abide in the Name, and the Name has come and abides in my heart (N. *Sri Ashtapadi*, 4:5).

2. Hear thou, O God steeped in sweetness,[2] my Beloved! Thou wellest up and overflowest in my mind and body without a moment's intermission. …Thou dwellest in heart and body and face; the Life of the world pervades my heart and body, at the Guru's word I experience love. …How could I forget thee for a moment?[3] I surrender [myself to thee][4], I live by singing thy glory! No one is mine, and to whom do I belong? Without God I could not exist;[5] having sought the shelter of his feet, I dwell there, and [so my] body has become pure (N. *Barah Maha*, 3, 14, 3). Nanak says: Persons who know love and devotion become pure[6] (K. *Sorathi*, 3:4).

---

[1] *Tūm thāni thanantari ravi rahiā.*

[2] *Rasa bhinne* ; *rasa* means the sweet juice of a fruit, so *delight, sweetness, love.*

[3] *Ghari*

[4] *Hau balihari* lit: I (am) a sacrifice, i.e., I give myself (for thee).

[5] lit: remain

[6] Kabīr here wrote 'perfect'; by a slight change Guru Arjan made it 'pure'.

Knowing and loving God, who is all, and in all, Nanak can no longer be apart from him for a moment. No more does he see the fish, the bird, the tree, the star, the silent hill at night, the restless river, and ever-moving waves—all is God, instinct with his enfolding love. God is in all that meets the eye; and in his own heart that little 'self', which hugged its wretched separateness so long, no longer usurps the throne but has yielded to that same God who now reigns in glory.

Nanak is still, at peace, resting in the arms of that perfect Love who rules his life. No longer can the fierce fevers of mind or body rise to disturb his heart's perfect health, pervaded as it is by the triumphant Beloved King. Never again for a moment can his mind wander from that endless peace which has atoned him with its own infinite blessedness, purifying him from the stains of long wanderings abroad. Being merged in God, his Life—as He is indeed the Life of all, though many know it not—Nanak shares God's perfect purity and finds all joy in a continual adoration of his infinite gloriousness.

8. GOD IS HIS HELPER

1. As the cowherd guards and keeps watch over cattle, so day and night [God] cherishes and guards the soul, keeping it in happiness.[1] Here and hereafter protect me, O Kind to the Poor,[2] and so satisfy with a gracious glance the one who seeks thy protection!

---

[1] An image certainly taken from Sri Krishna as the guardian of the cows, or souls, but recalling the 'Good Shepherd' of Christianity (GMC 28, CZ 55, GH 1)

[2] G. *Dīnadayālā*, a favourite name for God also among Vaishnavas

Where I look, there art thou pervading; save me, O Guardian [of souls]! Thou art the Giver, and the Enjoyer thou;[1] Thou art the Support of Life! (N. *Gauri Ashtapadi*, 17:1-2) No kingdom do I desire; I want no liberation, [but only] a love for the lotus feet in my heart![2] (Ar. *Devagandhari*, 29:1)

2. The Lord's Name tastes sweet [to me] (Ar. *Sukhmani*, 23:1); O my Beloved, I live by contemplating the Name; without the Name life could not be!...The mind is contented when it gets the Name, ... and now my true Guru has established the Name [in me]! (R. *Sri*, 2:1) God's Name is my father and mother, and God my relative and brother[3] (AD. *Gauri*, 17:3); I have put my trust in God, and God is my support; I rely on him because there is no other path but God[4] (R. *Āsa* II, 2:1).

God is always on the alert to protect his messenger and will not fail to look after Nanak. Indeed, so full is the Guru of his love for God that he can see none but him everywhere, pervading all things. Friend and foe alike are but forms of him, sent by his loving care to guide the soul

---

[1] It is God who gives; it is God also in the human soul who receives.

[2] cf. *Bhāgavata*. In his *Jagannādhāshtaka*, Sri Krishna Chaitanya writes: 'I do not beg for a kingdom, O Lord, nor for gold and jewels; nor do I ask for a beautiful bride, so eagerly desired by men. ....O mighty Lord of the universe, do thou reveal thyself to me!'

[3] cf. *Prapanna Gitā*, 'Thou art indeed mother, father, friend, comrade, knowledge,,wealth; thou art indeed my all, O God of Gods!'

[4] God himself is the only way that leads to him, as love alone can lead to love, and trust alone to trust.

home to him. The only treasure is a real love for this kind God; Nanak cannot be put off with any other gift but the gift of the Divine Person himself.

Nanak has found by experience how sweet it is to contemplate the beloved Name, the essence of that all-perfect Personality; he knows that life itself is involved in that kind of prayer, for without it life would be but the existence of a worm, empty of real happiness. He rejoices that God, through the inward Teacher of his heart, has put that love for Himself in the very centre of his being; in true religion—which is indeed 'the falling in love with God'—is man's only safety, only real friendship and consolation.

CHAPTER TWO

The Glory Of God

To that tortured age Nanak brought the old message of
the eternal God who loves us and in whose love alone we
can find our peace. It is he from whom at the beginning all
came; it is he who acts in all who act, who lives and loves
in all who live and love; who is at last the final refuge and
home of all. Though himself ever distinct from his creation, he pervades all that he has made—for apart from him
nothing could exist. Formless, and yet revealed by every
form that is; manifest and yet eternally unseen in his own
Self; beyond all thought and sense; whom no names can
name because all names are his—who can describe or
understand this Infinite, save his lover inspired by his own
grace? Omniscient, he knows our every need; all-generous,
he supplies it; all-good, his every act is for our welfare. At
his bidding religions arise, prophets speak out his will to
men; they die and are forgotten—but he remains, eternally
the King of all, adored by all creation, each creature
worshipping him through its own nature and abilities. How
can man's rituals avail to honour so universally adored a
sovereign of the universe?

9. THE CREATOR OF ALL THINGS

1. To him I bow who holds the arrow[1] in his hand; to the Fearless One I bow; I bow to the God of Gods, who is in the present and the future! (G. *Vichitra Nātak*, 1:3) I bow to the primal one Supreme Being who emanated [2] sea and land, the earth and sky, the First Person Unseen and Immortal, whose light shines forth in the fourteen worlds,[3] ...the inner Knower of all hearts, ...far from all, yet near to all.... He takes delight in the play of the fourteen worlds, and again mingles them within himself.... He is not absorbed in any one love but mixes in the light of all [beings], [4] ... the death of all and maker of all! (G. *Akāl Ustat*, 1-10)

2. In the very beginning of all was darkness;[5] no earth or sky, only the boundless Will; no day or night, no moon or sun, only the brooding in formless ecstasy![6]... Nothing else was there, only the One, ...nor can anyone speak of or describe a second. ... Himself unseen, he revealed [all]....He watched as

---

[1] The 'arrow' symbolizes God's purposive will which none can resist.

[2] *Pasārā*, lit: spread out

[3] Seven above, and seven below: *Bhūh* (earth), *Bhuvah, Suvah, Mahah, Janah, Tapah,* and *Satya;* together with: *Tala, Vitala, Atala, Sutala, Rasātala, Talātala and Pātāla*, the underworlds.

[4] God enters into, but is not caught up in, all thoughts and feelings.

[5] *Arabada narabada dhundhūkārā*

[6] *Sunna samādhi lagāida*; lit: he absorbs (himself) in featureless trance.

he kept making, and expressed the Will (N. *Maru Solhe*, 15:1, 4, 6, 13, 15). By the Supreme was the Creator produced,[1] the Supreme made what things are in the mind—from the Supreme arose the mountains and the ages....He created the whole world with ease (N. *Dakhni Oamkār*, 1:1-3, 2:1), forming it with careful thought (G. *Akāl Ustat*, 36), and he himself selected names [for all things]. Further, he made Nature,[2] then taking his seat [in her] he watched with delight (N. *Āsa dī Vār*, 1). He himself, having created [all], was pleased, and he himself received glory (N. *Maru Solhe*, 15:6).

3. At first, when God extended himself, the world was created by him (G. *Vichitra Nātak*, 2:10); he himself created [and then] recognized himself. Separating sky and earth, he spread out a canopy; establishing the firmament without pillars, he uttered the Word.[3] Having produced the sun and moon, he put light [in them]; he brought about the wonderful drama of night and day (N. *Mālār ki Vār*, 1).

4. [O God], thou actest and causest to act, establishing [all things] (Ar. *Mājh Ashtapadi*, 2:8);

---

[1] That even the Creator is secondary, derived from the One Unmanifest, has always been a commonplace of Asian religious thought; it entered the West, for a time, through the Gnostic schools.

[2] *Kudarati*, the divine creative power (*Māyā- śakti*)

[3] The meaning is clearly, as in other scriptures, that by uttering the creative Word he established sky and earth, etc.

pilgrimage and rites, meditations and ritual bathings—nothing else is worthy of thee [save love]! How am I to describe thee? Thou sittest on the eternal throne, while all else come and go! (N. *Mālār ki Vār*, 1) Everything created is thine, nothing at all is ours! (Ar. *Mājh*, 24:3)

5. Call everyone noble, let no one seem low to you; the One created [all] forms,[1] the One Light is in the three worlds (N. *Sri Ashtapadi*, 14:6). In the One is all, and in the all the One! (N. *Rāmkali Ashtapadi*, 8:5) Ever and always thou art One, creating thyself Two [as a] play! (N. *Mājh ki Vār*, 3) Thus from being One thou hast become endless, and in the One art reabsorbed, says Nanak (Ar. *Mājh Ashtapadi*, 2:8). Whatever is made is made by him, all that exists shall likewise be merged [in Him]; ... [O God], the various forms that are always appearing are thine and in thee shall they be resolved (AD. *Gaurī*, 15:1-2).

Nanak begins his message with a humble prostration to this great God, the Source and Goal of all, who resides in all. He tells us how all things evolved out of the Divine Will—even the Creator himself arose from that One Ineffable Infinite, who now enjoys the Play from his unchangeable seat in the heart of all that is. Such a God is far above and beyond all that we can say of him, far transcending any worship we may offer him; and because he who is in all is infinitely perfect, we dare not not regard

---

[1] lit: vessels (*bhānde*)

anything he has made as low or vile, unworthy of his boundless skill and goodness. Indeed, all is he, manifested as 'many' solely that he may enjoy the bliss of reuniting all in the eternal 'One'.

We may profitably compare Nanak's picture of the beginning with those in the Rig-Veda, the Egyptian and Babylonian texts, the book of Genesis, the writings of Hermes. In the infinite Darkness of the Unseen arose the eternal Light of God Manifest, wherein he brought forth the things which are, planning all, and rejoicing in their perfection (Gen. 1:31); He, too, it was who put 'names' to all things, and so breathed into them their essential being. It is he who does, has always done, all; and when our eyes are freed from the veil of ignorance we see only him in all around us.

10. IS HIMSELF THEIR GOAL

1. In a thousand pots one air;[1] the pots break and the same [air] remains (Ar. *Suhi*, 1:3). As from one fire millions of flaming sparks arise, though it be one by one, they will unite again in the fire;[2] as from one dust heap many tiny specks of dust fill the air and again mix with the dust heap; as millions of ripples are produced from one river [and] the ripples of water all become just water—so from the All-Form[3]

---

[1] *Ākāsa*, lit: 'ether' or 'space', but these words do not fit the context in English. The word is common in Vedāntic use.

[2] More than any other single passage, perhaps, this shows the predominantly *visishtādvaita* position of the Guru's thought.

[3] In Gurumukhī, *biswarūpa*

appear unconscious and conscious beings springing from him, and all are merged in him again [G. *Akāl Ustat*, 87].

2. One can know fully Him whose work this is if absorbed in the Guru's word (AD. *Gaurī*, 15:3), for without the Guru's word no understanding is gained (N. *Rāmkali Ashtapadi*, 3:6). When the Guru is met the Master is realized; that is, says Nanak, the door to liberation[1] (N. *Maru Ashtapadi*, 2:8).

The endless stream of individual souls (*jīvas*) come from God like sparks from the One Fire; they fly away from him, and then sink back again into the Flame from which they rose. Can sparks exist if there be no fire? Can the soul exist if there be no God? It is when the false separateness of the spark ceases, when the enclosing vessel of clay is broken and the enclosed air or space mingles with the limitless air or space around, when the wave sinks back into its parent sea—then the human soul finds its way back into the heart of the Divine, and the Truth is known.

And this realization of the truth comes to each soul, this 'blowing-out' or nirvana comes to each little spark, when the cool breeze of the Guru's teaching blows upon the aspirant. It is God's grace that brings the true teacher to the prepared pupil; one word from that teacher tears away all veils and shows the oneness of lover and Beloved—which is earth's final secret for all her children.

---

[1] *Mokha duāru*

11. GOD IS INFINITE

1. The Unseen, Infinite, Unattainable and Imperceptible has no time or destiny; Born and yet Unborn, Unaging and Self-existent, he has neither moods nor fancies[1] (N. *Sorathi*, 6:1). God is without birth and death (G. *Akāl Ustat*, 31), [being] infinite, only he can know himself (R. *Āsa Chhant*, 7:1). He has neither form nor colour, nor even outlines,[2] but is manifested by the true Word (N. *Sorathi*, 6:2); formless and yet with form, He is himself the one *nirguna-saguna*[3] (Ar. *Bawan Akhari*, 2). Unrelated and unstained,…God[4] is hidden within every bosom; in every breast there is the Light (N. *Sorathi*, 6:2-3); great is his glory when he in himself [is all in all]! (N. *Āsa dī Vār*, 2 Sl. 2)

2. Thou art the Maker of all, everything is thy glory—as thou pleasest, so [thou] makest it to

---

[1] *Alakha apāra agamma agochàri, nā tisu kālu na karama; jāti ajāti ajoni sambhau, nā tisu bhāu nā bharamā.*

In this striking couplet we find an attempt to describe some few of the qualities of the Supreme God; *kālu:* death, time, fate: *karamā:* binding actions which lead to effects which must be undergone: *bhāu:* the Skt. *bhāva,* mood, emotion, etc., *bharamā:* his own *māyā,* and so caught in the trap of illusion.

[2] *Nā tisu rūpa varanu nahĩ rekhiā*

[3] i.e., Without qualities and at the same time with qualities. There are no *two* Brahmas, as Śankara is falsely said by some to have taught: there is only *one,* but in that One are both the Unmanifest and the Manifest.

[4] *Brahamu,* the Absolute, to be known only in true yoga

move;…All is subject to thy Word! The Personal Lord art thou, the Almighty;[1] no one is so great as thou; the Word is thine and thou art the Mover of all (R. *Āsa Chhant*, 7:4, 3). All light is thine (N. *Sorathi*, 6:2); Nanak, the Blessed One is warp and woof [of all]![2] (Ar. *Bhairo*, 24:4)

3. Thy names are many and thy forms are endless; how many are thy virtues[3] cannot be told (N. *Āsa*, 33:1); but thy [real] Name is the Formless (N. *Āsa dī Vār*, 5). How many names! No end is known [to them]! There is no other like thee, O God! (N. *Rāmkali*, 3:3) Thou art One, the many others are thy forms; Nanak knows thy mysterious play! (N. *Āsa*, 25:4) There is the One; is there any other? Thou alone, only thou! (N. *Mājh ki Vār*, 13 Sl. 2)

God everywhere and always! Never was a time when he was not, never will time see his end; no possible spot in all the boundless universes unfilled with his glory! What form is his, of whom all forms are but veils to temper that glory to our poor feeble sight? He is formless in that all forms are his, no one alone; he is without qualities in that there is no quality not in him, no virtue which does not arise in and from his all-perfection. This universe is but the ever-changing waves dancing on the surface of his unfathomable deep; all obey his will, from whom comes

---

[1] *Purakhu Sujānu tūm paradhānu.*

[2] He is the infinite 'Ground' of all, as Tauler also taught.

[3] *Gunas*

the light and power in all that causes them to be. What name is exclusively his of whom all words are names? No word can fully describe the infinite, no names express the ineffable glory that is he. When he alone exists, has real and independent being, how can there be a name to mark him out from others? There are no others.

12. HIS GREATNESS IS UNTOLD

1. How many utter words from mere hearsay,[1] ...no one knows an end [of them]! (N. *Maru Solhe*, 12:6) Everyone hears, and calls God great, but has anyone seen how great [he is]? The extent [of thy greatness] can neither be grasped nor uttered; those who speak [of it] are held lost in thee! (N. *Āsa*, 1:1) Thou remainest aloof and none can attain to thee; that is why thou art called the Endless One (G. *Purānas Introd.*). O my great Master, fathomlessly deep and brimful of excellences, no one knows how great is thy extent! (N. *Āsa*, 1:1)

2. He to whom the Unseen has revealed himself can understand the ineffable story (N. *Maru Solhe*, 12:6); this is his quality: that there is no other, nor has there ever been, nor shall there ever be (N. *Āsa*, 2:3). God is as he is, and I remain rejoicing in singing his glory (K. *Śloka*, 122). If all were to join in trying to describe him, they could neither add to nor decrease his greatness (N. *Āsa*, 2:2); even if a hundred poets

---

[1] *Suni suni ākhai ketī banī.*

were found they could not complete a particle[1] [of the tale], even by weeping! (N. *Sri Ashtapadi*, 1:2) Let all the thoughtful meet and think their utmost, ... still they could not utter even a fraction of thy greatness (N.*Āsa*, 1:2).

3. All truth, all zeal, all goodness, and the great qualities of perfect persons—without thee no one can fully attain, and when thy grace is gained none can keep them away. What can the poor talker do? Thy treasuries are filled with thy praises; but what can he do whom thou givest this gift? (N. *Āsa*, 1:3-4) The world itself also comes and falls at the feet of those to whom God himself gives greatness; ... to those whom God himself protects how many others will come running. ...while who will not oppose the ones whom the Supreme has smitten? (R. *Gauri ki Vār*, 14 Sl. 2, 18 Sl. 1, 12) Nanak, it is the True One who arranges [all] (N.*Āsa*, 1:4).

Since man attained to speech he has vainly tried to express his sense of the infinite that lies all around him and within; but his feeble and halting words cannot reach even a shadow of God's glory. The mind itself falls back dazzled from that height, fettered to the earth, as the boy's kite cannot reach the blueness of the sky. Even the vast universe itself is but a tiny speck upon God's robe!

How then can we speak of him, or know him for ourselves? In our own power it is impossible; yet the

---

[1] *Tilu*: lit: a seed of *til*, one of the tiniest of all seeds

Omnipotent can reveal himself to his infinitesimal creature if and when he will. It is his grace that teaches man what he is—even though the skill of all his wisest cannot compass a tiny fraction of his glory with the boldest sweep of their united efforts. He alone conveys the beatific vision of himself to those whom he has chosen, and then strong in his strength these saints of God become invincible, before their quiet gaze the terrors of cruelty and sin fade away, and all joys hasten to their side. God's grace does all; he gives victory and defeat, life and death, day and night. None can resist his elect, none can save those whom he has doomed. And he is all good, all wise.

13. HE KNOWS ALL

1. [Seated] in the mind, [God] sees all and with a look of grace moves [all] (N. *Āsa dī Vār*, 16); the Great Sovereign, the Supreme Lord, made the universe to watch it (N. *Āsa Patilikhi*, 24).[1] The same who made now watches (N. *Tilang Ashtapadi*, 1:1); he knows everything which is happening (Ar. *Gaurī*, 2:2), he sees, understands and knows all, being everywhere within and without (N. *Āsa Patilikhi*, 24); he who made the creation, it is for him again to look after it (A. *Āsa dī Vār*, 23).

2. The Inner Knower of all bosoms (Ar. *Sukhmani*, 3:7) knows everything;...my Lord knows all states in advance (Ar. *Āsa*, 42:3, 128:1). The Kindly One indeed daily perceives secrets, yet does not in anger

---

[1] *Pātisāhu paramesaru vekhanako parapanchu kīā.*

withhold [men's] daily bread[1] (G. *Twaprasādi Sawwaiya*, 2); he knows every veil[2] of every bosom,[3] ...and takes away its disease, its grief and guilt (G. *Akāl Ustat*, 7, 10). Sad when his saints are sorrowful, he finds happiness in the happiness of the righteous (G. *Rahiras Chaupai* 12).

From his hidden throne in the heart of every creature in his universe God watches the Game that he has set in play, and knows everything that is going on everywhere. Being one with each soul he knows its needs, hears its silent prayer even before it can be put in words, sees the thought of mischief lurking in the depths of the wicked heart, and yet remains perfectly detached and impartial; like the sun he 'shines alike on the righteous and unjust'. Knowing the purpose of each incident in the age-long drama, he never interferes with its working; he allows the wicked to prosper until perhaps the very last act, and yet he silently guards from all real harm his chosen actors who are devoted to him and to his play, even when they seem to suffer grievously. For he is one with them, he shares their every feeling, He takes part in every joy and pain of theirs, as does the loving mother in her child's.

14. GIVES ALL

1. Glories[4] are in the hand of the Great One; He gives

---

[1] Most alliterative in the original: it reads: *rozī hī rāja bilokata rāzaka rohh rūhāna kī rozi nā tārai*. This is rather typical of the style of Guru Gobind Singh.

[2] Or curtain; the idea being that we cannot hide our hearts from him

[3] I have distinguished between *ghata* (bosom) and *mana* (heart).

[4] Or greatness (*wadiāīā*).

to whom he pleases (N. *Sri Ashtapadi*, 1:6); he himself gives the qualities of greatness, he also has the [good] work done (N. *Āsa dī Vār*, 16). If it pleases him he gives greatness, if he pleases he gives punishment [instead] (N. *Āsa Ashtapadi*, 11:4); but what comes from him is not evil (Ar. *Sukhmani*, 23:7)—whatever God does, that being done by God is pleasing to devotees (Ar. *Gauri*, 1:4), **they** consider the Lord's doing as sweet[1] (Ar. *Āsa*, 88:1). 'O Lord,' [they say], 'from thee do I receive this;…what thou givest I take as happiness![2] (Ar. *Mājh*, 33:3) Thou art the gratifier of all the heart's desire' (Ar. *Mājh Ashtapadi*, 3:3).

2. That which pleases him takes place; Nanak, what can man do? (N. *Āsa Ashtapadi*, 11:7) Living creatures are upheld by thee;…bad [or] good, we are thine! (Ar. *Sorathi*, 93:1-2) What can those who serve thee [really] give to thee?[3] (N. *Mālār*, 1:2) **They themselves** remember Thee [in their need] (Ar. *Mājh*, 21:3); they never cease from begging and taking [from thee]; thou art the Giver of Life, thou art indeed the Soul within the lives of all (N. *Mālār*, 1:2).

---

[1] *Prabhū kā kiā mīthā mānai.*

[2] This is the doctrine of the French school of the seventeenth century, as typified by *Abandonment to the Divine Providence*, by Fr de Caussade; it is also the 'Little Way' of Saint Thérèse de Lisieux.

[3] cf. the glorious hymn in GH 24:1, and 'We give thee but thine own, whate'er the gift may be!'

3. He is the Spring, and all the world [is his] garden (AD. *Basantu*, 17:4); wherever the King is, forest and glade burst into blossom, the beauty of spring everywhere is spread abroad[1] (G. *Akāl Ustat*, 268). Nanak, the Giver is one, there is no other besides (AD. *Sri Ashtapadi*, 2:8), and the Lord's chief function is kindness to devotees[2] (Ar. *Gūjari*, 12:1). My merry Friend is called the 'friend of all'; all consider him their own, and he saddens no heart (Ar. *Maru ki Vār*, II, 7 Sl. 2); he cherishes and fondles people like [his own] children (Ar. *Gūjari*, 12:1), [saying to them]: 'If thou remainest mine, then all the world is thine' (F. *Śloka*, 95).

He is the King Omnipotent; he is the director and allots parts to each player in his cast, and when the curtain falls it is he who gives rewards to those who have played the best, or reproofs to those whose shyness or forgetfulness have spoiled their acting. Knowing him as the author of the whole drama, the actors welcome whatever he may say or do to them, for it is certainly for their good. So God's saints are always happy, even in the midst of dreadful suffering, because they know they are still in the Beloved's tender hands, and it is he who lovingly cuts away from them the abscess of sin which destroys their spiritual health.

---

[1] In Guru Gobind's original:

jaha taha mahipa bana tana praphula,
sobhā basantu jaha taha pradula.

[2] *Bhagati-vachalu*, a favourite title of Sri Krishna also. But that Sri Krishna is the same One Lord whom Guru Arjan praises here.

Indeed, those who cannot thus surrender to his will and find it in all events of daily life, must pass through endless misery in this world; for he is sovereign, and there is no escaping what he chooses to send to each of us. He is King; yes, but he is also the joyous Lord of Beauty, the generous Providence who gives at every moment exactly what each child of his requires—friends, books, joys, pains, quarrels, losses, gains, all circumstances of his life. He is the source of all we have, of all we are, and there is nothing which is ours that has not come from him. That we know he is kind and good, being the very heart of our heart, inseparable from ourselves and sharing in all that comes to us, helps us to welcome all events of life, knowing that they cannot but be for good. He is indeed our loving Friend; one who has him, who is all, has all the world and more.

15. AND PERVADES ALL

1. In every single place thou art, the One present everywhere alone (Ar. *Mājh Ashtapadi*, 3:2); all comes to be seen by the gracious look as real when the spirit has become detached[1] (K. *Maru*, 3:3). If he throws his look of grace,[2] when I gaze intently there is no other besides (N. *Āsa Patilikhi*, 13), yes, my Lord is immanent in every

---

[1] *Jau ātama bhayā udāsu*; the connotation of *udāsu* is almost 'disillusioned or disgusted' with worldly things, and so 'withdrawn' into spirituality.

[2] Nanak everywhere insists that realization can come only by the grace of the Guru, who is God manifesting to the devotee.

place! (Nd. *Prabhati*, 1:1) Steeped in love, my Master is immanent, pervading everywhere (N. *Sri* 25:1), whose [very] form is Love [and in him] is no spot of anger....[He is] eternally in every place (G. *Akāl Ustat*, 124, 164), whose body is all things [of the universe][1]...He, being separate, is yet immanent (in all)[2] (Ar. *Sukhmani*, 23:6, 10:4); Nanak, everything is God outspread![3] (Ar. *Mundavani*, 1)

2. Whom shall I call evil when there is naught but he? (F. *Śloka* 75) I declare that no one seems bad [to me] (N. *Maru Ashtapadi*, 10:8), for the One resides in the heart [of all] (N. *Āsa Patilikhi*, 13). In every heart of creatures born from eggs or wombs, from sweat or mud,[4] the Light is found (N. *Barah Maha*, 14); the Light in all of us takes many different colours (N. *Āsa*, 37:4), but in every heart, at the inmost of all, there is only the One God (Nd. *Āsa*, 1:4). Behold him who is within outside as well, for there is no other besides; receiving the vision of

---

[1] We meet again the familiar thought that the universe is God's 'body'.

[2] A clear statement of the *visishthādvaita* position—distinct and yet not different

[3] Or has emanated from God; *sabhu Nānak brahama pasāro*. Note that the word here used for 'God' relates to the Absolute, not to the manifest and personal.

[4] *Andaja, jeraja, setaja, utabhuja*: the 'four kingdoms' of living nature as represented by birds, mammals, lice and worms.

oneness from the Guru's presence,[1] behold the Light enshrined in every bosom! (N. *Sorathi*, 11:1) In the eyes of saintly folk all is God;[2] ...and on beholding that vision all are entranced![3] (Ar. *Sukhmani*, 23:4)

3. Wherever I look, there is thy light, thy wondrous beauty! (N. *Sorathi*, 4:1) Within, without is God the One Lord[4] (R. *Suhi Chhant*, 2:2). I look with both eyes, but I see none but God; the eyes remain fixed in love [on him], and now no [other] subject can be spoken of (K. *Sorathi*, 4:1). [My] love is attached to that True One...who, even if I separate [from him] will not be separate [from me], being immanent in all (Ar. *Sri*, 13:1). All is God, all is God! There is naught but God! (Nd. *Āsa*, 1:1)

4. This world is the little chamber of the Real, wherein is the True One's dwelling (A. *Āsa dī Vār*, 2; Sl. 2). He who is absorbed in love for the real Master [sees] the Inner Light and [hears] the Inner Word (N. *Sorathi Ashtapadi*, 1:1). [O God,] though

---

[1] *Gurumukhī*: lit. from the mouth of the Guru, but often used simply for contact as when sitting in his presence or serving him. Asians have always held that association with a saint, even a distant sight of one, may be enough to clear the vision and enable swift realization of God.

[2] *Brahama*: here again the word for the Absolute

[3] It is not possible for the God-seer to see other things at that moment; his vision becomes wholly turned upon the One, so that to the world he seems asleep, or mad, or blind. The senses are still.

[4] *Antari bāhari Hari prabhu eko.*

thou art unseen thy Light is seen! (5:31 6 G)

When we detach our minds from blinding egoism we see that in all alike is only God, that this universe is but the curtain behind which he plays his shadow play, that in all we see and hear there is really nothing but him. Yet this is no vulgar pantheism, for God is not bound or limited by his creation; the Divine Actor does not forget his real Self for all the varied parts he may play in this wondrous drama. He assumes so many roles, disguises himself in so many forms, and yet remains apart from all of them, transcendent as well as immanent in all.

Realizing that all we see is really our Beloved playfully disguised, we shall no longer be able to condemn or criticize another—for he too is God, playing perhaps the villain's role in the drama; and how can there be interest in a drama if there is no villain to complicate the plot and so prolong the play?

God within the heart, God in all the universe outside! God everywhere at every moment! An ecstatic ocean of all-pervading bliss; nothing but perfect love on every side! An ocean in which we, his little fishes, play and live our lives immersed in him. He who sees thus can see no evil, can never turn his mind away from the One all-good. Being the centre of each heart, never can God be apart from any of his children; he is the eternal Companion, enlightening and gladdening all alike. This beatific vision is to be enjoyed not only by the sainted 'dead', but equally by those in this world of ours whose eyes are opened by the grace of the true teacher sent to those made ready by God's holy will.

16. HE IS THE ONLY ACTOR

1. Thyself the tablet, thyself the pen, thou art also the writing upon it (N. *Mālār ki Vār*, 28 Sl. 2). Thyself the fish, thyself the net (N. *Maru Solhe*, 1:11), thyself the fisherman and the fish, thyself the water and the net, …thyself the bait within it! (N. *Sri*, 25:2) Thyself [thou art] the water, dry land, ocean and tank;… Thyself the cow, thyself the herdsman.…Thyself the yogi and thyself the enjoyer![1] (N. *Maru Solhe*, 1:6, 11, 12) Speak of the One, O Nanak, why of a second? (N. *Mālār ki Vār*, 28 Sl. 2) He is himself the maker of his own play,…of whose play there is no limit (Ar. *Sukhmani* 13:8, 16:3).

2. My Darling is himself playful[2] in many ways! (N. *Sri*, 25:3) Being himself the Actor, he makes [others] act (N. *Sri Ashtapadi*, 1:4); as the Lord pleases, so he makes them dance…When one thinks: 'Something has come through me,' then for him there can be no happiness;…**our** hands can do nothing at all (Ar. *Sukhmani*, 11:7, 12:4, 6:8). To whatever [duty] thou assignest [man], to that he must apply [himself] (Ar. *Gauri*, 9:4). Thou thyself performest the whole play, Creator, why speak of or mention a second? (A. *Mājh ki Vār*, 2 Sl.)

---

[1] *Āpe jogi āpe bhogi*: the force lies, of course, in the contrast between the renouncer who unites with God, and the hedonist who seeks epicurean delights in worldly things.

[2] *Rangulā*: suggesting the loving tricks of a playful child

3. At his will all come into being, at his will they carry out [their] work, at his will [man] comes into the power of death,[1] at his will he is merged in the Real. Nanak, what pleases him takes place; there is nothing at all in the power of creatures[2] (N. *Sri Ashtapadi*, 4:8); this is the good pleasure of the True One (N. *Maru Solhe*, 15:12). He himself ... beholds [his own] glory; the one whom he inspires serves the Guru (N. *Āsa Ashtapadi*, 18:7-8).

4. Thy Shadow overshadows in everything, (even) fancies[3] are thy making; having formed fancies, thou thyself leadest men astray, while those meet the Guru [on whom] thy favour [falls] (N. *Āsa Patilikhi*, 10). Thou who madest the day hast also made the night[4] (N. *Āsa*, 2:4); dying and living are in the hand of the Lord to whom I have given this heart [of mine] (N. *Barah Maha*, 8). Demolishing thoroughly, [he then]

---

[1] *Kālai vasi*: lit. into the power of time, fate, death

[2] i.e., creatures have no power at all.

[3] *Bharamu*, i.e., illusions, errors, superstition, vagary. It should not be understood from this that God wilfully misleads or deceives his creatures, but that he permits them to wander into falsity so that they may in time perceive and love the truth. The ignorant cannot gain wisdom, but even the world of illusion is his world.

[4] God rules *all* things. Nanak does not shrink from the logical consequences of this truth, even where it suggests to the careless that *all* includes evil. As Julian of Norwich rightly said, 'Evil is no thing.' Darkness is but the absence of light, and evil the turning away from God. Isaiah sang: 'I Yahveh made the light and darkness.'

uproots; but he is himself the Adorner at his will (N. *Alahania,* 1:3). He does that which pleases him (A. *Āsa dī Vār,* 24), and whatever he does, I consider well done (N. *Āsa,* 37:1). He himself does it; to whom shall I complain? There is no one else who acts; go and complain to him if anything goes wrong! (N. *Suhi Chhant,* 4:4) But he knows all without our speaking (N. *Dhanasari,* 5:1).

5. If ever he inspires some service, that will indeed be done; he does it, of whom [are we to] speak? (N. *Āsa Ashtapadi,* 18:7) Thou art the Doer, I do nothing; when *I* act, it comes to nothing[1] (N. *Āsa dī Vār,* 12 Sl. 1), but when thou thyself actest, that comes to pass (R. *Āsa Chhant,* 7:3).

God is all; he is the slayer and the slain and the act of slaying; the author, pen, book, reader, characters and plot of the story. There is nothing anywhere that is not he, that does not draw its very being from him and exist solely by his will. It is he who prompts the actors in this lovely world-play of his, it is he who wrote the drama, it is he again who sits in the auditorium and enjoys the show. We think ourselves so clever, we human beings, with our aeroplanes and submarines, our radio and our atom bombs —yet we are nothing at all, only shadows dancing at his will. Only when we come to know this do we ourselves begin to enjoy the great Play, and then we realize his supreme Wisdom designed it all for our welfare. He sends

---

[1] How true it is that what we think *we* do turns to ashes! Gandhiji believed he was liberating India from corruption.

us into birth, guards us from the countless accidents which might destroy our bodies before we have played to the end of the part allotted to us; and when the last words are said, when the curtain sinks slowly over the fading scene of our earthly life, it is he who receives us and leads us home.

When we know that all life's events, its joys and sorrows, its friendships prompted, guided, worked out by that divine and its bitter treacheries, are prompted, guided, worked out by that divine hand—how can we be angry or hate, feel enmity or contempt? All are but his instruments, taken up one by one to work his perfect will. Even our wanderings, our sins and failures, our despairs—are part of his design, planned that we may learn from the agony they cause that peace and happiness are in naught but him, so that we may resolutely turn from all else to him alone and so find unending bliss.

It is when we delude ourselves by thinking it is we who act, who earn merit, perform vows, make pilgrimages, give charities, serve the nation—then it is that we, by thus enslaving ourselves to petty egoism, invite ruin on our ideals. True victory can come only when it is God who acts through us, when we regard ourselves as his tools, passive to the workings of his will; from him come all urges to noble action, and from him alone comes its success.

17. HE ALONE IS TRUE

1. *The first name is God's; how many prophets [stand] at his gate !*[1] *[1:123 N] There are tens of thousands of Muhammeds, but only one God; the*

---

[1] Tradition says this was the Guru's reply to Sheikh Farīd (II) when the Muslim saint invited him to honour the name of Muhammed.

Unseen is true and free from care, and many Muhammeds stand in his court, so numberless they cannot be counted! (1:121 N) How many saints and prophets beyond counting![1] They came into existence from the soil and were mixed with the soil again (G. *Akāl Ustat*, 77). The Teacher of teachers is one; many are the disguises [he assumes] (N. *Āsa Sohila*, 2:1), *Prophets have come into the world when sent; whenever he pleases he has them seized and brought before him* (1:121 N). Nothing is unmoving save the Name of God (AD. *Gūjari ki Vār*, 22 Sl. 2).

2. Serve only the One, the very Divine Teacher of all;[2] know that his real nature[3] is only one, the One Light in all (G. *Akāl Ustat*, 85). He is, and ever shall be; he has not gone, nor will he go;[4] eternal is the Creator....Nanak, know that the Real is eternal, ...everything else is false (N. *Sri,* 28:3, 5:1, 4). The

---

[1] Such sayings as this, current in the days of the Gurus, inflamed the anger of orthodox Muslims who felt them disrespectful to their great prophet. But Muhammed himself said such things in the *Korān*. Great is the Prophet indeed, but what is he before his Lord? How many worlds are there in God's universe, where his children live, to whom he must send his messengers from time to time! The words used are *pīr au pikāmbara kete*.

[2] *Eka hī kī seva sabha hī ko gurudeva eka.*

[3] *Sarūpa.* In his true Self God is only One; yet he manifests as many.

[4] A hard passage; the text reads; *haibhī hosi jāi na jāsi*; it may mean, as M. has it: 'He was not born, neither shall he die', but it does not say so much.

whole world [is like] a dream drama;[1] [God] causes the whole play of the drama to be enacted (R. *Kanre Ashtapadi*, 5:5).

3. What pleases him, the Almighty, that indeed takes place; this world is an illusion (N. *Alahania*, 1:3), this world is all a dream[2] (Ar. *Bawan Akhari*, 40). Yet everything is true to the one who understands, for, Nanak, the Lord is altogether true[3] (Ar. *Sukhmani*, 17:1). The whole world must pass away [in time], the Compassionate[4] is the only permanent Abode. By day the sun moves, the moon moves by night, tens of thousands of stars pass by; he is the one perpetual Abode, O Nanak—this is positively true (N. *Sri Ashtapadi*, 17:6, 8), whose bliss-form is ever blessed (Ar. *Sukhmani*, 16:2).

Countless saints and devotees, countless prophets and messengers at his command—but only *one* Lord, only one who is eternally true. The greatest of men, even *avatāras*, appear in the world, do the work God gave to them, and vanish again at his call; he alone is real and everlasting,

---

[1] 'All the world's a stage,' said Shakespeare

[2] We must be careful not to exaggerate what the Guru says here and fall into the error of the *māyāvādin*. The world *is* there, but 'things are not what they seem'; looking at the rope we take it for a snake.

[3] The essence of perfect truth, Brahman, could not produce what is false; the truthful does not lie or deceive. God is real, so the universe that comes from him must be real also—in a sense. Its 'reality' is relative and depends wholly on God's sustaining will.

[4] *Rahīm*, one of the beautiful names for God in the *Korān*.

always omnipresent. There is no wisdom, then, in adoring men, in raising saints and prophets to the throne of our hearts where he alone has the right to sit. The very greatest are *nothing* before him; it is not only foolishness but blasphemy and treason to exalt his servants to his place; they are but dreams that fade away in the first light of the real spiritual dawn. The whole world is real to our eyes while we live in it, but it is fundamentally false because impermanent. To rely on the fleeting, the unreliable, is the utmost folly; the eternal alone is a strong support, the source of everlasting security and happiness. He alone can be our real Home, who ever was, who is now, and evermore shall be, changeless and serene; resting in him, we shall find him in all, and so be at home in everything.

18. ALL NATURE ADORES HIM

1. Stars, moon and sun[1] meditate, earth sings and sky (Ar. *Āsa Chhant*, 5:3), all creation serves Thee day and night (Ar. *Sri III*, 2:12), [while] tens of thousands of devotees adore, repeating, 'Beloved! Beloved!' (Ar. *Āsa*, 106:1) God in the water, in the dry land God, God in the bosom, in the forest God, God here, God there,...God timeless, infinite God....God without disease, the griefless God, God without fancies, God without [the effects of] action, God invincible, God fearless, God undifferentiated, God without defect!...[O God], thou art indeed Space, indeed thou art Time, thou art the Occupant,

---

[1] *Nakhiatra sasi ara sūra.*

14

thou art indeed the Place [as well]....Thou in truth art Thou, Thou, Thou; thou in truth art Thou, Thou, Thou![1] (G. *Akāl Ustat*, 51-69)

2. In the sky [is thy] paten,[2] the sun and moon are turned to lamps,[3] the circle of stars are the inlaid[4] pearls; the fragrance of sandalwood is thy incense, the wind thy chowrie-fan;[5] all the forest flowers for the King of Light[6]! (N. *Dhanasari Sohila*, 3:1)

3. What an *ārati*[7] is this, O ender of births and deaths,[8] Thy *ārati*! The music of the uncaused

---

[1] Another typical piece of the Tenth Guru's style; in the original, it begins: *jale Harī thale Harī, ure Harī bane Harī*, and ends in a shout of ecstasy, untranslatable in English: *tuhī tuhī tuhī tuhī, tuhī tuhī tuhī tuhī.*

[2] *Thālu*, the silver plate in which offerings are made to God during Hindu worship; I have used the word *paten* to convey the religious sense.

[3] *Dīpakabane.*

[4] i.e., inlaid in the plate.

[5] *Pavanu chavaro kare*; the chowrie is a 'fly-whisk' of peacock-feathers, or other soft material, kept waving constantly over the head of a king or of the divine images. Sikhs wave it over the Book while reading their *Guru-Granth Sahib*.

[6] Or, is flowering with light for the King.

[7] *Ārati*, the worship of God through an image, with blowing of conches, ringing of bells, waving of lights, and public adoration. There is no exact English equivalent.

[8] *Bhava-khandanā*, a name for the redeemer of man from the woes of repeated entry into this world of birth and death.

sound[1] is thy blowing of horns. A thousand[2] eyes are thine, and yet thou hast no eyes; a thousand forms, yet not one is thine; a thousand holy feet, and yet not one foot; without an organ of smell, a thousand organs of smell are thine! I am fascinated by this play! (N. *Dhanasari Sohila*, 3:2)

4. The light in all is this very Light [of thine] through whose radiance there is a brightness in everything; the Light has shone forth in the Guru's witness! What pleases **God,** that is the [real] *ārati.* [Like] a bee maddened with desire for the flower, [so] day and night [my] heart becomes entranced with thirst for God's feet! Give the water of grace to the Sāringa[3] Nanak so that he may dwell in thy Name! (N. *Dhanasari Sohila*, 3:3-4)[4]

When the entire universe adores God and glorifies him by its unquestioning obedience to his laws, how small it seems for us to try to worship him in temples with our

---

[1] *Anāhatā,* the mystic sound heard in the heart *chakra* when the soul draws near to spiritual illumination. Materialists explain it as the 'beating of the heart', which explains nothing of its description in the scriptures of experience.

[2] The word is vague, meaning and indefinite large number.

[3] The bird *cuculus melanoleukos* which is said to drink water only when the moon is in Arcturus and to sing at night before the rains commence. On hearing it, love's wounds 'bleed again' and the lover longs for the beloved. It is another name for the *chatrika* of *GGS* 7:3.

[4] These three paragraphs form the song of Guru Nanak when invited to take part in the *ārati-ceremony* at the temple of Sri Jagannāth (Krishna) at Puri.

lights and flowers, with curling wisps of incense smoke and muttered prayers! God is everywhere, to be adored in every place, in every form; how can we be separate from him even enough so as to worship him, as outside ourselves? The whole of nature is his temple, the stars his altar lights, the soft forest odours are the incense ceaselessly offered him, the wind-waved branches are the royal fan above him, the 'voice of the silence' mystically heard in each heart is the uplifted chant of adoration. Everywhere is he, in everything adoring and adored, himself the object of his own worship, truly served only by the doing of his holy will. What a God is this of ours, my brothers! Who but is lost in wondering love at the very thought of him!

———————

CHAPTER THREE

Mortal Man

Though destined for immortal bliss, by the delusive pleasures of the world the soul of man is trapped in the false belief that the body is his self, its wants his needs, and so he forgets the Lord in whom is all his good. Clinging to the perishable things of the world, he shares their fate and is subject to mortality (cf. GH 3:4); the victim of sin, he is dragged again and again into physical birth by his own deluded choice. This must go on until by God's grace the Guru awakens in him the purifying love for God which destroys his egoism and sets him free from illusion. Bodily death is common to all who take a body, but it cannot affect God's lovers, who dwell not therein but at his feet, spending their lives in continuous memory of him and self-identification with his will.

19. THIS WORLD IS FALSE

1. The mortal round world[1] was created like a house of sand (Ar. *Bilawal*, 31:1): what is seen must

---

[1] *Mrita mandala jagu.*

perish like the shadow of a cloud (T.*Gaurī*, 2:2), so one should think continually of the Unseen (K. *Bawan Akhari*, 24). Taking as real a body false as a dream of the night (T. *Gaurī*, 2:1), O man, why do you pamper the body? It will vanish like a cloud of smoke. Worship God, the One Friend (Ar. *Sorathi*, 4:2). [He who] in his soul takes the world for reality shall not meet the Beautiful even in a dream (K. *Gaurī*, 23:2); the disciple sees and remembers the truth that save for the Reality [within it] the world is impermanent (N. *Dakhni Oamkāru*, 2:4). O heart, worship God and give up imagination;[1] God is the Life of the world,…so do service to God within the heart (K. *Bilawal*, 10:1, 3).

2. This world is all [mere] water, from water alone everything has come[2] (AD. *Mālār ki Vār*, 11 Sl. 2). Between fire and drops of water we came into being; for what purpose did we obtain existence? For how long have we a mother, how long a father? From whence have we really come? (N. *Gaurī*, 17:1) With whom should we make friendship?[3] The whole world is fleeting! (N. *Āsa dī Vār*, 10 Sl. 1). Through

---

[1] Or illusion, superstition, and the like (*bharamu*)

[2] A revival of the old Greek doctrines of Thales 640-550 BC but of course the idea goes back to ages beyond him, to the Vedas and elsewhere.

[3] These rhetorical questions recall the style of Zarathushtra in the Gathas. (cf. GZ 66-68)

how many ages this mind[1] has wandered! It does not finally remain [anywhere] but comes and goes. When God wills, then he causes the wanderings—he creates the play of the universe![2] (AD. *Gūjari ki Vār*, 13 Sl. 2) Those who have not met the true personal Guru are unfortunate and in the power of time;[3] again and again they wander into the womb and are placed in appalling filth (R. *Sri*, 2:3). Living creatures are all thy Play (R. *Āsa*, 1:2); all the Play is thine, O Lord! (R. *Gaurī*, 12:4)

This body, part of a perishable world made of unstable materials subject to incessant change, is wholly unreal—if by 'real' we mean 'eternal'. All save God is fleeting, unreliable, so it is wise to attach the heart to him alone, turning it away from this fickle world. Those who set their heart on earthly things are doomed to disappointment, to constant misery; never can they hope to see God while looking away from him. Only they who devote themselves to him can know the exquisite joy his service infallibly affords.

World and body alike derive from 'water', the most unstable of the 'elements' (cf. Gen. 1:2); our earthly relationships are momentary and of little meaning, for our real relationship is with God, and that is religion. For ages

---

[1] The word used here is *manu*, mind or heart; note that the wanderings are 'in' the *mind*; they are in a sense therefore fictional, as taught in the Advaita.

[2] *Parapanchu.*

[3] *Kāla*, time, death, fate

and ages through birth after birth of wandering, the soul has sought for happiness in this welter of human things, never realizing that real joy can be found only in the One Source of Bliss himself—until at last the true Teacher comes to him, and the long search is ended in the rapturous vision of the Beloved Lord. It is he who in his wisdom caused that sad wandering, so that the restless longing might grow to fever heat and the soul melts and dissolves in its love for him.

20. SIN

1. The pleasure of gold, the pleasure of silver, the pleasure of women and the scent of perfume, the pleasure of horses, the pleasure of the couch and palace, the pleasure of sweets, and the pleasure of meat! Such being the pleasures of the body, how can the Name [find] a dwelling in the heart?[1] (N. *Sri*, 4:2) The false one is by his affections attached to the false,[2] forgetting the Creator! (N. *Āsa dī Vār*, 10 Sl.) All the senses are intoxicated with their own pleasures and feel no interest even in their house![3] (Ar. *Gaurī*, 20:2)

2. The Bridegroom gave me these things, and on them I fixed my mind;…in these luxuries I forgot my Spouse and did not sit near him. …O Husband, I withdrew from thee, and so stored up misery [for

---

[1] Strictly: bosom (*ghaṭi*)

[2] *Kūl kūlai nehu lāgā*. Like attracts like.

[3] i.e., the welfare of the body itself, in which they dwell, is neglected.

myself]![1] (N. *Suhi Kuchaji*, 1:8-14) God, graciously pardon me, for I am a sinner very full of guilt! (AD. *Śloka* 29:2) By my not obeying his command, even though [God] is within the house he **seems** far away (AD. *Gūjari ki Vār*, 6 Sl. 1). But even if I have gone astray [I am] a child, O God, and thou [art my] father and mother! (Ar. *Sri*, 27:1) In the true Master are all virtues, but all demerits are in us (N. *Sri*, 10:1); we commit many sins, no end of them! (AD. *Śloka*, 29:1) Yet if **we** let God's feet dwell in the heart our transgressions shall be blotted out (AD. *Gūjari*, 6:2).

3. Through ignorance is man involved in worldliness; if he knew he would save himself [from it][2] (Ar. *Sukhmani*, 11:3). Now are my faults as overflowing as the waters of the sea and ocean;… my defects cannot be counted (N. *Gauri*, 17:5, 1). When there is impurity in the heart and impurity in the body, the tongue must also be unclean;…how can it be made pure? Without the heart the word cannot be cleansed—truth arises from the true[3]

---

[1] Habitual disobedience to God destroys the intimacy wherewith he may be constantly perceived as present; it alienates the soul from all good.

[2] *Aanajānata bikhia mahi rachai*; 'They know not what they do!' cried Jesus as his torturers drove in the nails. Knowing God, how could one sin against him?

[3] 'By their fruits ye shall know them.' One with a pure heart has pure thoughts and utters pure words; how can the words be pure when the heart is full of foulness and every filth? Only contact with purity can purify, as the magnet magnetizes the steel it touches.

(N. *Sri Ashtapadi,* 5:1). If one freely sings [God's] glory day and night, all one's offences are erased (AD. *Suhi Chhant,* 1:3) but if he forgets the Real for one instant that time goes in vain; with every breath he must remember [God],[1] and then He himself gladly pardons him (AD. *Gūjari Ashtapadi,* 1:9). Intoxicated with God's presence, he becomes pure (Ar. *Gaurī,* 109:4).

4. Cleave to God the Treasure, worship the true Guru, leave all wickedness; (Ar. *Sri,* 25:1); through devotion get rid of the [petty] self;…such a man becomes pure (AD. *Basantu,* 5:1-2). Having seen the vision [of God] he becomes holy and uplifts all brothers and friends (Ar. *Mājh,* 16:2). O Nanak, then falsehood is ended, truth at last prevails![2] (N. *Rāmkali ki Vār,* 13 Sl. 2)

The pleasures of the world for a time distract the seeking soul from its agelong quest and hold it back from the passionate search within which would unveil the Hidden One in the heart. So all-absorbing are these worldly delights, worthless though they be, that they leave the soul no time to think of its true needs; the senses are so busy tasting them that they forget that their very function is really to set God on the throne within the soul.

---

[1] cf. G.N. 16:6, etc. It is impossible to point out in detail the parallels between these two 'Gospels'; they are so close that they may be regarded as one, in two forms; Sikhism is indeed a Vaishnavism purged of 'image-worship' and 'caste'.

[2] Almost verbally the same as in the *Korān* 34:49 (GI 34:3).

So the soul forgets God, intoxicates herself with pleasures that turn to misery—ashes in a mouth that thought to relish sweets. By turning to him with a cry for pardon and a humble admission that the agony of separation from all that is good is caused by her own fault, the soul invokes his aid, pleading for God's paternal love to replace her own sins with his infinite virtues. It is only this attraction to the world of sense which plunges man in sin, and as that comes from ignorance, its cure is knowledge—the knowledge that God is all and God is Love. Only his entry into the heart in the manifested form of the Divine Name, can take sin away and make the soul in a moment wholly pure, plunging it into a sea of entrancing bliss.

One who would be free from sin must cling to God, obey the Teacher sent to him, and through his devotion transcend the egoistic self; then 'the pure in heart shall see God', and such a one saves himself and all in contact with him too.

21. BONDAGE AND LIBERATION

1. In many forms this world has bewitched [men] in many ways (Ar. *Sri*, 21:4); by imagining an illusory[1] body to be real, in this way is the self bound (T. *Sarang*, 3:2); those who practise falsehood and deceit [fall] into birth in the world (Ar. *Āsa Chhant*, 13:3). This soul has dwelt in many wombs;[2] being plunged into a sweet

---

[1] *Mithiā*, the same word as is used in the famous Advaita dictum *brahmasatyam jaganmithya*.

[2] *Garbh*, the Skt: *garbha*.

fascination, it was trapped in the womb.[1] This *māyā* has brought the three worlds into its power and set its lure in every bosom (Ar. *Bawan Akhari*, 7). [Brother,] you are clinging closely to the unreal;…desire, anger, greed and illusion[2]—to these pleasures the senses cling… So the [Divine] Person the Creator[3] has caused you to wander again and again into birth (Ar. *Āsa*, 126:1, 3).

2. Accursed be this love for the lure of worldliness; no one [who has it] is seen [to be] happy! (Ar. *Sri*, 13:1) The Creator takes to himself no blame [for this][4] (N. *Āsa*, 39:1). Bound by the fetters of his own 'I, I', the blind one imputes blame to others [for his misery] (Ar. *Bawan Akhari*, 2). When this one thinks anybody bad, then all join in a plot against him; when he ceases to say: 'Mine, thine', then they no longer feel enmity for him.[5] … He who attaches himself to God is the friend of all (Ar. *Gauri Ashtapadi*, 1:2, 6:1).

---

[1] *Joni*, the Skt: *yoni*; in English it is difficult to distinguish with exactness these two words for womb.

[2] *Kāma krodha aru lobha moha*; the usual four in Skt. works; they are not pleasures to *us*, but the 'senses' (or the 'physical elemental') finds great pleasure in the excitement they provide (cf. C. W. Leadbeater's books).

[3] *Bidhāte*, Skt.: *Vidhāta*, i.e. Brahma the Creator

[4] *Āpe dosu na deī, kartā*; no sorrow can be caused by God, but he allows man to suffer the unhappy results of foolishness, so that he may become wise (cf. GH. 31.1).

[5] This teaching is typical of that of modern Theosophists.

3. The world is pervaded with the intoxication of desire, anger and egoism (Ar. *Sri*, 25:2); the heart's infatuation increases [the trend to] birth and death (Ar. *Bawan Akhari*, 2), [and thereby the soul] has [only] received the fruits [of its own acts] recorded in the past (N. *Sri Ashtapadi III*, 1:8). When such men entangle themselves in the infatuation [of worldliness], coming and going[1] [in the world] they are always sought by death (Ar. *Gauri Ashtapadi*, 1:4); bound by death's rope and the love of sweet worldliness, deluded by error, they do not realize that the Lord is always with them (Ar. *Bawan Akhari*, 9). When a man harbours pride in the heart, then he madly roams about away [from God]; but when he has become the dust of all [feet], then in every bosom he perceives the delightful Lord (Ar. *Gauri Ashtapadi*, 1:1).

4. The service of the Lord (Ar. *Sukhmani*, 19:4) and the service of a good man breaks the bondage of birth and death,[2] and one attains to happiness.... He takes the name of the One and strings it in his

---

[1] *Āvai jāi*, the usual phrase for rebirth in the physical world—a doctrine fundamental to Sikhs as to Hindus of almost every school.

[2] The power of service done to a saint with a pure heart is also fundamental to Sikh doctrine; the saint's grace is the channel of God's grace, and this instantly frees the faithful soul from bondage. The personal lives of the Second and Third Gurus specially proved this truth.

heart,[1] and then he will not be swept again into birth....Nanak, the coming and going is at an end for him in whose heart God is (Ar. *Bawan Akhari*, 27 Sl., 14, 7 Sl.). When all errors have been destroyed in him, there is no difference [in him] from the Supreme God (Ar. *Gauri Ashtapadi*, 1:4) The errors are cut away by the Guru, and then all is considered God! (Ar. *Sri*, 25:4) He who is given to love interiorly is a liberated [soul] (AD. *Majh Ashtapadi*, 20:7); when he recognizes the Creator, then for him there is no more burning [of desire][2] (Ar. *Gauri Ashtapadi*, 1:3).

5. Graciously unite [with those], O God, separated [from thee] by past deeds; wearied by wandering in the four quarters and ten directions,[3] they have now come for the kind welcome of the Lord! (Ar. *Barah Maha*, 1) Mother, father, son, brother, friend, there is none but he;...He fulfils the heart's desire [of one who] repeats [the Name of] the Sea of Happiness[4] (R. *Kanre ki Var*, 13-14).

It is by taking this changing body to be real that man is caught up in the toils of worldliness, which are so alluring and so crafty that few can escape its snare. Caught in their

---

[1] i.e., lets the heart hang on the Name as a bead upon the thread of the *mala* or rosary. When the Name pierces and supports the heart, it lies at the centre of the man's life and he is merged into its bliss.

[2] i.e., of the pain of separation from God, source of all good.

[3] The four cardinal points, east, north, etc.; the four intermediary points, north-east, south-west, etc.; upwards, and downwards.

[4] *Sukha-sagar*, familiar name for God throughout India

beauty, the soul passes age after age in physical bodies, being deceived into the belief of their essentiality so that almost without question she yields to all the demands of sense and passion. So long as these prevail in the heart, man lies chained by *māyā*, and cannot escape from rebirth.

Now in this slavery there can be no real happiness, for man is meant to be free. This is the fault of no one but the silly soul herself, though she tries to throw the blame for her sorrows on others, even on God himself—but in vain. Indeed, so long as she attributes her woes to others, she brings down their cruelties and injustices on her own head and surrounds herself with enemies. When she renounces the petty self which has caused all the trouble, she is at once free and finds in all the world a friend.

So long as the soul is subject to the passions and desires of earthly things, so long must she fall into earthly bodies and endure the sorrows of the unstable and unsatisfactory earthly life, which have already been earned by earlier actions and desires. It is the proud belief that she acts on her own which has entangled her in this snare, and it is only the humility which sees God as the inspirer and doer of every action which frees her for ever and shows her God enthroned in every being everywhere.

This humility arises from the contact with a saint of God; it grows from the act of surrender to God, which is symbolized and manifested by prayer and by repetition of the holy Name. When God takes the throne, rebirth, sin, pride, egoism for ever vanish, the barrier between Creator and creature disappears, and the 'light is merged with Light'. In this union alone lies peace, full satisfaction of the heart's long desire for happiness; the soul enters into God and knows him as in real essence not other than herself.

22. DEATH

1. The world is a perishable home—my heart has known this truth[1] (N. *Tilang*, 1:1); everything that comes into the world must depart again; all but the Name is under [the control of] time[2] (N. *Sri Ashtapadi*, 16:4). Like the guest of a night you will arise and go away at dawn;[3] [my brother], why are you attached to the family? All are garden flowers![4] (Ar. *Sri*, 22:2) As many as [there are] souls, so many are wayfarers; when the summons comes there can be no delay (N. *Rāmkali ki Vār*, 11 Sl. 2).

2. When [God] sends [a man] he comes [into the world], he goes when recalled (N. *Rāmkali Ashtapadi*, 7:10); leaving in the world his raiment[5] and pleasant beauty, he must go (N. *Āsa dī Vār*, 14); he came naked, and naked he will go[6] (Ar. *Āsa*, 38: 3). No one brought this wealth when he came here,

---

[1] *Duniā mukāme phanī tahkika dila dāni:* which is Arabicized Urdu. We find a good deal by the First Guru in this dialect, for he mixed much with Muslims to whom he spoke in their own tongue.

[2] Or death (*kāla*)

[3] This metaphor of the night's visitor at an inn, who packs up and goes early in the morning, is a favourite one among Muslims of all lands, as it was with the Manicheans long before.

[4] We blossom for a day or two, fade, and fall.

[5] i.e., body—a metaphor derived from Gnostic and Hermetic usage through Persian literature, as much as through the Hindu tradition. The parallels between the *Granth Sahib* and the *Gītā* are too numerous to indicate; their writers moved in the same tide of inspiration. (cf. *Gītā*, 2: 22)

[6] cf. Tim. 6:7.

no one will take it when he goes (K. *Sarang,* 1:2); save only for God's Name all will be lost in the future [1] (Ar. *Barah Maha,* 3).

3. Why is the foolish mind proud? It will have to depart when the Master wills,…it will have to leave the house, for none can remain [here] (N. *Maru,* 2: 1-2), and that day has drawn very near [for you] (Ar. *Sri,* 22:4). You weep for others, but who will weep for you?…They will not at all hear, [though] you would make people hear [your cries]. O Nanak, the One who made them sleep awakens them; if you realize your [real] home, then there will be no [more] sleep (N. *Āsa Ashtapadi,* 13:3-5).

4. Those who wander from the Supreme Lord are filled with every disease (Ar. *Barah Maha,* 9); forgetting God, **they are** already dead (Ar. *Āsa,* 149: 1), for death seizes on him who has become an unbeliever[2] in the Lord; not perceiving the blissful Self,[3] he will be born and die in many wombs (Ar. *Bawan Akhari,* 21).

5. The fish did not understand the net [spread] in the unfathomed briny lake;…like that fish, so the net will fall unawares on man. The whole world is

---

[1] *Agai,* i.e., after death on the road to judgement.

[2] *Sākata,* Skt., *Śakta,* worshipper of *Śakti,* power; it is curious how this word came to mean in Punjabi almost 'atheist'. The absence of God *is* death.

[3] *Ātmārām.*

bound by death; without a Guru death is invincible,[1] but those escape who are imbued with the Real, having left doubt and wicked desires[2] (N. *Sri Ashtapadi*, 4:1). So give up [mere] pleasure, and spontaneous happiness[3] will come (N.*Maru*, 2:2).

6. When the body falls and the soul leaps away, what will be the state of evil-doers? (N. *Sri Ashtapadi*, 16:4) Azrail[4] grabs me by my hair,[5] yet my heart does not know it; there is no wife, son, father, brother to take my hand[6]—no one [to stop] me falling when at last my [hour of] fate arrives (N. *Tilang*, 1:1-2). [Yet] if one takes care not to forget the Master, then it is easy to die;[7] ...Nanak, he who dies such a death shall live for ever! (AD.*Bihagale ki Vār*, 17 Sl. 2)

All earthly things are fleeting and doomed to perish; all friendships and relationships last but for a little, and when death calls, the soul must at once leave them all behind. All its cleverness and learning, all its bodily beauty and

---

[1] Or death swallows all but the Guru.

[2] *Vikāra*, i.e., *vāsanā, doṣa,* guilt, evil traces of desire

[3] *Sahaja sukhu; sahaja* means 'easy', natural, unopposed, habitual, etc.

[4] The Muslim name for the Angel of Death

[5] lit: shame; to be pulled by the hair or beard is an unspeakable disgrace, but death pays no heed to the dignity of men.

[6] i.e., as a helper (*dastangir*); this passage is in almost pure Persian.

[7] That death is a joy to the believer who 'falls asleep in the Lord' has been declared a thousand times in every religion.

strength, its wealth and courtliness, its noble ancestry, its lands and houses, proud balances in the bank—all remain behind and pass into other hands; the soul must enter the unseen as naked as it came into the world at birth. One thing alone remains; the Name of God—that is, as much of him as the soul has been able to perceive in life.

Death is always on the doorstep for each one of us, and it becomes us to think how much of that precious Name is really treasured in our heart, so that we may not go altogether empty to that world beyond. Those who profess love for us here will soon forget us when we die; only one Friend is ever constant, and in him alone can we find a real and eternal home.

Not the death of the body is to be feared, but the greater death, which is forgetting of the Lord and which dips us again and again in the hell of earthly wombs. Forgetfulness of the Real is the snare which catches us and hands us over to death; leaving aside all evil and worldliness, filling the heart with the nectar of God, we shall find that life eternal is our birthright that none can take from us. One whose body dies while his soul and mind and heart dwell in the Lord of Life will certainly find that death is but the gate to eternal life and joy.

23. JUDGEMENT

1. The Master,[1] seated in judgement with his book, will call for the reckoning (N. *Rāmkali ki Vār*, 13 Sl. 2) of every moment.[2] He will take an account, the soul will get bad and good [returns] (N. *Tukhari*

---

[1] *Rabu,* the Arabic word *Rabb,* that is, God

[2] *Ghali,* strictly the short space of twenty-four minutes

Chhant, 2:5); what she has earned here, that she must receive yonder (AD. *Bihagale ki Vār*, 19 Sl. 1), each must get the very same bad and good that she herself has done (N. *Āsa dī Vār*, 14). In the next [world] no authority avails; everyone fares according to his deeds[1] (N. *Alahania*, 1:2); he may have done [his own] will to his heart's content [down here], but in the future he must walk on the narrow road[2] (N. *Āsa dī Vār*, 14), [and there] he is judged exactly according to the work *he has done* (N. *Suhi*, 7:3).

2. The work of all creatures is written on their head,[3] and the judgement will depend upon their actions (N. *Basantu*, 3:4). Without [good] action[4] no one can pass [the test][5] (N. *Rāmkali ki Vār*, 11 Sl. 2), [and] no one can blot out the written record[6] (Ar. *Bawan Akhari*, 17). As he sows, so he eats

---

[1] *Agai hukamu na chalai mūle siri siri kiā vihāna.*

[2] The 'narrow road' is described also in Muslim and Parsee books, often as being narrow as a razor's edge (cf. GZ 41:1).

[3] This looks like fatalism, but such is not the meaning of the law of karma; fate has nothing to do with it, for each makes his own karma and then reaps the effects of what he has made. He can change it as soon as he wishes.

[4] This reminds us that mere pious dreaming is not enough; there must be virtuous action in the world to earn the grace of the Guru, which alone can give true piety and so lead to enlightenment and spiritual freedom.

[5] The word is *tarai*, i.e., 'be saved'.

[6] The terror of the judgement is mitigated by the assurance that the Judge knows also all compensating circumstances and, in weighing up our failures, considers also our difficulties and the efforts we made to overcome them.

(R. *Āsa*, 2:5). God ever watches and hears everything; nothing can ever be hidden from him (R. *Gaurī ki Vār*, 16 Sl. 1). From whom do you try to hide, when he is always present watching? (Ar. *Sri*, 16:3) Misled by error you keep a curtain, but will [have to] confess the secrets of the soul;[1] ...how can you hide from him? (Ar. *Āsa*, 128:1, 42:3)

God, who dwells as the conscience in each heart (*antarajāmi*), judges every soul after death, taking account of every action, thought, feeling and desire, and giving an exact return for all. In that life we find the perfect fulfilment of our life down here; all incomplete plans are worked out, all sins meet their unpleasant consequences, all deeds of merit bring their own happy fruits. There is absolute justice in that judgement; there is no partiality, no favouritism; each receives exactly as he gave, by the infallible and inevasible **law of karma**. No matter how much a rich or powerful man on earth may have escaped the fruits of his deeds here, in that life which follows he finds them awaiting him and there is no road for his escape. Nor can he hope that his secret lusts and hates will be unknown to that dreadful judge for he is omniscient, and the stern words of sentence will ring out like thunder on his ears as he goes away to his punishment.

We meet here the same kind of metaphorical picture of judgement as we find in G1 49, GH 28, GZ 38, GMC 48-49; the tradition goes back to the 'weighing of souls' in the Egypt of 1500 BC along one line. Banno's *Granth Sahib,* which is

---

[1] *Brahma ke mūse tūm rākhata paradā pachai jīa ki māni.*

regarded as apocryphal by orthodox Sikhs, gives us many lurid extra details which bear resemblance to the descriptions of hell in various scriptures; but as these can no longer awaken respect in the minds of readers we shall not print them here. They are translated in part in Macauliffe's Vol. I, pp. 124-127.

24. HELL AND REBIRTH

1. What is the use of bathing in holy waters if the filth of pride [remains] in the heart?[1] (N. *Sri Ashtapadi*, 12:4) He who feels no love for the Name in his heart will go to hell even if he perform millions of ceremonies...He who does not adore God's Name in the heart shall be bound in death's city in the manner of a robber[2] (Ar. *Gauri Ashtapadi*, 10:5-6); he asks for happiness but misery will come hereafter (K. *Gauri Ashtapadi*, 1:1). Him who slanders [another here]...there [Death] seizes and throws into a terrible hell—a pit of misery is that ! (R. *Gauri ki Var*, 16 Sl. 1) Those who forget my Master, for them there is extreme pain (N. *Sorathi*, 1:1); the haughty in mind who have still something left [to pay],[3] over them Azrail will be placed in charge, and they will see no way to come or go,

---

[1] This is a frequent refrain of the Guru, who saw the Hindus of his time putting almost all their faith in such external rites.

[2] *Chora kī nyāi Jama-puri bādhā.* The name is more familiar in its Skt. form of Yama.

[3] *Talbā pausan ākiā bākī jinā rahī.* This passage seems to suggest an idea akin to the Catholic Purgatory and the Parsee Hamastakan(GZ 50:1, 46:7-8).

being trapped in the narrow street (N. *Rāmkali ki Vār*, 13 Sl. 2).

2. One utters nectar in the mouth while poison [lurks] in the heart, he undergoes a beating[1] while bound in death's city; [another] commits sins behind many curtains, in a moment he is exposed to the world (Ar. *Gaurī*, 71: 2-3). The habitual slanderer[2] [becomes] a dweller in hell and is separated from the Inner Self;[3] (N. *Maru Ashtapadi*, 7:3); naked is he sent to hell, and then it seems very terrible [to him] and he repents of the sins he has committed[4] (N. *Āsa dī Vār*, 14), Nanak, he has as many chains on the neck as sins; if he [acquires] virtue his chains...are cut off (N. *Sorathi*, 1:4). What happiness can there be for the one without virtue?

---

[1] Let us not be misled by these metaphors into crude imaginations about life in the spirit-worlds. Swedenborg's account of conditions found there, confirmed by later research, shows that the Guru here describes what he actually *saw*, in the only words which could convey anything clear and definite to his audience.

[2] *Nindā kari kari;* lit: 'slander making [and] making', a common idiom for continuous action.

[3] A striking thought, agreeing with the doctrine that hell is separation from God, combined with despair.

[4] The Catholic dogma that repentance is impossible in hell is contrary both to common sense and to the defined nature of God. What, then, is the *soul* subject to time, so that after death its whole powers and nature are changed and it loses both free will and moral life? Then the soul is *dead* along with the body. And no thinking person can believe that God who, in all worthy creeds, is defined as Absolute Love, could create souls for *eternal* suffering. A wicked blasphemy.

(N. *Sri Ashtapadi,* 5:1). Nanak, the Creator is gracious to him who is drunk with the sweetness in the True Name within (Ar. *Gaurī,* 71:4).

3. [Man] reaps the [fruits of] acts performed in a past [birth]; the happiness and woe thou givest to every individual is just, [O God]! (N. *Barah Maha,* 1) As he made a sowing in the past life, so he reaps now (R. *Gaurī ki Vār,* 16 Sl. 1). Impute no blame to anyone, [my brother,] the blame belongs to your own karma; say, 'What I have done, that have I suffered [now]! I give no blame to another person!'[1] (N. *Āsa Patilikhi,* 21)

No ceremonies can cleanse the heart—nothing but the love of God can avail for that. The only way, therefore, to escape from hell and rebirth in this unsatisfactory world is found in 'the practice of the presence of God', feeling him always within and without, around, and permeating every atom of the soul's life. Sin inevitably leads to hell and to the misery of another incarnation; the forgetting of God — worst of all sins and intensified by the harbouring of egoism in the heart—puts the unhappy soul in the clutches of merciless Death from whose 'realm' he can find no escape.

Useless then are the elaborate pretences of piety so cleverly kept up by sinners in this life; in the beyond all veils drop away, all curtains fall, and each soul stands naked as he really is before all mankind—glorious with the assumed merits of the Lord conferred as an act of pure grace, or foul and stinking with the loathsomeness of sin which drags him

---

[1] What joy for the believer in karma; it makes life sensible and puts it in our own control!

down to its own home in hell. There he must repent at leisure amid frightful torments which exactly correspond to his sins and are their precise results.

So too in the past. Before this present birth, each has lived many times and earned merit or shame by his actions; according to these earnings of the past so are his opportunities, talents and circumstances today. All is absolutely just, for each has exactly what he has deserved and lies on the bed he himself has made for his own use.

25. THE CONQUEST OF DEATH

1. Madmen, you remain asleep! Drunk with the pleasure of worldliness, family and sense objects, you embrace fleeting delights[1] (Ar. *Āsa*, 142:1); while [a man] sleeps in sin and worldliness,[2] no perception or understanding comes to him; when Death seizes his hair and lifts him up, only then does he go home[3] (Ar. *Āsa*, 152:1). [Now] he rises eagerly for some bad work, but at the time for [repeating] the Name he lies sleeping! (Ar. *Suhi*, 8:1)

2. From what an origin has this thy mighty power made man! (Ar. *Sarang*, 81:1); [and yet] the body is a temple[4] (P. *Dhanasari*). [My brother,] keep far from

---

[1] The language here is striking, it reads: *bāvara soi rahe; moha kutamba bikhai rasa māte mithiā gahana gahe* (*cf.* GH 8:2).

[2] *māyā*

[3] i.e., according to M, 'come to his senses'. God is the real home. The same idea is common to Gnostics and Manicheans.

[4] *Devāla*, i.e., 'house of God', an idea current among Christians first, so far as I have read.

passion and guilt (Ar. *Suhi Chhant,* 11:3); press to your bosom [God's] lotus feet [resting] in the heart (Ar. *Sukhmani,* 19:1), for there is no impurity for those who in the heart think of God, (K. *Gaurī Ashtapadi,* 41:3), who fashioned you, and made the earthly body, who is the aforesaid Light bringing thought and discrimination, who protected you in the mother's womb—remember that Protector, O man! (Ar. *Rāmkali Ashtapadi,* 2:1)

3. What comes into being is destroyed by death; but God has preserved us by our study of the Guru's word....Death cannot trace out the one in whose heart God's true Name dwells and who sings his glory (N. *Gaurī Ashtapadi,* 14:1, 9). On meeting such devotees, man Nanak,[1] what can Death do to them? (N. *Rāmkali,* 4:4). Nothing can injure the one whom God has caused to love Him[2] (AD. *Anand,* 28:3), while if anyone is very egoistic, he is mixed with the dust in a moment (Ar. *Gonda* 20:3). As a fish perishes without water, so does the unbeliever die of thirst...without God (N. *Sorathi,* 7:1). [O God] thou art the ocean of water, we thy fishes! (Ar. *Mājh,* 14:1)

4. O dear one, enjoy [God's] love while youth is still fresh, the days of youth are few (N. *Sri,* 24:1); the

---

[1] *Jana Nānak;* the word *jana* means, 'person' then 'man' in the sense of 'slave' or 'servant', and finally 'man of God'.

[2] We recognize the confidence of St Paul here (cf. Rom. 8: 28).

home is a whirl of entanglements, brother, and the stone of sin cannot go [across it]; embark the soul on the raft of the fear [of God] (N. *Maru*, 2:4), for in whose heart fear is in their heart is also love (N. *Āsa dī Vār*, 5 Sl. 2). When it pleases **God**, then [man] feels love,[1] the deception of error departs from within [him], wisdom spontaneously arises, and intelligence awakens; by the Guru's grace he then experiences [real] love.[2] In such a companionship [with God there is] no dying; recognize his will, and then you must meet the Master (K. *Sri*, 1:3-4).

5. Make a prayer before the true Guru to let you meet that Friend; on meeting the Friend one finds happiness and Death's messengers take poison and die....Death enters not there where the light is merged in Light. Thou art the Friend, thou the beloved Lord,[3] thou the uniter with thyself! [Brother,] in the words of the Guru praise [him who has] no end or limit;[4] death does not approach there where is the Guru's infinite Word (N. *Sri Ashtapadi*, 4:5-6).

---

[1] *Bhau,* i.e., felt or emotional love, to be clearly distinguished from *liva,* or *prema,* which may have little of the emotions in it but acts as a goad to heroic action. Western mystics also stress that one need not *feel* the love for God in order that it may be real, and sanctifying.

[2] *Liva lāgai,* i.e., absorbs himself in devotional love; cf. note 1 above: the force here is that a fiery love is the fruit of the long cultivation of the emotional love which is nearer to the surface.

[3] Sujānu, so translated by M.

[4] Or praise God with the Guru's word without end or limit.

How foolish to drowse away the precious hours of life, careless of the future thus infallibly and inevitably earned! Intoxicated with the sweets of the present and eager for more of such pleasures, many forget altogether that their life is to know and love the infinite and eternal God, and to give all they have as sacrifice in his dear service. Until the last moment they give no thought to what follows death, and so when the call comes they are taken unawares.

Made from the humblest of materials as it is, man's body is yet the holiest thing on earth, God's very temple, meant to enshrine his infinite sanctity. It must be kept clean and holy, that therein the precious feet of the Beloved may be lovingly treasured and adored. The lover of God is always holy, the real saint, for his mind is ever bathed in the pure water of remembrance of him who is the source of love and wisdom and goodness.

Death is the forgetting of God; one who lives always in the thought of God can never die, even when his body falls away into the dust from out of which it came. How can one living in the eternal fall under death's power? Death is the fruit of sin, of adherence to the petty ego which is impermanent, unstable; it is the natural fate of those who turn away from God their Life but can never touch those who are filled with love for him.

Brief is life, and the world is a trap from which it is hard to escape; nothing can save the soul but love for God. This should be our aim even in early youth, for none knows certainly how long he is to live. This love is God's own gift; it drives out all false ideas and clarifies the vision of the Truth and so infinitely deepens the attachment to it. The lover finds the Beloved, and in his arms forgets the long fever of separation. To this end then let all our prayers be turned, that God may in his mercy give us grace to love him truly and, with the teaching of the Guru as our guide and inspiration, burn away the ego which is the veil that hides him from our eyes.

———————

CHAPTER FOUR

The True Guru

Unaided man cannot come to God. He needs the awakening word of the real teacher sent to him by God himself. Such a teacher must be himself a saint, wholly devoted to the Lord, sincere, kindly, and of good repute. It may not be the recluse or anchorite who is near to God and able to lead others to him, but the guide must be detached from worldliness in order to be able to save others from the world and bring them safely to infinite bliss.

26. THE DIVINE TEACHER

1. One path and one door — the Guru, the ladder to one's own home![1] (N. *Mālār ki Vār*, 1 Sl. 2) Without the true Guru, the path is not found

---

[1] I have kept here the clipped pithy style so characteristic of the Guru in his own *Gurumukhī*, though often barely intelligible when copied too exactly in English. It reads: *heko padharu heko daru gura pauli nija thanu.*

(B. *Prabhati*, 1:5); no one has ever found it by pleasing himself[1] (R. *Kanre ki Vār*, 3 Sl. 2). Without a Guru no one has obtained [God], for all his talking; it is he who shows the way and fixes true devotion [in the pupil] (N. *Āsa Ashtapadi*, 18:4).

2. Some go here and there babbling a great deal, but no one has found God by talk (AD. *Anand*, 16:4); Nanak, there are no virtues in the one without a Guru;[2] one who turns his face away [from a teacher] has a lying mouth (N. *Saran ki Vār*, 7 Sl. 1). In the absence of a Guru there is only dust;[3] without his word no understanding is gained (N. *Sri Ashtapadi*, 4:6). If a hundred moons went up and a thousand suns rose, even if such a light were given, there would still be intense darkness without a Guru (A. *Āsa di Vār*, 1. Sl. 2); light comes from the Guru's teaching, and then one remains absorbed in the love of the Real (N. *Sri Ashtapadi*, 4:6).

3. When God wills, [then man] meets the real Guru and magnifies the One Name (K. *Kedara*, 4:3); it is he who applies himself to the service of a saint on whose brow this destiny is written[4] (Ar. *Todi*, 8:2), and it is he

---

[1] i.e., by going his own way, following his own ideas

[2] It is interesting to compare these passages with those on the same topic in the *Gospel of Narada*. They are equally insistent.

[3] M. reads 'darkness' here, but the word *gubāru* is equivalent to *dhūl* in Hindi.

[4] This shows clearly how what is 'written on the brow' is the direct result of previous actions; there is no partiality or 'fate' here, but simple justice.

who lovingly serves the Guru to whom [the Lord] has shown kindness (Ar. *Bilawal,* 4:1), [but one who] has never done good to others does not think of serving the true Guru (Ar. *Todi,* 3:4). [Who is the Guru?] He is the true Guru in whose heart is God's Name;...and one who has served him without desire always obtains the Lord (Ar. *Sukhmani,* 18:3, 2).

4. The Invisible, having now been revealed, is obtained from the Guru; Nanak, he is God's favourite[1] (Ar. *Āsa,* 145:3). Through the Guru the soul wins [real] life, through the Guru she goes to God's house. Nanak, the disciple[2] is merged in the Real (N. *Prabhati,* 6:4). **God** cannot be seen by anyone without the true Guru, but graciously causes himself to be revealed by the Guru (AD. *Mājh Ashtapadi,* 10:5). Today in our house is spring;...it is always spring when the Divine Teacher is met (Ar. *Basantu,* 1:1, 3). [Today] through the Guru I have lost error and fear, and my eyes behold the Blissful Form in all (Ar. *Āsa,* 68:4).

5. When the Guru is met, the fear [of God] dwells in the heart (N. *Sorathi Ashtapadi,* 2:7). Nanak, I will go to ask my Guru and will depart to wherever the Lord is;...the true Guru has become the

---

[1] *Cholhk,* dainty titbit, sweetmeat. God loves the Guru best, so he always rewards those who serve him faithfully.

[2] *Gurumukhī,* lit: 'at the mouth of the Guru', so one who obeys the Guru.

go-between[1] for my meeting the Beloved (N. *Barah Maha*, 10, 11). If [the Guru] makes the disciple[2] perfect, then he gains the secondless Reality; …Nanak, if the perfect is [really] met, how can virtue decrease? (N. *Sri*, 9:1, 4)

6. God [lets] one meet the Guru [according to] his past earnings (N. *Rāmkali Ashtapadi*, 4:5); without the help of a saint God's companionship cannot be gained; without a Guru the body [remains] filthy with dirt. …There is no love without devotion to the Guru, nor does a saint give his company without the Guru (N. *Basantu*, 5:2). By the Guru's kindness God dwells in the heart; in no other way can he be drawn (R. *Suhi*, 10:1); by the perfect Guru is God's Name fixed [in the heart]; without the Name life is useless (R. *Jaitsari*, 1:2). Nanak, by [repeating] 'Rāma Rāma Ramu Rāma Rāma,'[3] the [supreme] state[4] is achieved; when the true Guru is met, he establishes the Name, and then one is united to God's Name[5] (R. *Kalyan Ashtapadi*, 6:8). God has kept himself [hidden] in the

------

[1]Marriages are usually arranged in the East with the help of a mutual friend of the two families; so the Guru brings his disciple into touch with God. The Gopi in Sri Jayadeva's *Gita-Govinda* plays this role.

[2] *Gurumukhī*, lit: 'at the mouth of the Guru', so one who obeys the Guru.

[3] Different forms of the Name of God (Rāma).

[4] Or the goal (*gati*)

[5] Experience confirms that the practice of repeating God's Names can succeed only after the mantra has been imparted regularly by one who is regarded by the practitioner as his Guru. Then only does it 'stick'.

true Guru (N. *Āsa dī Vār,* 6); the Guru is God, and God is the Guru[1] (R. *Āsa Chhant,* 1:4); there is no difference between the Supreme and the Guru (Ar. *Bhairo,* 24:4).

None can win his way to God by himself, however much some may talk of independence and equality; only with the help of the Guru can light shine into the heart's dark places. It is the good man who meets this heavenly guide, and it is by serving him his grace is won and the road to God is thrown open. Who is the Guru? The devotee who loves God with *all* his heart. He who *has* God can share him with another, can introduce a friend to him and so fill that friend with surpassing joy.

The very meeting with the Guru awakens that joy in the heart and makes it blossom with bright spring flowers, for the sight of him disperses fear and anxiety, tells of freedom to come, and reveals the Beloved Lord. All obstacles disappear; the aspirant has now only one thought—to hasten to that Lord in whose presence he will become perfect.

There is no shortcut to God, no easy way. He is found through his own appointed means, the contact with a saintly devotee, to be gained only as the reward of past good actions. Devotion is infectious; it arises in the heart even at the first contact; it becomes a flame which burns away the dross and purifies the golden nugget there. In the pure heart God himself comes to dwell in the manifest form of his Name; it is true to say that where the Guru is, there already is the Lord. So close is the union between the saint and God that we cannot say which is acting at any moment; they are as it were the same.

---

[1] A clear enunciation of the same thought as in the *Guru Vandanam*: *Gurur Brahma, Gurur Vishnu...* etc. It is impossible for the pious to exaggerate their debt or the honour due to one who reveals God to them.

27. THE REAL SAINT

1. No one but the devotee is accepted [by God] (G. *Akāl Ustat*, 38), and he who dwells upon God's Name is the devotee; Nanak, from age to age greatness[1] lies in the Name (AD. *Rāmkali*, 1:6). Those who please him are the good; what further explanation to make? Those possess wisdom, honour and wealth in whose heart It remains merged;[2] what sort of further praise is possible for them? (N. *Sri*, 4:3-4) The Lover of devotees,[3] God, keeps company with them (N. *Āsa Ashtapadi*, 9:8).

2. Signs appear on the faces[4] of those in whose hearts is the true Name (N. *Sri*, 6:2); he who makes [good] use of *māyā*[5] knows the One God immanent [therein]; and the sign of him is known—he stores up the wealth of patience[6] (N. *Basantu*, 11:3). Nanak, the true Guru is known thus—that he mingles freely with all[7] (N. *Sri Ashtapadi*, III, 10); those who are

---

[1] i.e., true spiritual greatness like God's, or glory

[2] cf. *Gītā* 18 : 78, the last verse

[3] *Bhagati-vachlu*, lit: beloved of devotees

[4] A certain spiritual glow (*tejas*) is visible, a radiance which shines out almost like a beam of light and is reflected on the faces of those around.

[5] i.e., who is not ruled by *māyā* but has it well under control

[6] Or contentment, modesty *(khimā)*

[7] Seeing in all the One he loves, how can he be exclusive or draw curtains round himself? Openness of heart is a certain sign of true spirituality.

engrossed in their Lord like every one (N. *Wadhans*, 1:1); he who dwells throughout the eight watches of the day[1] in the Lord's presence, that man, says Nanak, is perfect (Ar. *Sukhmani,* 17:7); perfect in the world is he in whose heart there is no one else (K. *Gaurī Ashtapadi*, 38:5).

3. [He has][2] the mantra of God,[3] God's Name, and broods on [the One who is] fully [present] everywhere;[4] the wisdom to look equally on pain and happiness, a life pure and free from enmity; he is kind to all living things and has expelled the five vices; his nourishment is hymns to God,[3] remaining untouched by worldliness like the lotus in water; his teaching is for friend and foe alike, and he delights in devotion to the Blessed One; he will not listen to criticism of others, but giving up egoism [he becomes] the dust of all [feet]; being filled with these six signs, Nanak, a person has the name of a perfect saint (Ar. *Sahaskriti Ślokas*, 40).

The real Guru is the saintly devotee, the one devoted to God's Name and trying always to please him, for He is always near to those who love him in this way. The devotee can be easily recognized: he sees God in all acts with all in a spirit of reverence and affection, in joyful

---

[1] A watch consists of three hours; the ceaseless practice of the Presence is here given as a sign of perfection.

[2] In the original this paragraph is in Prākrit.

[3] God is here called 'Rāma', 'Govinda', and 'Bhagavān'.

[4] *Sarvatra pūrnah.*

patience endures all that comes, knowing it is from the Beloved's own hand, is easily pleased by the smallest kindness from another, and is at all times aware of God's loving watchfulness over him. Unshaken by joy or sorrow, wholly free from anger and dislike, virtuous and kind, delighting in the worship of God, without the least taint of worldliness or egoism, eager for humble service of the lowliest of men—such a Guru can guide us to the Lord he loves.

28. THE TRUE MUSLIM AND YOGI

1. To be [rightly] called a Muslim is hard;[1] when one is [surrendered], then he can call himself a Muslim. First let him find sweet the religion of saints, then remove the rust of pride and give away his wealth.[2] When he is resigned [to God], making religion the pilot of his boat and putting an end to the false idea[3] of death and life, let him heartily obey God's[4] pleasure, honouring the Creator and facing the [petty] self. Having then, Nanak, become

---

[1] The language in this paragraph is full of Arabic words suited to the Muslim audience to which it appeals.

[2] *Avali aulī dīnukari mīthā masakala mānā malu musāvai;* this line, which even M. found hard to translate, is full of the alliteration in which the first Guru delights. I have followed Professor Jodh Singh here.

[3] *Bharamu;* not 'life and death is to be put away', but our wrong understanding of their real nature. The word means also 'fancy, error, superstition'.

[4] *Rabb,* the Arabic term for God, the Master

kind[1] to all living beings he can then be [rightly] called a Muslim (N. *Mājh ki Vār*, 8 Sl. 1).

2. [Make] good works the Creed[2] you repeat, then shall you be a Muslim (N. *Mājh ki Vār*, 7 Sl. 3). Practise the books [like] the *Korān*;[3] put the wick of the fear [of God] in this body of yours, and burn in it the understanding of truth.[4] In this way the lamp will burn this oil, and having made a light you will then find the Master. When God's words are impressed on this body, happiness follows and service is done. All the worlds come and go; do service in the world,[5] and then, says Nanak, you will get a seat in Court and swing the arm![6] (N. *Sri*, 33:2-4)

3. The knower of God[7] is the Brāhman; have no

---

[1] Kindness to others is here rightly shown as the effect of selflessness.

[2] Kalamā, the profession of Muslim faith: '[I believe that] there is no God but [the One] God, and that Muhammed is the Prophet of God.' But no profession of faith can equal the doing of righteous deeds, which alone proves the sincerity of such a profession.

[3] So reads M. But in my copy of the *Granth Sahib* I read 'Purānas'. Of course, there is little practical importance in this, for both Muslim and Hindu require the same moral code, the same prerequisites for spirituality.

[4] Guru Nanak delights in such metaphors.

[5] The stress here on active service in the world is important; no true religion ignores our duty to man, which is not apart from the duty to God. So too the Parsee scriptures.

[6] i.e., be able to do whatever you like in the future, being wholly free.

[7] 'God' in this context is almost always 'Brahma', the infinite Absolute.

caste pride, you stupid fool, for from this pride many evil results proceed (AD. *Bhairo*, 1:1). What advantage in cleansing this [body] when there is impurity within the heart? (K. *Sorathi*, 8:1) The [real] Brāhman bathes in the gnosis[1] of God; his leaves for worship[2] are God's glories: one name, one God,[3] one Light of the three worlds! (N. *Maru*, 11:2) The Name of God [established] by the Guru's grace in the house of the body captures your Lord God[4] (AD. *Rāmkali Ashtapadi*, 1:8); he is to be called a Brāhman who day and night is rapt in the love of God (AD. *Gūjari ki Vār*, 10 : Sl. 1).

4. O Yogi, this will not be yoga to leave the family and make a home elsewhere! (AD. *Rāmkali Ashtapadi*, 1:8) In the house itself [there may be] renunciation (AD. *Sri*, 1:4); in the house itself is always the beloved, the Child;[5] He ever remains in

---

[1] This word, the Greek equivalent of Skt. *jnăna*, seems the best translation of it in most places, for it includes the idea of *love* as well as mere *knowledge*—the union of which is true *wisdom*.

[2] In several forms of Hindu worship leaves, e.g. of tulasi and bel plants, play a part.

[3] *Nărāyana*, 'human' God

[4] cf. the saying of Thăkor Haranăth in GN.

[5] *Ghara hi mahi prītamu sada hai bālā*. This may also be: 'The beloved Child is always in the very house.' Every human child is as it were a form of the Divine Child, Sri Krishna or Sri Rama; how then can family life divorce God's lover from the sight of him? Rather is it the easiest way to him.

bliss the giver of happiness[1] (AD. *Mājh Ashtapadi* 27:2); living in your own home, you can obtain him (AD. *Basantu,* 9:3). Making the house in every way your forest, understand in the heart [that you are a] hermit (G. *Hazare Shabad,* 1:1); why should **you** go searching in the jungle when there is a green wood in the house? (N. *Āsa Ashtapadi,* 17:1)

5. Regard all activity save the one supporting Name as delusion. (G. *Akāl Ustat,* 50) Nanak, the [real] yogi is the friend of all in the three worlds (N. *Rāmkali Ashtapadi,* 2:8); when the true Lord himself throws a look of grace [on a man], then he becomes the servant of servants;[2] then he does service to the true Guru, day and night, and never leaves his presence; as the lotus remains untouched in the water, so is he renounced in the family (AD. *Rāmkali ki Vār,* 7: Sl. 2).

6. Nanak is the servant of those who live in solitude with the One dwelling in the heart, without expectations in the midst of [those full of] expectation, seeing and showing forth the Unattainable and Imperceptible! (N. *Sidh Goshti,* 5) When there is expectation, then there is also anxiety; how can one do [this and] speak of the One? When [a man] remains desireless amid

---

[1] So he will not treat unkindly those who depend on him in the family by leaving them for selfish retirement and meditation.

[2] cf. the Latin name beloved by the Roman Pontiffs, *servus servorum dei*

desires,[1] Nanak, then he finds the One; in this way he crosses over the ocean [of the world] and thus 'dies' [while still] alive[2] (N. *Rāmkali,* 3:4-5). He does not chatter or speak but gathers a wealth of contentment and burns up passion with the [fire of the] Name. ...He who fixes the mind on God's feet, who remains desireless [amid] desires[3] and is in love with the One—he is a *sannyāsi*[4] (N. *Maru Ashtapadi,* 7:7-8); he causes fear to no one, nor does he fear any;[5] Nanak says, 'Hear, O mind, you may call that man a sage'[6] (T. *Śloka,* 16).

7. He treats happiness and sorrow as both the same and regards honour as dishonour, stands aloof from exultation and grief,[7] and recognizes the Real [hidden] in the world (T. *Gauri,* 1:1). The knower of God[8] is purer than pure,...higher than high, yet in his own mind lower than all;...the glance of God's knower rains down nectar...and he delights in helping

---

[1] Or hopes, expectations; cf. *Gītā,* 2 : 70; *nirāśā parama sukham*

[2] i.e., becomes a *jivanmukta,* whose 'ego' is dead that the Self may live

[3] cf. *Gītā* 2 : 24

[4] lit: 'renouncer of all'

[5] cf. *Gītā* 2 : 15

[6] Or Gnostic *(jnāni)*

[7] cf. *Gītā* 12 : 18-19, etc. The whole passage is parallel to *Gītā* thought.

[8] i.e., the *Brahmajnāni* or Gnostic

others;…[yet] the knower of God loves [only] the One,…so **he** is free from care…and possessed of all, [because] **he** is himself the Formless One (Ar. *Sukhmani*, 8:2-8).

We boost ourselves with high-sounding titles, we call ourselves Christians, Muslims, Brāhmans, and the like; but how often do we ask ourselves how far we are really followers of the Christ, wholly surrendered to God, or knowers of the Divine? The true Muslim is indeed the perfect saint; the name 'Muslim' is of no value if it does not bear its full significance of resignation to God's holy will and abandonment of the petty selfishness of man. It is not enough to wear a label and demand admission to heaven on the strength of that label—God looks into the heart where our deeds and thoughts are written, and judges us only on that infallible record. If we really do what the Prophet teaches, if we really follow the Sermon on the Mount, if we really perceive the Immanent in all and treat all with love and reverence as His manifestations—then we need claim no label, for as we step before the judgement seat of God our hearts in triumphant joyous tones will name us his.

How foolish to rely on the 'caste' of ancestors and to claim, 'I am a Brāhman, because they too were Brāhmans born!' God is known through devotion to his 'Name', as St Bonaventura (quoted by Tanquerey, op. cit. p. 464) says, 'The best way to arrive at a knowledge of God is to taste the sweetness of his love.' He who thus knows God, the devotee, is the only real Brāhman, and he bathes eternally not in Gangaji or any other holy waters, at Kāśi or elsewhere, but in the nectar of his presence.

Nor is it 'yoga'—union with God—to wander from the house and beg from others here and there. God is everywhere, in the house as much as in the forest, in family duties as much as in sacrificial fires or silent meditations. One who runs from him in the household where he has placed him will certainly not find him after deserting his God-given duties. No earthly work or duty can ever come between the true aspirant and his Lord; it is as easy to practise the Presence while washing clothes or scrubbing floors or keeping office ledgers, as it is while standing on one leg in holy places far from human haunts and amid Himalayan snows. Indeed it is far easier, for God has willed the first while man's pride prefers the second, and God loves humble obedience more than pride and self-will. Wherever he may be at the time, it is when God calls the aspirant to his feet that his grace descends and he draws nearer and nearer till the state of perfect union becomes possible; presumption on our part does not win grace but rather merits God's stern reproof. Dwelling in the midst of worldly duties, among worldly folk, the true devotee remains always immersed in the wordless bliss of God's love which surges round him like a mighty sea of nectar, and he is there a shining light to all his neighbours.

Such a devotee is the greatest of men; free from all attachment, he quietly does as a sacrifice to Him the work God gave him to do, turning everything he touches into a sacramental grace by his total inward absorption in the will of God. Without thought of personal reward, without passions or overmuch talk, undisturbed by the whirl of worldly thought around him—such a one is the real *sannyāsi,* and not the egotist in orange robes exploiting the simple piety of village folk and boasting of his great renunciation. Such is the real Brāhman, the knower of his God, the enlightened Gnostic, whose very presence is a blessing to the world and who in himself manifests the Lord of all.

29. BROODING ON THE WORD

1. The Lord is not found by egotistic argument,....nor is the truth[1] obtained by setting up the 'I, I';...he who studies the Guru's word gets rid of egoism (N. *Gaurī Ashtapadi,* 12:4, 13:1, 3). Yes, the Lord is found when the mind is happily engaged upon the Word (N. *Barah Maha,* 6). Beloved, thy Words are nectar, most beautiful dear Charmer[2] in the midst of all, yet distinct![3] (Ar. *Devagandhari,* 29:1)

2. I direct the words of my mouth to all, but hold my soul near to the Lord (Ar. *Āsa,* 54:2). We have come [here] to listen to and read his Word (Ar. *Sarang,* 79:1); for giving the mind [to that we] shall obtain the delightful Name (N. *Gaurī Ashtapadi,* 12:4); and it is always spring for him in whose heart is the Name (Ar. *Basantu,* 3:1); yes, he shall meet with greatness in whose heart the Word pervades (N. *Rāmkali ki Vār,* 12 Sl. 1). By means of the Guru's word egoism is lost from within, and God himself

---

[1] Or the Real One *(sachu)*

[2] *Manamohana,* a common name for Krishna; lit: fascinating the heart

[3] The *visishtādvaita* position also: God is immanent in all, yet also transcendent over all; one with creation, and yet not identical therewith.

comes to dwell in the soul and heart, which are ever plunged into peace and spontaneous happiness.[1] He is near, and he is far; by the Guru's word one sees him always present (AD. *Basantu*, 5:2, 6:2).

3. The True One, the Creator, is invisible and secondless, no end can be found of him; their coming [to the world] has become fruitful who have pondered on that One in the heart (N. *Alahania*, 3:3-4). The owners of wisdom, meditation and virtue[2] please the Lord, and then they are pleased [in turn] (N. *Barah Maha*, 13).

Not by much talk or clever discussions among philosophers and logicians can the truth be known or the Lord found, nor by meditative silence apart from the stream of life, but by the active contemplation of the Guru's teaching —holding the heart on God, the mind on his Word, the hands upon his work among men. 'If you love me you will keep my commandments,' said Jesus; and for this we have to be wholly dedicated to the Lord and keep the egotistic self altogether out of sight.

This is the purpose of life; holding firm to this, we find the heart will blossom into divinity while God takes his seat therein amid deep peace and overflowing joy. We

---

[1] *Sada santi sukhi sahaji samai.* Teja Singh always translates *sukhu* as 'peace'; e.g., *Sukhmani* (Psalm of) [mental] peace; but passages like this show that the usual Hindi meaning of 'happiness' is to be preferred.

[2] *Gianu dhianu guna*: i.e., knowing-love (of God), quiet contemplation (of him), and the ensuing good qualities of virtue; these three are here given as qualifications for success in the search for God.

who can thus enthrone him over our lives find him everywhere around and know nothing in the world but him.

30. TRUE RELIGION

1. Yoga[1] is not the patched cloth, yoga is not the staff, yoga is not the smearing of ashes; yoga is not the earrings and shaven head, yoga is not the blowing of conches:[2] remaining unspotted amidst impurity, thus is contact with yoga gained![3] (N. *Suhi,* 8:1)

2. Yoga is not mere talk, but the yogi can be called the one who looks upon all equally with one regard; yoga is not [going] out to tombs and burninggrounds,[4] yoga is not the adopting of postures;[5] yoga is not roaming in foreign lands, nor is yoga bathing in holy waters:[6] remaining unspotted amidst impurity, thus is contact with yoga gained! (N. *Suhi,* 8:2)

---

[1] This section is a complete hymn which Guru Nanak is reported to have sung to a group of 'yogis' who criticized his unconventional dress and ways. It is a useful lesson to us all.

[2] Or horns; to attract attention, mendicants make such sounds as they enter a village.

[3] The rhythm of the song will be well shown by the first paragraph, which reads: *jogu na khinthā jogu na dandai; jogu na bhasama chalāiai; jogu na mundī mundī mudayai; jogu na sīngivāiai;* and the refrain repeated at the end of each paragraph: *anjana māhi niranjana rahīai; joga jugati iva pāiai.*

[4] Many 'yogis', specially those of various Tantric schools, make a practice of living in cemeteries, etc., where it is said that they were guilty of nameless outrages on the dead.

[5] *Tali:* so translated by M. specially as '*padmāsana*'

[6] i.e., going on pilgrimage to Kāsi, Rameswaram, etc. (*tīrthnāīai*).

3. When one meets the true Guru, then are doubts broken up and distractions brought under control; a gentle rain [of grace] falls drop by drop,[1] one listens attentively to spontaneous music,[2] and the very house obtains happiness, remaining unspotted amidst impurity, thus is contact with yoga gained! (N. *Suhi*, 8:3)

4. Nanak, remain 'dead' while living,[3] practise such a yoga! The horn sounds without being blown,[4] and then you attain the fearless state, remaining unspotted amidst impurity, then[5] is the contact with yoga gained! (N. *Suhi*, 8:4)

This is true religion—devotion to God amid the whirling waves of the world-ocean, imbuing it too with a love for the holy Name, and filling every heart with joy and peace. This is yoga, and not the outward show which so delights the conceit of the egotistic mind.

---

[1] cf. § 1:1

[2] *Sahaja dhani lāgai..*

[3] cf. § 28:6 and the note thereon

[4] i.e., the 'voice of the silence' in the *anāhata-chakra* of the heart.

[5] In this place the usual *iva* changes abruptly to *tau,* then.

CHAPTER FIVE

The Divine Name

Finite man cannot directly see or know the infinite and ineffable God; it is only when He deigns to reveal himself by taking some manifest form that the creature may become aware of him, and that 'manifest form' is called the 'Name'. The Name is God himself, adapted to our powers of perception, and it is the only path through which we may approach him. Without this contact we are as good as dead; with it we are full of blissful life and soon come to merge in him, the beloved Source of Life.

31. GOD'S NAME IS SAVIOUR

1. Without God's Name who has ever attained the Goal?[1] (K. *Gaurī*, 4:4) There is no purity without the Name of God (N. *Basantu*, 5:2); what can the Yamuna do for those whose tongues [already] love God's Name?[2] (K. *Āsa*, 5:1) Why, Ganga, Yamuna, Triveni

---

[1] *Gati:* the supreme state of union with God, or at least of blissful enjoyment of his presence, which is the purpose of life

[2] cf.§ 24 : 1. The theme constantly recurs in the *Guru-Granth Sahib* as a natural protest against the prevailing external ceremonialism, which is pure superstition.

Sangam, the seven seas, charities and worship are all contained [in the Name];[1] in age after age I have known the One Supreme Lord; repeating God's Name with great delight, I bathe in the sixty-eight holy waters [of pilgrimage][2] (N. *Barah Maha,* 15). The disciples who brood [on it] receive nectar, and it is they who are really pure. Day and night repeat the Name, O mortal, so that your impurities may be washed away (N. *Mālār,* 1:3), for by remembering God again and again trans gressions are destroyed (N. *Āsa Ashtapadi,* 9:4).

2. The poisons of greed and lying are spread throughout this body; but, Nanak, the disciple who continually drinks the nectar of God lives in health;...disease does not enter [even] the dream of those who love the medicine of the Name (Ar. *Bawan Akhari,* 45 Sl.), and when there are very serious

---

[1] Neither the Ganges, nor the Jumna (as they used to be called), nor the place where their waters mingle near Prayāg (Allahabad), can wash away sin. Only God, the source of all purity, can do that by his grace, which is given through the Name. Nor all the waters of the ocean, nor any kind of righteous action, can avail to this end—it is an unearned gift of God.

[2] *Mahā rasu Hari japi athasathi tiratha nātā*: I have not found a complete list of these 'holy waters' wherein pilgrims are to bathe; it would obviously include Gangotri and Yamunotri, Prayāg (Triveni Sangam), the union of Gangāji with the sea, Pushkara Lake, Badrinarayan, Mānasarowar Lake, Nāsik and Tapoban, Paithan, Alandi and Dehu, Brindāvan, Dwāraka, Udipi, Bhadrāchalam, Rameswaram, Kanyākumari, Dhanushkoti, Tirupati, the Kāveri near Srirangam; but the list would doubtless vary from time to time according to the preferences of different sects.

17

difficulties God's Name in a moment takes them away (Ar. *Sukhmani*, 2:1). It is the Lord who in a moment saves and carries [us] over the very fierce world-ocean (Ar. *Gauri*, 83:2); we cross over the world of darkness by clinging to his feet (Ar. *Mundavani*, 1:5). The One Name saves [us from] the world; by the Guru's grace the Name is dear [to us, for] without the Name no one has attained to liberation (AD. *Basantu*, 10:3).

3. I gathered the fruits of sin and filled my heart, so that my heart forgot the Lord, the Supreme Person (D. *Āsa*, 1:2). [Now] my only lamp is the Name, I have put in it the oil of suffering; by its flame that oil is now exhausted and I have escaped the meeting with death. Thousands of logs collected together, one spark is applied! (N. *Āsa*, 32:1) Darkness is effaced, wickedness given up, and the heart is reconciled with God [1] (Ar. *Suhi Chhant*, 4:4). O Infinite One, if I had committed no sin, how couldst thou have the Name of 'Purifier of the Fallen'? [2] (Rd. *Sri*, 1) With every breath Nanak sings [God's] glory, and the true **Guru** has drawn a curtain over **his** sins (Ar. *Mājh*, 17:4).

---

[1] So M. *mite andhāre taje bikāre Thākura siu manu mānā.* The music in this line is obvious even to those who do not understand Gurumukhi. It is typical of that true poet, Guru Arjan, and almost demands to be sung.

[2] *Patita-pāvana,* a favourite name of Sri Rāma as the Redeemer.

4. Everyone rests in hope of thee (Ar. *Mājh*, 2:3); and those imbued with the love of God's Name have no load of error [to carry]; great is the gain of repeating God's [Name, they are] fearless [because] God is in their heart (N. *Sri*, 23:4). He whose inmost heart is pure,…in that person all fear is cut away (R. *Bihagale Chhant*, 5:3).

5. Man Nanak, so ponder always in heart and mind on God's Name that at the last moment it may bring you rescue [from shame] (R. *Gaurī*, 13:4); by honouring and praising the Name honour arises and a true 'thread'; in God's court [man] obtains a pure 'thread' which will not break[1] (N. *Āsa dī Vār*, 15 Sl. 3). Though he makes many efforts yet the heart does not melt—how can such a one go to God's Court?[2] (Ar. *Sukhmani*, 12:3) They know not the secret of themselves, but give a verbose description of heaven![3] When the mind is attached to the hope of heaven, then

---

[1] The 'sacred thread', as a sign of social superiority as belonging to one of the upper castes, awoke the Guru's scorn even as a boy when he was to be invested with it. The true 'thread' which ties us for ever to God, is love for him and repeating of his Name. This alone wins his favour.

[2] No matter what a man does, if he acquires no gentleness and sweetness of character, he cannot hope to be received by God as his own.

[3] Ignorant of their own nature and defects, how can they presume to speak of transcendent things? cf.CMC 30:3. The Sikh equivalent of Gk. *gnōthi seauton,* 'know thyself'.

it cannot be attached to dwelling at [God's] feet[1] (K. *Bhairo*, 16:1). Mortal, brood on the One Name and go to your [real] home with honour! (N. *Mālār*, 1:1)

6. Where no pain of separation arises in a body, deem that body a burning-ground (F. *Śloka*, 36), for without the Name egoism goes on burning[2] (AD. *Basantu*, 12:3). Nanak, the whole world is in pain; the one who obeys the Name obtains victory—no other action is of any account (N. *Rāmkali ki Vār*, 14 Sl. 1). Those who are without the Name will be rejected, no one will keep them company (N. *Sri Ashtapadi*, 4:3); they will not get liberation, for the disciple wins liberation only through the Name. Without the Name of God useless is birth in the world (N. *Bhairo*, 8:1). He who pleases God meets the Guru, and then he ponders on God's Name (AD. *Sri Rāg dī Vār*, 10). God, O God, thy Name is the remover of pain![3] (R. *Tilang Ashtapadi*, 2:4)

7. When the heart is thrilled on hearing the Name,[4]

---

[1] A striking warning to those who hold out the hope of heaven as the main attraction to the spiritual life; it is an unworthy aim.

[2] In the body of one who does not even miss or feel the need of a God, there is indeed a perpetual fire of passions and desires.

[3] *Hari Hari terā nāmu hai dukha metanahārā.*

[4] This idea frequently appears in the *Bhāgavata,* and was insisted on by Sri Rāmakrishna as a sign of the nearness of God's grace. But such thrills and even tears of love may not appear in certain souls who are even nearer to God; it depends on the temperament of each whether these 'signs of Bhakti' appear openly or not.

then is the door of liberation won (N. *Āsa dī Vār*, 10 Sl. 2). Golden the body and spotless the soul in whom the stainless and shining Name [abides]; all sorrow and disease are driven away; Nanak, it escapes by means of the true Name (N. *Mālār*, 7:4). So let him who is called a Sikh of the true Guru[1] arise early and ponder on God's Name. Let him bestir himself at early dawn and bathe in the nectar tank [of the Name]; taught by the Guru, let him constantly repeat God's Name,[2] and all transgression, sin and guilt will be taken away. At sunrise let him again sing the Guru's hymns and...brood over God's Name. He who at every breath in and out meditates upon my God is a Sikh of the Guru and pleases the Guru's heart (R. *Gaurī ki Vār*, 11 Sl. 2).

God alone can purify and remove the stain of sin. From him all holy things derive their holiness; he is their source, the unfailing fountain of perfect purity. Spiritually washed in the holy Name, the disciple becomes infinitely pure as the immaculate God himself; for with him no sin can cohabit, no evil can share the heart with his holy Name. So full trust in his saving power is the certainty of salvation, the highest gift of the Divine Guru to suffering men.

From life in this fallen world we gather up many sins, but not one can remain when the water of God's Life flows over

---

[1] i.e., a pupil of the true Teacher. I have kept the original word for obvious reasons—this being the source of the pious custom of *nāma-smarana* and the singing of the Guru's hymns by Sikhs for the three hours before dawn, during *brahma-muhūrta*.

[2] *Hari Hari japu*. The Name is given twice to suggest the repetition.

them. That spiritual baptism washes away every spot in the heart; fires of love consume the dead twigs of failure fallen from the trees of our life. Before the infinite light of God's presence the black darkness of ignorance and error flees away, for he is our redeemer and raises every child of his into the radiance of his presence.

This is our only hope, and it banishes all fear of sin, of hell, of rebirth in this unhappy world where we may feel separated from his love. For perfect love casts out fear, and love is the natural fruit of a sight of him gained through the heartfelt 'chanting' of his Name. It purifies the heart and adorns the soul with the 'sacred thread' of the true Brāhman or God-knower; it is the passport into heaven.

The soul without the Name is lost in the raging fires of egoism and passionate desire, unable to win her way from that misery to God's company in which is peace and joy. When God would save a stricken soul, he sends his messenger with His Name, revealing himself thereby, and sets the love of himself in the poor sinner's heart. The inner glory shines out through the disciple's body as he dwells constantly upon God and is slowly transformed into his likeness; all defects are burned away from him as he grows in his love for God and clings more and more to the worship of him at every moment. Thus he draws nearer to the 'door of liberation', and so becomes a 'Sikh' indeed and not in the mere name alone.

32. IT IS LIFE

1. What have we but the Name of God?[1] (N. *Āsa Ashtapadi*, 9:1) My brother, our body and property

---

[1] lit: What is ours... *Rāma nāma binu kavanu hamāra.*

are not [real] companions, God's Name is stainless wealth,[1] (N. *Sri Ashtapadi,* 15:1), accompanying and helping us (N. *Āsa Ashtapadi,* 9:1); wherever we go, there it also goes (AD. *Gūjari,* 2:3). When the body perishes, whose is its property called? (N. *Āsa Ashtapadi,* 9:1) All other capital[2] than God is deceptive;[3] it goes not with us when we are made to depart (AD. *Gūjari,* 2:3). Some charitable gifts, many kindnesses, do not equal the Name in weight (N. *Wadhans Chhant,* 1:4), but he to whom [God] is gracious comes to obtain that [Name] through his own good deeds (N. *Sri Rāg dī Vār,* 18 Sl.1).

2. Nanak, on our departure hence all false friendships are snapped [asunder][4]...Those who have been regarded as kings and lords come to be seen as mere ashes;[5] when they have passed into the future life they realize that without the Name [their titles] are vain (N. *Sri,* 6:4, 3). As useless as husks without the grain are mouths empty of the Name (Ar. *Gaurī,* 65:1). It is hard to repeat the true Name (N. *Āsa,* 2:1); it is the Lord who has it given by the Guru;...if the real Giver gives, then there will in the future [life] be no question of the

---

[1] i.e., possession which has no such defect as instability

[2] *Rāsi,* lit: the stored-up wealth

[3] *Kūli,* lit: false, unreal

[4] This is the consistent teaching also of the 'spirits'.

[5] *Sultāna khāna ho de dithe kheha.*

one whose comrade is the Guru, the Creator[1] (N. *Sri Ashtapadi*, 15 :1-2). O heart, make that beloved God your friend, and always keep the mind on the support of your life! (Ar. *Gauri*, 39:1) Remain alive,[2] Nanak, and worship the Name of God continually with love! (Ar. *Bawan Akhari*, 26 Sl.)

3. Only the Name of God can delight the heart; in return comes nectar filled with the essential Reality (J.*Gūjari*,1:1); he whose heart and body are lovingly attached to the Name is drenched with nectar (Ar. *Suhi Chhant*,10:4). The one who is united with the Name remains ever in love with the [Divine] Void[3] (K. *Maru*, 4:4) [God's] servant is intoxicated through and through with his presence[4] (Ar. *Mājh*, 18:1); on remembering the Lord's Name, heart and body dissolve [in love] and he drinks God's nectar (Ar. *Sri Chhant*, 3:3). Of what sort are those who forget not the Name? Realize there is no essential difference between God[5] and them (Ar.*Āsa*, 108:1).

---

[1] Note the identification of the (Divine) Guru with the Creator: God is not other than his saints, and the Guru is his saint.

[2] Forgetting God is death, so to remain alive is to remember him (cf. § 32 : 4).

[3] 'Void' (*sūnna*) may be understood as the 'Divine Darkness' of Dionysius; it is not quite the teaching of a *sūnyavāda* like that so violently denounced by Vaishnavas.

[4] *Oti poti*, lit: 'warp and woof'; cf. § 13 : 2.

[5] *Sāni*, the same as the well-known name Sāi

4. Forgetting the Name, the blind has neither this [world] nor that (N. *Sri,* 3:1); forgetting the Name, he loses honour and intelligence[1] (N. *Gauri Ashtapadi,* 11:4), and by forgetting God his virtue also slips away into dissolution (N. *Maru,* 3:1). O heart, if your breath goes in vain, then without God you will die (N. *Sorathi,* 7:1); dying is the forgetting of God, while living is the dwelling upon God's Name (Ar. *Gatha,* 15). Lord, this is my heart's desire:…that with every breath I may remember my Lord and remain always in the company of saints! (Ar. *Devagandhari,* 26:1-2). Thou forgettest those who wander [away from] thyself; if thou forgettest [me], then must I die indeed! (AD. *Gauri,* 7:1-2). So let me gaze upon thy face without blinking and not for a moment turn the mind away! (Ar. *Jaitsari ki Vār,* 12 Sl. 2)

5. O darling God, kind and loving,[2]…high, un-fathomable, infinite Lord! I live by continually remembering thee! (Ar. *Mājh,* 9:1) Without the Name, how could I live, O mother?[3] Night and day I keep repeating it, putting myself under His protection[4]

---

[1] *Pati mati khovahi nāmu visāri.*

[2] *Lāla Gopāla dayāla rangile;* the beloved names of Sri Krishna are often used in this way for the One Supreme God, and rightly so, for Krishna is He, to those who correctly understand the Vaishnava texts.

[3] These songs were actually addressed by Nanak as a boy to his own mother when she urged him to become worldly like other boys.

[4] *Teri saranāi,* in the original; i.e., Thy

(N. *Gaurī Ashtapadi*, 12:8). While I utter [the Name] I live; if I forget it I must die.... Then how can I forget it, O my mother? (N. *Āsa*, 2:1)

All things in this world are unstable, unreliable; on God alone and on his sacred Name can we depend with absolute certainty of faith. Even our virtues are worth little, the noble qualities we may have gained, if they be not enriched by that infinite Grace of God which is their crown and purpose. At death we have to leave everything else and stand as it were naked before God and all mankind; the only covering in that hour is our faith in him, His Name is our only refuge then. And it is not easy to acquire this greatest of all gifts, for it is *not* the mere verbal utterance of mystic syllables or dearly-loved names—that would be superstition, childish and absurd; it is the loving self-gift of the whole heart to the unseen Lord, putting oneself in his presence with an act of surrender, of adoration and aspiration; it is the very essence of true prayer, and not a mere prayer of words. Words may or may not accompany this prayer.

So great a gift as the Name can come to us only in a worthy way; God confers it through the Guru, the saintly devotee whom he sends to us when we are ready to receive him. And then, because our yearning is at fever heat, we find in his presence an upwelling fountain of bliss, a ceaseless flow of nectar, whose sweetness inebriates and inspires until we are filled with godliness, and even our bodies shine with something of our Father's glory. With what joy we drink that nectar of God's love! A long desert tramp on a hot day over soft sand, the burning sun overhead, the mouth as dry as leather—and then the deep shade of great trees, the music of running waters, great draughts that cool and delight the whole heart and soul! Such is the coming of the Name to those who receive it from the God-sent teacher; its melody turns them into gods and all the world into a garden.

Without that nectar we die of thirst; apart from God we cannot live in the parching heat of worldliness. But for God it would be impossible to endure this world, lost in the agony of folly, vice and shame. How then can we bear to lose sight of him even for a moment? Let us cling to the society of saints day and night, so that we may always have him in mind and heart, and so enjoy the sweet delights of Life Eternal!

33. AND JOY

1. Pure, pure, pure and holy![1] Nanak repeats that Name with love in the heart, ... for all happiness lies in love for the Name; ... the Name of God is the glory[2] of man, through God's Name man obtains beauty,[3] and the Name of God is for man both **delight** and **union** [with Him][4] (Ar. *Sukhmani,* 12:8, 5; 2:6). God[5] is beautiful (N. *Mālār ki Vār,* 1 Sl. 2); good and beautiful is the hut in which his glories are sung, while the mansion where God is forgotten is nothing worth

---

[1] M. translates this with a Trisagion, 'Holy, Holy, Holy,' but those words connote something not in the original; *pavitra pavitra pavitra punīta.*

[2] *Vadiāī,* lit: greatness. [3] *Sobhā,* splendour

[4] *Bhogu jogu,* lit: enjoyment and union with God, i.e., earthly and spiritual pleasures alike

[5] *Thākuru*

(Ar. *Suhi*, 41:1). Once this sweetness [has been] enjoyed, it cannot be left again;[1] no other sweetness can compare with it (Ar. *Gaurī*, 15:4). I have tasted all other flavours and the heart has seen that God's sweetness is sweeter than all (Ar. *Mājh*, 15:1).

2. [Man] is born and dies in many births;[2] on repeating the Name he obtains rest (Ar. *Sukhmani*, 2:3). [When his] hunger attaches itself to the true Name, then he satisfies the hunger therewith[3] and the pain departs (N. *Āsa*, 2:1). I have listened [in vain] to the songs, music and poems of poets, but at the Name of God all sorrow flees away (N. *Barah Maha*, 3). The moment wherein he does not enter the mind, that moment goes in vain.[4] Then I would sell this body to a buyer if I could find one; Nanak, the body in which the Name is not, has no value (N. *Suhi*, 7:3-4). A pauper indeed is he in whose heart is not the Name (K. *Bhairo*, 8:4). [So, my brother,] urge the mind to repeat it with every breath you take (N. *Sri Ashtapadi*, 1:1).

3. If one were to live and eat a hundred years, that day would be acceptable when he realized the Master (N. *Āsa*, 4:2). I surrender, my soul surrenders to those

---

[1] *Iha rasa rāti bakuri na chode*

[2] *Jonī*, lit: wombs

[3] So St Augustine: 'Our hearts are ever restless till they find their rest in thee' (*Confessions*, 1 : 1).

[4] cf. GN 30 : 1

who have caused the nectar Word to dwell in my heart,[1]...who ponder on the honey-sweet Name...and are drunk with love in that nectar-sweet Love [of God]. This nectar is obtained by the Guru's grace ...at his command accepting the nectar, at his command they drink the nectar too (AD. *Mājh Ashtapadi*, 16:1-4). If anyone sings or hears the Names of God with attentive mind,...he most certainly attains at last the supreme state[2] (K. *Gaurī*, 55 : 4); if anyone knows him in the centre of the heart—he who speaks becomes Himself![3] (K. *Bhairo Ashtapadi*, 1:8)

God is our only real delight; from him come all beauty and all joy. The very sound of his Name recalls the enchantment of that infinite beauty which is his, and which he has so lavishly scattered abroad through his creation. Indeed his is the only beauty; those without him are hideous to the clear-sighted, whatever be their outward shape or form. The humblest cottage where he is loved and honoured is more than the palace of worldliness; to his lover nothing can be so sweet as his silent presence, his soft touch, his vibrant song. Once known, he will never let it go. Even when all spiritual efforts have ended in success, when God is owned in all his fullness—still the

---

[1] *Hau vārī jiu vārī amritu bānī manni vasāvaniā;* i.e., I adore them.

[2] *Paramagati*

[3] M. greatly weakens this striking passage; it is clear; *jo bolai so āpai hoi*. The Guru's hymns repeatedly teach this final mergence with, identification with, God, and not only a vague assimilation to him—'like Him'.

saint clings to his Name and loves to utter it, singing in all melodious tunes the praises of his Beloved.

Only these songs console a heart wearied with the long roads of earth. Age after age rolls past the pilgrim as he struggles on towards the light; friends come and go, delight gives place to pain and hope to misery—but the loving thought of God is a constant joy. Without it, even one moment seems an age of agony; its possession is a treasure for which his lover would gladly barter all he has, a pearl for which he would give away his whole wealth. Only the moments spent with God are life; those of forgetfulness are worse to him than death.

This inebriating sweetness comes from God through the Guru; he alone can carry it in the chalice to the thirsty disciple that he may drink it to the fill. Wise indeed—the wisest of the wise—are they who love this intoxicant, who pass their hours imbibing the honeyed nectar of God's presence, for this intimacy assures the ultimate union with him who is their all in all and their unending joy.

CHAPTER SIX

The Way to God

The Guru now tells us how that final goal can be attained. When God calls the soul to him, the Guru acts as go-between, and the soul learns from the Guru how to surrender his heart wholly to the Lord. God's lover cannot but love all his children, so the devotee is kind and gentle, wise and patient—the treasury of all goodness derived from him on whom he ever meditates, humble and generous, looking on God as an infinitely loving Mother. A life of perfect consonance with his will, misled by no superstitious beliefs, a life of prayer and faith in his grace, seeking him as the only aim and treating all other attractions as irrelevant, a life of ceaseless abidance in God seen now in the heart as in all else—rejoicing in the company of others of his lovers whose sole delight is in him, learning to sink quietly into his arms, holding nothing back from him, yielding to him all personal desires and feelings, and yet manfully standing in the world for Right—such a life swiftly carries the soul to God its Home.

34. THE NEED FOR A GUIDE

1. Without a Guru liberation is not won, my brother (Ar. *Gond*, 7:4); nor [can man] escape from karma without a Guru (N. *Sri Ashtapadi*, 5:7). Even if you perform thousands of [good] deeds,[1] [there is still] darkness without the Guru (N. *Gaurī Ashtapadi*, 18:1). [When God] gives grace then is the true Guru found (R. *Suhi*, 6:4); to those for whom the meeting with the true Guru is written he comes (AD. *Sarang ki Vār*, 31:1), yet in this world few repeat the Guru's mantra[2] (T. *Śloka* 56). Man Nanak, among millions only a few find how to worship God (T. *Gaurī*, 3:2), who become disciples and realize him[3] (T. *Dhanasari*, 2:2).

2. The one to whom God himself gives love and devotion is very rare in the world[4] (Ar. *Gond*, 17:3); if the true Guru is met thus he satisfies the [demands of] grace (AD. *Gūjari ki Vār*, 3), and by serving the true Guru infatuation is consumed and in the house itself there is renunciation (AD. *Sri*, 8:1); then is the sweetness of God obtained (R. *Suhi*, 7:4). He who immerses the heart in the immortal

---

[1] *Karama;* this may mean, as M. has it, 'ceremonies'. cf. *Gītā* 18 : 66.

[2] This lament is found in most of the world's scriptures, for it is the experience of all God's lovers.

[3] *Kinahū guramukhī hoi pachānā.* cf. *Gītā* 7 : 3.

[4] *Jaga mahi virale koi koi.*

water of gnosis carries with him the sixty-eight holy places; ...there is no holy place equal to the Guru, so that Guru then becomes [for him] a tank of consolation (N. *Prabhati,* 6:1).

Nanak here again insists that those who would seek God absolutely must take a Guru, but he comforts us by saying that when we are ready for him he will certainly appear. It is by ordinary goodness in our daily life, by the faithful discharge of our duties, by longing for God, that we are made ready for the teacher whom God sends to us the moment we can benefit from his teaching. Few really desire that teaching; blessed indeed are we if among those few!

Having met the Guru, it is then our joy and privilege to serve him in lowly humility and with all devotion. Then we shall find his very presence a purifying stream which washes out the countless dust stains on our spiritual garments, stains gathered during the long wandering over earth's scorching desert of separation.

35. THE NEED FOR DEVOTION

1. That is prayer,[1] mortification,[2] service[3] and attendance[4] which pleases the Master (AD. *Sarang*

---

[1] *japu,* lit: repetition (of the Name), which is the highest form of prayer (see Introduction).

[2] *tapu,* lit: penance, i.e., all practices aimed at forcibly gaining control over mind, body and passions.

[3] *seva,* i.e., clinging to and enjoying the presence and service of God or a great man, or a holy place.

[4] *chākarī,* i.e., doing lowly personal service.

ki Vār, 27:2), and those are devotees, those are knowers of the Essential, who honour [God's] command;[1] ... without service there is no devotion (AD. *Gūjari Ashtapadi*, 6:6-7). He is the good man and an anchorite[2] who has caused the Name to dwell in his heart (AD. *Sri*, 8:3).

2. God,[3] the Guru, is won by devotion (N. *Maru Solhe*, 21:11), for those who have gained love and devotion do not burn in wickedness (Ar. *Barah Maha*, 14). Because of the Truth impurity [cannot] get a hold, and the heart [grows] pure by brooding upon God (AD. *Sri*, 7:2). Without worshipping the holy Blessed One,[4] or delighting in the Unity, even kings have no [place] in the record [of honour][5] (G. *Sawwaiya Mukhavak*, 4:4), for in the heart [the two] earrings are surrender to God and the Guru; Nanak, a man is saved by devotion to God (N. *Rāmkali*, 11:4). By devotion I myself have attained, by becoming simple[6] I have met God the King![7] (K. *Gauri*, 6:4)

---

[1] *se bhagata se tatu giani jinakau hukamu manāe.*

[2] *sādhu bairāgi.*

[3] *Gopāla;* Krishna as the protector of souls.

[4] *Sri Bhagavān bhaje binu.*

[5] i.e., can find no niche in the hall of real fame.

[6] Or: foolish (*bhole bhāi*).

[7] *Raghu rāyā*, i.e., Rāma, the Divine King of Ayodhya.

If we would please the Master, we must do gladly what pleases him, trying to anticipate his desires and not to serve ourselves by doing what we ourselves think best. Having thus pleased the Guru we shall find we have also pleased God, and then he will rain down his grace on us and fill us with the nectar of his love. Never again shall we fall into the sins which displease him, for there can be no darkness where the Infinite Light has shone forth, nor filth amid the cleansing streams of boundless holiness. Where God is, there is no impurity. And God is always with his devotee. So only the devotee can be really pure.

36. KINDNESS AND GOD'S GRACE

1. Keep no feeling of enmity for anyone; God is contained in every bosom (Ar. *Bawan Akhari,* 46), and on the head of the one who stirs up enmity against the man who has no enmity all the world's sin falls[1] (R. *Gaurī ki Vār,* 13 Sl. 2), while he who looks equally on foe and friend...comes to liberation (T. *Śloka* 15). Enmity and opposition are removed from the heart of him who listens to hymns about God from the Guru's mouth (Ar. *Bawan Akhari,* 46), *[but still you should] give your head rather than forsake those whom you have promised to protect*[2] (4:391 T).

---

[1] Evil leads to evil in return; if the victim of slander has no slander in his own heart the slander returns with a redoubled force upon him who sent it forth.

[2] This beautiful sentence is not in the *Guru-Granth Sahib;* it may be by some other Sikh giving the purport of the last words of the Ninth Guru, suggests Professor Jodh Singh. Guru Tegh Bahadur himself gave his life to save those who relied on him.

2. Beloved outside Him who is within,[1] there is no other besides (N. *Sorathi,* 11:2); do not utter even one unpleasant word,[2] [because] the True Owner is in all; give no pain to any heart, for all are priceless jewels; yes, that hearts of all are jewels, it is bad to injure them in any way (F. *Ślokas* 129-130). So be angry with no one but think of your own [defects]; remain humble in the world, Nanak, [and you will] cross over by his grace; becoming the dust of all [feet], give up egotistic pride,[3] and your remaining [sins] will vanish (Ar. *Bawan Akhari,* 44).

3. God becomes the sugar spilled in the dust, which the elephant cannot pick up; ...dropping [pride of] family, caste and descent[4] become the ant, pick it up and eat (K. *Rāmkali,* 12:2). Those whose hearts become the dust of [the feet of] everyone perceive the Name of God in every breast, they drive out evil from their own hearts and regard the whole of creation as friends (Ar. *Sukhmani,* 3:6).

---

[1] *Jo antari so bāhari dekhohu.* We are in him, and he is equally in us.

[2] Or : curse *(fikā)*

[3] What is impossible for the great and lordly becomes very easy for the little ones who creep in the dust: St Thérèse's 'Little Way'. Such can enter heaven under the door!

[4] *abhimānu.*

4. Nanak, cherish his body who remembers the Lord, in whose bosom the lotus feet abide, [and whose] tongue repeats the [Name of] God (Ar. *Bihagale ki Vār,* 14 Sl. 2). The person who has realized his Lord becomes able to give all things; …Nanak, ever worship the feet of that person! (Ar. *Sukhmani,* 17:8) God ever remains aloof from those who indulge in wrangling and in pride (G. *Vichitra Nātak,* 6:13); having escaped from the 'I', there is bliss, for where the 'I' is not, there is He[1] (Ar. *Bawan Akhari,* 51).

5. He in whose bosom God remains as dweller comes to sing the glories of God (N. *Āsa Patilikhi,* 18); understanding manifests and honour results when he imbibes the fear [of God] from the Guru's talk; Nanak, the true King[2] then takes him to himself (N. *Sri,* 10:4). [When] by the Guru's grace he comes to dwell in the heart, pain and darkness go from it (N. *Āsa,* 3:3), but those who are absorbed in the Master and enjoy the bliss of his embrace are dependent on his strength and remain humble (N. *Sri Rāg dī Vār,* 7 Sl. 2). Always, always are we thy children[3] and thou art our Master, O Lord; Nanak

---

[1] *Hau chutakai hoi anandu tiha hau nāhī taha āpi.* Hereby the Guru declares what is essentially the *sādhana* of Advaita, as of Christianity and of every other path to God. cf. GP. 28:1.

[2] *sachā pātisāhu,* a title often given to the Guru, here to God.

[3] Or: boys; here pupils before the master, (*cohare, mīrā*).

says, thou art the Mother and Father of us children;[1] [put] the sugared milk[2] of thy name in our mouths! (Ar. *Todi,* 5:4) We play, and thou caressest all [of us]![3] (Ar. *Rāmkali,* 6:3)

How can we hate one whom we see only as our heart's Beloved? It is only the blind who hate; those who throw stones at the sun get them back on their own heads, and those who cast enmity or slander at God's children are struck by their own returning missiles. Seeing God everywhere, the devotee can never be angry with anyone, nor can he be unjust or proud; how could he, who is swimming or drowned in God, pour out rudeness, hate or evil? To such the whole world is God, seen reflected in his smile and loved as his creation. Such souls are the perfection, the crown, of our humanity; blessed are they, and blessed those who keep their company. They are known as free of egoism, for God and selfishness cannot live together, the one or the other must go, as light and darkness cannot together occupy the same place.

Those who surrender to God as tiny children, who drink the nectar of his grace from the love-full breasts of the Divine, are the real saints of God; absorbed in him, they humbly rest in his unconquerable might.

37. THE STRAIGHT PATH

1. Vain is the life of the unbeliever[4] (Ar. *Sukhmani,* 5:6); [you may] regard all [false]

---

[1] *bārika,* little children before their parents.

[2] *khīra, payasam* cf. GN. 37:7.

[3] *hama khelaha sabhi lādalādavaha*

[4] *Birathī sākata kī ārajā.*

religion[1] as fruitless (G. *Akāl Ustat,* 50). Without truth how can one become pure? (Ar. *Sukhmani,* 5:6) Call no one evil so as to get into a quarrel (N. *Wadhans Chhant,* 1:3); whom **are you** to call bad when [there is but] one Master of all?[2] (A. *Sarang ki Vār,* 2 Sl. 1)

2. If anyone knows the fear [of God], the one word of all words (A. *Āsa dī Vār,* 12 Sl. 2), the chief work of this body…is to hymn the Name of God (K. *Basantu,* 2:3). Without [acquiring] virtue the birth is ruined;… if the pure Name be not forgotten, man becomes the recipient of virtue (N. *Sri Ashta-padi,* 6:1, 11:7). The Formless One goes on creating creation, and action in the Lord's heart is good action[3] (N. *Barah Maha,* 1). Honest action is the very essence of God's Word (AD. *Mājh Ashtapadi,* 8:4), so the world praises those who walk in the path of honesty (Ar. *Barah Maha,* 12).

3. Never do at all such an action as you will

---

[1] *Sabha dharma;* the word cannot here mean, as often, *duty* or *righteousness,* nor can it mean that one creed is false and another to be chosen instead—the Gurus lived in no such narrow bigotry; rather we may compare it with the *sarva dharman-parityajya* of the *Gītā* 18:66 and understand it thus: all self-relying ways to God are fruitless because based on egoism; we have to rely on him and surrender wholly to him, for no other act can avail and he alone can save.

[2] The same idea as in §§ 12 : 2, 36 : 2, etc.

[3] Or: the act of obeying the Lord is good action, for that is good which pleases him (cf. § 35 : 1).

have to be sorry for at the last[1] (AD. *Anand*, 11:4); in the soil of duty sow the seed of truth and so practise tillage;[2] then you will know good business and carry off the profit (N. *Āsa Ashtapadi*, 13:8). Let a man make a free gift of the body [in service];[3] if he realizes the field and sows gifts in it, that tiller will be accepted in Court…for he will receive what he has himself done (N. *Śloka* 17). Having under the Guru's teaching given up evil, he will become equal to the Perfect One (N. *Sri Ashtapadi*, 6:1). But to him who calls himself good goodness does not come[4] (Ar. *Sukhmani*, 12:3).

4. Eat that which he gives, says Nanak seriously (N. *Gūjari*, 1:4), but by putting spices in forbidden food it will not become lawful (N. *Mājh ki Vār*, 7 Sl. 2). Those whose Guru is blind eat the uneatable and give up and leave what may be eaten. [We are] conceived from flesh, from flesh born; we are masses[5] of flesh. Pundits understand nothing at all of gnosis[6] or meditation, but are called clever. Meat

---

[1] *aisā kamu mūle na kīchai jitu anti pachotāiai.*

[2] *dharama bhūmi satu bīju kari aisī kirata kamāvahu.*

[3] Or: the body makes charitable gifts (*punna dāna*)

[4] How can one be good who is filled with egoism and pride?

[5] lit: vessels (*bhānde*).

[6] *giāna:* I have generally preferred so to translate this word, which has no exact English equivalent but is cognate with the technical Greek term.

was used in the Purānas, and meat in the books[1] of the four ages; crying 'Meat, meat!', fools quarrel, but they know neither gnosis nor meditation, or what is meat and what is called vegetable, or in what the sin consists.[2] You arose from the [blended] bloods of mother and father but eat no meat! All living creatures come from flesh and take their abode [therein]; if you come to give up such tastes you will be a *sannyāsi*, says Nanak with deliberation (N. *Mālār ki Vār*, 25 Sl. 2).[3] *Those who realize the First Person as the One God let no other belief[4] enter their hearts; they who cherish any other belief shall be debarred from meeting the Friend* (5:308 G).

Silencing the least breath of criticism in his heart, the devotee gives his whole energy to maintaining there the presence of God, 'repeating his Holy Name' by day and

---

[1] Note. 'Muslim' books, as M. has it, for there were no such books during the 'four ages': Satya, Treta, Dwapara and Kali, but only in the last. The Guru tells us that meat-eating has been allowed from primordial time, and hints that even the greatest of Rishis who gave us our scriptures were meat-eaters themselves and did not forbid meat to their disciples until the days of the Buddhists and the Jains.

[2] The 'sin' consists in needless cruelty to sensitive creatures, and not in the material from which the digestive organs subtract what the body needs as food. Nothing is really *impure* save what is forbidden by the Guru, i.e., by God. And that differs for each soul.

[3] Somewhat rearranged.

[4] Such superstitious beliefs, throwing emphasis as they do on the unessentials, act as barriers to true spirituality and increase pride and the tendency to criticize others who do not share our own customs.

night, never letting the mind for a moment stray into blind imperception of the All-Pervading. This is the only true religion, the essence of spirituality—not the performance of empty ceremonies, the offering of cruel sacrifices, or the muttering of surface prayers through heedless lips. Nothing but Purity can purify, nothing can make true but the Truth, nothing implants love but Love himself; God is the only means, the practice of his presence the only real *sādhana*, which can avail to bring the soul to him. Charity and honesty, humility and righteousness, blossom naturally where he, the source of all fruitfulness in virtue, dwells; nor are they possible in his absence.

All he gives us for our earthly needs is pure. The Guru does not here advocate that all should eat flesh, but warns us against the superstitious belief that by abstention we can become pure, that spirituality is based on diet, that what goes into the man can defile him. And in brief that *moksha* depends upon the contents of the stomach. So we have absurd arguments about whether fish or eggs are vegetables; whether eating eggs violates the law of ahimsa, whether eggs are sensitive to pain, and the like, wasting life's precious moments in childishness instead of learning how to love and worship God. Experience proves that in fact it is perfectly possible for even the foulest eater to tread the highest path in spirituality, while the most punctilious abstainer from flesh, alcohol and nicotine is not infrequently a very sink of materialism and lust. The man who conceived the horrors of the Nazi camps at Belsen and Auschwitz was a strict vegetarian, a teetotaller, and a non-smoker.

38. PRAYER AND FAITH

1. The Master is the strength of the strengthless (Ar. *Sri Ashtapadi,* 1:1) and the support of the helpless[1] (Ar. *Sri,* 13:2); *so when your own strength does not avail, clasp your hands and worship God, saying* (1:33 N): 'Carry me across, O God, carry me across! I am an ignorant fellow and know not how to swim; Father Vitthal,[2] give me an arm' (Nd. *Gond,* 3:1). [He is] the wise Giver, gentle, pure, beautiful, infinite;...What one asks of him, that one obtains (Ar. *Sri,* 13:2). O my heart, abide ever with God;...He will cause all sorrow to be forgotten, he will welcome you and arrange all your affairs (AD. *Anand,* 2:1-3). [When] God the King[3] is the shelter [you seek, then] service of the Lord is your gain (Ar. *Barah Maha,* 11).

2. Those persons who truly offer devotion to thee, thou arrangest their work, [O Lord][4] (D. *Dhanasari,* 1:1); whatever [such] may do is done for love of the Lord, (Ar. *Sukhmani,* 14:8), and that work is pleasant which is for Thy sake, [O God]! (Ar. *Mājh,* 2:1) Nanak, the far-sighted gains

---

[1] cf. the favourite Hindu title for him: *anātha-nātha*

[2] *Bīthula,* apparently a form of the name of Krishna as known and loved by the Mahratta saints, among whom Nāmdev was one of the greatest.

[3] *Govinda Gopāla raī*

[4] cf. the famous *Gītā* verse, 9:22.

happiness and his heart [becomes] patient through the Guru's word (N. *Barah Maha,* 3); the Lord being kind to him will give his grace, [and then] he will cause God's work to be done (N. *Āsa dī Vār,* 15). Spring is theirs who have sung God's glories (AD. *Basantu,* 16:1), and a flood of nectar rains down in delightful drops when the Friend of kindly[1] nature meets them and love for God is built up [in their hearts] (N· *Barah Maha,* 4).

3. What shall a silly girl do when the bride pleases not her Spouse?[2] She may make supplication and many attempts, but she [cannot] win [entry] to the palace;[3] without grace[4] she can obtain nothing, even if she receive much [else] (N. *Tilang,* 4:2). God comes into the house[5] when it pleases the Lord, [and then] the woman stands up and remembers his glories (N. *Barah Maha,* 4).

---

[1] Or: intimate, natural, easy, (*sahajī*)

[2] This metaphor for the soul's relationship with God is extremely old; we find it fully developed in the book of Canticles; it is present in the Manichean Psalms: 'Take me into thy bride-chambers that I may chant with those who sing to thee'; it appears in the Song of Solomon: 'Like the arm of the bridegroom over the bride, so is my yoke over those who know me'; in the Babylonian ceremonies: 'He may give me the holy exalted bed-chamber'. We find it even before literature in the whole complex of Mediterranean rites as the *'hieros gamos'*, and it is still the favourite metaphor for mystics of our own day, as for the Tamil saints.

[3] Or: bed-chamber *(mahalu).*

[4] Or: good works *(vinu karama).*

[5] Or: comes to his temple *(maudarī).*

4. The mortal imagines, 'This body is mine,' and clings to it again and again; snared by sons, wives and household, he finds no [chance of] becoming God's servant (Ar. *Gaurī*, 13:1). If anyone prays false prayers,[1] it will not take him a moment to die (Ar. *Mājh*, 43:1); when you pray then you pray for worldly things, from which no good comes to anyone; if you ask for any need, ask for one thing only, Nanak, from which[2] salvation comes (Ar. *Bawan Akhari*, 41). The Beloved's desire should be your own desire[3] (S. *Bilawal*, 1:1).

5. If you would strive for the Beloved, cut off your head and make it a ball; playing and playing [with it][4] reach the state (of feeling): 'Whatever is, is He!' (K. *Śloka* 239) Nanak, giving his head [for God] a man escapes [from worldliness] and receives honour in [God's] court (N. *Āsa Ashtapadi*, 18:8).

It is the Almighty on whom we are to depend, an all-powerful Lord who is the very acme of mercy and kindness and never refuses a prayer for help. He undertakes for them the business, the responsibilities, of his devotees and carries it through to completion, so that all they do in his

---

[1] *Jhūthā Manganu*, M. reads: prays for worldly things.

[2] Or: for the One from whom. . .

[3] *kāmārathī suārathī vā kī paija sawārī*.

[4] In this mood one of the early Babi martyrs about to be beheaded recited the Persian verses; 'How joyous the lover who knows not if it be a rose or his own head which he throws at the feet of his Beloved!'

name and for his sake in this world is sheer joy because they love him.

Nothing the devotee may do has any pleasure in it if it be not pleasing to his Lord; only by giving him delight can he hope to enjoy his company, without which his own life is vain and purposeless. When the mere utterance of the heart's desire before its Beloved ensures its being granted, will not the devotee take care that his heart's desire be only for such things as may honour his Beloved? God will give whatever he asks for; let him then ask only for spiritual grace, for the welfare of his Church, the *Khālsā*, for the power to offer up for him his very life and all he has. The countless martyrs who died with unflinching courage for the faith, even in our own days in the Punjab, have now 'received honour in God's court'.

39.   SEEK GOD ALONE

1. What comes into being is all destroyed (T. *Sarang*, 3:1), the whole world is like a dream[1] (T. *Sorathi*, 8:1); so the pursuit of worldly [business] is a stupid and wicked act (N. *Prabhati Ashtapadi*, 3:2), and it is good to break from the obstinate[2] who love the glamour of worldliness (AD. *Bihagale ki Vār*, 2 Sl. 1). If he break not that glamour he will find no place [hereafter] (N. *Āsa*, 23:5), [for only] the renouncer can

---

[1] *Sagala jagatu hai jaise supanā;* this sounds like *advaita,* and in fact comes very near to it.

[2] Or: pig-headed, following his own opinions, *(manamukhā),* the opposite of *guramukhī,* the one who follows the Guru's advice.

serve God[1] (Rd. *Gond,* 1:2). The Lord becomes his who has no one else (Ar. *Āsa,* 162:3); the Lord is his one Friend, Companion, Comrade (Ar. *Gaurī,* 87:4).O Lord, how can sorrow reach him over whose head thou art [as Protector]?...Death cannot come near to him! (Ar. *Suhi,* 57:1) That love which is directed towards any other shall fade away (Ar. *Jaitsari ki Vār,* 4 Sl. 2).

2. God[2] is the death of the glamour of worldliness; when death comes, is it *then* [we are to] remember him? (N. *Āsa Patilikhi,* 28) God shows grace and then his glamour goes; Nanak, then one remains absorbed in God (N. *Āsa,* 23:6). In God [he finds] all the loves which delight the heart[3] (Ar. *Barah Maha;* 4); one whose affection rests in any other than God[4] feels ever miserable (Ar. *Dhanasari,* 2:4). Unless he meets God the Friend, how can he find rest?...Know that to live even one moment without him [makes] the birth vain (Ar. *Barah Maha,* 1-2). No more birth will take place if he once realizes the True One; the disciple speaks of, the disciple understands, the disciple knows only the One (N. *Āsa Patilikhi,* 29).

---

[1] *Mukundā,* the giver of liberation.

[2] *Madhusūdhana,* the slayer of the demon Madhu, i.e., sense-intoxication.

[3] *Ranga sabhe Nārāinai jete mani bhāvani;* a most beautiful thought.

[4] *Govinda,* the protector of souls.

[Brother], with both eyes I gaze, but I see no other than God alone (K. *Sorathi,* 4:1).

3. My daily occupation is to earn God[1] (Ar. *Dhanasari,* 23:1); my heart has become an unattached renouncer in the fever for seeing my Friend (R. *Āsa,* 15:1). As the bee cannot remain without the lotus, so I cannot remain without God (R. *Āsa,* 15:1); without God I cannot remain a moment, just as the fish must die without water (R. *Āsa,* 10:1). If I break with thee, whom am I to join?... I have joined thee in true love, and to join thee have broken all other links. Wherever I may go, there thy service is, there is no other God like Thee, O God[2] (Rd. *Sorathi,* 5:1-4); Nanak says: Father [a man] may be held to have wept if he has wept for love; if he weeps for worldly things, father, all the weeping is wickedness (N. *Alahania,* 1:4).

4. In what way shall I obtain the Lord of Life? Fire is in my heart, vegetation is in bloom, I have gained an ocean in the intellect; both moon and sun are within the very house—have I not gained such wisdom [as is needed][3] (N. *Basantu,* 11:1-2). Thou

---

[1] *Hari-Hari,* i.e., the Saviour, whose Name is repeated constantly.

[2] *Thakur,* the supreme owner.

[3] A very mystical verse, whereby the Guru declares that he feels himself ready for the vision of God; his heart is aflame with longing, the flowers of virtue have blossomed, and the mind has become wide and deep, while night and day he receives light from within his own heart, needing no *outer* guide. These are the qualifications. M. misses the point.

remainest immanent in all, ...the Beloved of all dwells always near [them, and] by the Guru's grace a few are gratified by his glance (AD. *Mājh Ashtapadi,* 6:8, 4:5). Thou art the Giver, we are beggars; O God, give us a sight [of Thee]! (N. *Āsa Ashtapadi,* 15:1)

5. Offer up all the body, heart and wealth, surrender [to him] the whole of his life (Ar. *Sri,* 13:4); look for nothing [in return] but the Name; make worship and love into the burning of worldliness; see the One, seek no other! [Such a devotee] perceives the essential Reality at the tenth door of the sky (N. *Āsa,* 20:2-3). Look at the state of one slain by the sword: becoming righteous, he goes straight to the Truth and, Nanak, at the door [of Heaven] is lost in the vision [of God]! (N. *Rāmkali ki Vār,* 19 Sl. 2)

In this illusory and impermanent world only one thing merits our attention and our love. Those who renounce worldliness and seek that one thing, the love of the Infinite Lord, our Friend, have the best that life can give; resting secure in that undying friendship, they are free from death and fear, while those poor fools who cling to unstable worldly objects are doomed to desolation and despair.

One sight of God in a moment destroys the attraction of these worthless things; must we not then seek that vision of him while we are still young, so that our lives may be fruitful and full of real joy? We abandon them for God, but in him we find again all that we have given up for him—for all are

19

in him, and finding him we have all else besides; he is all. The wise therefore seek him alone and never for a moment turn away to other things apart from him. Making him their sole business in life, they soon find in him the utmost joy their hearts can hold—for he is life and joy; wherever we may go we shall find chances to serve him and so draw nearer to his beloved Heart.

This is Nanak's own choice; his whole heart is aflame with longing for God, the only Good, for the Infinite can never be wholly attained; we find ever deeper riches in him to reach. Nanak finds God's lights aflame in his inmost being, guiding him to their Source. He calls us too to surrender all we have for God, keeping nothing back, and promises us that God will surely free us from all error and give us place at his side in the heavenly court.

40. THE SECRET OF HAPPINESS

1. I am happy on rising, happy at sitting; fear cannot come when I thus understand that the One Protector, our Lord, is the Inner Dweller of every heart. No anxiety in sleeping, no anxiety in waking —O Lord, thou art everywhere pervading! I dwell happily at home, I find happiness abroad; says Nanak, the mantra has been planted firmly by the Guru![1] (Ar. *Bhairo*, 2:1-3)

---

[1] This beautiful little verse is sung by pious Sikhs when they first wake in the morning. In the original it reads: *ūthata sukhīā baithata sukhīā; bhau nahī lāgai jān aise bujhīā; rākhā eku hamarā suāmī; sagala ghatā ka antarajāmi; soi achintā jāgi achintā; jahān kahān prabhu tūm varatantā; ghari sukhi vasiā bāhari sukha pāyā; kahu Nānaka guri mantra drilāyā.*

2. There is no happiness, O [heart], without devotion to God;...it is he whose wealth is God that is happy (Ar. *Gaurī*, 139:1, 12:5), while without devotion life passes in vain (K. *Gaurī*, 59:1). So if you wish to have always happiness of every kind then plunge deeply into the sweetness of God (G. *Hazare Shabad*, 3:3); Nanak suggests that one who recognizes God's command[1] will be happy day and night (N. *Gaurī*, 17:6). Serve him, and then receive the happiness which remains immanent in the very centre of all [hearts] (N. *Āsa Patilikhi*, 16). If you realize the Supreme God, you will have no expectations;[2] if you turn yourself to devotion to God, you will keep the heart free from anxiety (Nd. *Āsa*, 5:1). Having come to love the One, your other desires pass away (K. *Śloka* 25), and the command of the Beloved is felt to be sweet! (Ar. *Āsa*, 95:1)

3. When the veil of falsity is taken away from within[3] (AD. *Gūjari*, 1:3), the disciple breaks his egoism and **then** broods upon the Name of God; he repeats the Name, adores the Name, and by the Name is merged in happiness (N. *Mājh ki Vār*, 4 Sl.2).

---

[1] Or: will. To see the Beloved's will in everything that comes is naturally the source of continuous happiness and peace of mind.

[2] lit: you will not look for pleasure from hope: *āsā te na bhāvasī*.

[3] i.e., seeing everything through the dark glasses of ego.

If anyone would remove his own sorrow, let him always sing God's Name in the heart (Ar. *Sukhmani,* 3:5); never can sorrows [stay] near him who loves the praise of God (Ar. *Āsa,* 160:2). If he be devoted [to God], he sees him always present; my Lord remains ever omnipresent (AD. *Basantu,* 4:3). 'Know the One without and within!'—this is the wisdom the Guru has taught (T. *Dhanasari,* 1:2).

4. Nanak, beautiful is he who repeats the Name of the Lord[1] (Ar. *Gaurī ki Vār,* 4 Sl. 2), but the beauty is ruined when pride is in the heart (Ar. *Āsa* 12:1). Beautiful are the feet when turned towards thee, beautiful the head which bows to Thy feet; the mouth is beautiful when it sings thy praises, and the soul when it falls in surrender to thee (Ar. *Rāmkali ki Vār,* 15 Sl. 2). Beautiful are the faces of those who remember the Lord; they remember the Lord and pass their lives in happiness, . . .filled to overflowing with love's sweet delight (Ar. *Sukhmani,* 1:6, 20:2).

5. From the Guru's teaching to the disciples comes the thought that the Kind One saves with a look of grace (N. *Āsa dī Vār* 5 Sl. 2). No love awakens without the Guru, nor does the impurity of egoism depart (N. *Sri Ashtapadi,* 11:9); there is no

---

[1] *Sāī:* cf. the English proverb: 'Handsome is as handsome does.' The same theme has often been treated by English poets.

giver greater than the Guru, ...for without the true Guru the way is not found...If [God][1] gives his own gracious glance, then he in the very glance the true Guru is obtained. ... If he grants his grace, then [the disciple] makes use of the Guru's word;...controlled in this way, trouble departs (N. *Āsa dī Vār*, 4, 14 Sl. 2, and A. 7 Sl. 2).

6. Nanak, when God's glories are spoken of even for a moment, then a man becomes happy (R. *Āsa*, 11:4); resting or rising up, continually brooding [on him] he becomes ever and always happy (AD. *Mālār kī Vār*, 7 Sl.1). By considering the Self one becomes a gnostic[2] (N. *Gaurī*, 4:1); realizing the self to be God (*SOHAM*), he comes to be satisfied in the Mystery through the Word.... When a disciple realizes the Self,[3] what else is he to do or have done [for him]? (N. *Sri Ashtapadi*, 11:9) He who has obtained the Treasure through love fixes his mind on **God's** feet (N. *Tilang*, 4:3). Night and day become pleasant once egoism is dispelled; I got rid of the heart's infatuation when I pleased him; [now, Lord], graciously come into my house![4] (N. *Barah Maha*, 16)

---

[1] Or: (the Guru)

[2] *jnānī* in Sanskrit.

[3] Or: when with the Guru's help he realizes the Self.

[4] i.e., heart

7. Happiness is not for those who make many friends in the world; it is those who keep the mind on the One who ever enjoy happiness (K. *Śloka* 21). The servants serve [Him] who uplifts [them] by kindness; dewy[1] is the night of those in whose heart is a yearning [for Him] (N. *Āsa dī Vār*, 5 Sl. 2). Bliss is in the heart which delights in love [N. *Barah Maha*, 16], so there is always bliss for devotees; they are put into ecstasy by singing the excellences of God[2] (Ar. *Āsa*, 10:2).

Realizing God as always present, Nanak is always filled with joy; whatever he may be doing, God is there at his side, and in his presence he can never know what it is to be afraid. He advises us also to dive deep into this delightfulness of God's continual presence and we too shall find in it perpetual happiness. All anxieties, all desires, fade away when we are with him who is himself the fullness of all blessedness.

Freed from egoism, ceasing to rely on his own efforts and leaning on the Omnipotent instead, the disciple finds him everywhere and so is bathed in ceaseless waves of bliss. Such a one is truly beautiful in whom the Lord resides, from whom the stains of selfishness and pride have gone. It is the fulfilment of God's purpose in creation that all things should live in him and thus 'glorify his name'; those who employ their limbs in his service and unceasingly ponder upon him are always shining with his beauty.

---

[1] i.e., cool, happy.

[2] lit: jewels: *Hari Kīratanu gāi bigasāvai*. The last word means literally 'blossom like a flower', but is used for great joy.

It is the God-given Guru who can give us the strength thus to consecrate ourselves to God; so it is he who gives us that immortal joy we find in such surrender, and one glance from him may be enough to turn us into saints—if we are ready for his grace. True happiness is found in the anchoring of the heart in the still waters of the Beloved's presence by means of love and constant remembrance. It is unknown to those who seek for worldly friends, but lifts to ecstasy those who find the One true Friend who deserves that name and can fill their hearts. Their love for him makes even the darkest night ablaze with the radiance of deathless joy.

41. HOLY COMPANY

1. Wherever a devotee may go, that place is beautiful (Ar. *Phunahe*, 18); the company of good men is heaven[1] (K. *Gauri*, 10:4), for God is the Companion of devotees and the devotees adorn his court (Ar. *Maru*, 1:4); there always ... the devotees abide sustained by hymns (Ar. *Gauri Ashtapadi*, 4:7); in the assembly of the righteous[2] there is bliss and rest (Ar. *Dhanasari*, 23:3). Nanak, in a million there are few in whose mind God[3] [dwells] (T. *Śloka*, 24); among tens of millions

---

[1] *Baikunthai*, at no time to be confused with 'Swarga', the 'summerland' of Spiritualists.

[2] The word here translated by 'good', 'righteous', is *sādhu* lit: one who is making definite efforts (*sādhana*) to attain perfection. It is not synonymous with *sant*, which may be rightly rendered by 'saint', or with *bhagata*, more correctly rendered as 'devotee', M. assimilated all these.

[3] *Nārāina*.

few saints appear; Nanak, one is saved in their company, and if a man be fortunate then he gets a sight of them (Ar. *Prabhati Ashtapadi,* 2:8). The society of saintly people is won by [acts of] great merit (Ar. *Jaitsari ki Vār*, 17).

2. The servant of a man [of God] is very fortunate; in the company of such a man he is lovingly attached to the One; ...the Lord is remembered in the company of the righteous[1] (Ar. *Sukhmani,* 16:8, 1:2). The homes where good men[1] are not served, and where no service of God is, are like burning-grounds (K. *Śloka*, 192); without the company of the righteous[1] the fear [of God] does not arise, and without that feeling there is no devotion to **Him** (Rd. *Dhanasari,* 2:2), while in the company of good men[1] love is doubled day by day (K. *Śloka*, 100). [Nanak tells us:] 'By serving a saint I developed love and affections for my darling Masters' (Ar. *Āsa*, 153:1).

3. God, God, God[2] charms [my] heart, and I sing the glories of God, God, God! (R. *Gūjari,* 2:1) In my heart there is a thirst for the vision [of God] (Ar. *Jaitsari ki Vār,* 15); the disciple who utters his praise is my friend, (R. *Sri,* 3:1), one who tells me

---

[1] The word here translated by 'good', 'righteous', is *sādhu,* lit: one who is making definite efforts (*sādhana*) to attain perfection. It is not synonymous with *sant,* which may be rightly rendered by 'saint', or with *bhagata,* more correctly rendered as 'devotee', M. assimilated all these.

[2] *Govinda Govinda Govinda.*

anything of my beloved God, he is a brother, he is my comrade (R. *Gond,* 6:2). Moment by moment I worship the feet of those who have made God sweet [to me] (R. *Jaitsari,* 3:3); I am the dust of the lotus feet of those in whose bosom God remains immanent ! (K. *Gaurī,* 26:2) God's people are an excellent tank of nectar; by very good fortune one can bathe therein.... O God, drown me in the nectar of the Name![1] (R. *Rāmkali,* 4:1, 6:1)

4. According to the company one keeps, so is the fruit one eats, ... so keep the company of a good man, he will take care of you at the last; do not associate with an unbeliever, whose [company] will become your ruin. ... The unbeliever is a black blanket; [even when] washed he does not become white (K. *Ślokas,* 86, 93, 100); one should not speak to an unbeliever even by mistake (K. *Āsa,* 20:1). By associating with the righteous[2] and remembering God,[3] even the fallen becomes purified (T. *Sorathi,* 1:1); by singing the glories of the Lord all the eight watches [of the day], evil desire and anger depart from this body (Ar. *Bilawal,* 84:1).

---

[1] *Hari amrita nāmu samhāre;* M. renders *samhāre* simply 'bathe'.

[2] The word here translated by 'good', 'righteous', is *sadhu,* lit: one who is making definite efforts (*sadhana*) to attain perfection. It is not synonymous with *sant,* which may be rightly rendered by 'saint', or with *bhagata,* more correctly rendered as 'devotee', M. assimilated all these.

[3] *Mādho,* i.e., Mādhava.

5. Impurity evades the company of good people, and the Supreme becomes their Companion (Ar. *Sorathi,* 65:2); God the King meets that person who has entered the presence of the righteous[1] (Ar. *Bilawal,* 46:1). The holy Lord dwells on the tongue of a good man,[1]... God[2] shines forth on the saint's[3] brow (Ar. *Sukhmani,* 1:4, 24:3). In the company of the righteous[1] a man is honoured by meeting the Guru, (R. *Gūjari,* 2:1); there is true bliss in the house of devotees (Ar. *Bilawal,* 3:4), so rejoice on meeting the company of righteous [folk, my brother]! (Ar. *Sukhmani,* 22:5)

6. He whose heart is cooled in the company of a saint finds coolness in all[4] (Ar. *Sorathi,* 6:2); the Lord becomes gracious to the one in whose heart he has implanted the Name; Nanak, such a man longs for the company of the righteous and obtains the sweetness of God (Ar. *Todi,* 4:4). From God's Name are gained [good] memory, under-standing, and thinking power,[5] and the beloved Guru

---

[1] The word here translated by 'good', 'righteous', is *sādhu,* lit: one who is making definite efforts (*sādhana*) to attain perfection. It is not synonymous with *sant,* which may be rightly rendered by 'saint', or with *bhagata,* more correctly rendered as 'devotee', M. assimilated all these.

[2] *Gupala*

[3] *mahānta,* the word used commonly for the abbot of a Hindu monastery

[4] cf. 'Unto the pure all things are pure' (Titus, 1:15).

[5] *Sudhi budhi surati nāmi Hari pāiai..*

from the company of a saint (N. *Mālār*, 5:2). Where God is adored, there is God the Friend and Helper (R. *Suhi*, 10:1); the Lord is with those souls who hold God dear[1] (R. *Tilang II*, 2:7).

7. Thy whole creation, my Lord, all yearns after the dust of the [feet of] the righteous (R. *Mālār*, 2:4); for on meeting a saint the True One is found (N. *Sidh Goshti*, 1). Whatever is God's belongs to his servant (Ar. *Mājh*, 18:3); Nanak, the glory of the righteous merges into the Lord; …brother, there is no difference between the righteous and the Lord![2] (Ar. *Sukhmani*, 7:18)

8. Saints of God, repeat the Name of God! Saints of God, let us walk with God! Those who repeat God's Name become God, they meet God the playful Child.[3] To repeat the Name of God is my dearest desire; God, dweller in the forest, graciously let me meet God in the company of the righteous [and become] the dust of the feet of good men (R. *Dhanasari*, 4:3-4).

The skin is blackened by pitch and whitened by chalk, disease spreads by contact, holiness awakens from the touch and very sight of a saint. Hence the importance of *satsang* in the spiritual path.

The saints are always in God's presence, and where God

---

[1] *Jinā Hari seti pira hali tinā jīa prabha nāle.*

[2] *sādha prabha bhedu na bhāi*

[3] *Jinā Hari japi se Hari hoe Hari miliā kela kelāli.*

is there is heaven; so the neighbourhood of a saint is itself heaven, and his occupation is that of heaven—the eternal glorifying (not by words alone) of his beloved God. The lover is happy in thinking of the beloved, so the saints are always happy, and those who cling to them share that supernal and infectious happiness. There are few indeed who are really devoted to God (cf. *Gītā* 7:3); almost all seek some reward for themselves and so are self-seekers rather than seekers after God. Those who have selflessness enough to enjoy saintly company get that blessing and are happy in serving God in the person of his lover. This service makes their rudimentary love grow stronger day by day until it sweeps through the whole heart in one vast wave. The bliss of this total surrender is due to those who first started it; the disciple is filled with gratitude to his blessed Guru who has led him to this joy.

Good comes from the good; so those who wish for goodness must seek the company of good folk and avoid the wicked, the worldly and the egotistical. God reveals himself through the very body of his devotee (cf. GN 16:7) while the unbeliever's company is a deadly danger—near him wickedness increases, just as sin flees before the saint.

It is the rudimentary love for God which brings the aspirant into saintly company, and there he finds that the tiny spark of love is fanned into a roaring flame which burns away all evil and warms the heart with all sweetness of self-sacrifice. With how much eagerness, then, the sincere aspirant longs for such company, in whose midst he will find the Guru who unites him to the Lord! That guru, the saint, lives in the Lord, as he in him—there is no barrier between, there is as it were no difference between God and his devotee; one who finds the one is equally in the presence of the other.

42. THE LOVE OF GOD

1. From age to age God has brought forth devotees and has continued to keep his promise [to them][1] (R. *Āsa Chhant*, 13:4); from age to age the devotees are dear to God (AD. *Gaurī Chhant*, 4:4). God the Master protects his own devotees (R. *Gaurī ki Vār*, 14 Sl. 2), removes the pain and sorrow of the poor, and is the true delight of his servant (Ar. *Sri*, 13:1). To be kind to devotees is God's very nature;[2] God protects their honour (R. *Āsa Chhant*, 8:4); he himself adorns them,[3] himself draws them to devotion (AD. *Gaurī Chhant*, 4:4).

2. Devotion to God is the love of God, if the disciple were to consider this carefully; ...he may be called God's servant who keeps God pressed to his bosom[4] (AD. *Sri*, 6:2-3). When this love for God has been built up within, then whatever a man does is pleasing to God, my Lord (R. *Gūjari*, 7:7). When the Beloved is seen at the gate, what [more] can liberation or heaven do? Intoxicated with praise and always renounced, [the disciple] does not lose

---

[1] This promise is given in *Gītā*, 6:30; it is also found in Zoroastrianism, Christianity, Islam and in countless other places in a hundred scriptures.

[2] *bhagati vachalu Hari biradu hai.*

[3] cf. § 47.

[4] There can be no steady service save where love is the motive; the mind soon wearies of it unless spurred on by the holy feeling.

his birth in the game [of life] (N. *Āsa*, 38:3-4). Once the very sweet love of God is secured, everything else is forgotten; ...then indeed is the heart contented, for he comes to dwell in peace in the heart! (R. *Sarang*, 4:1-2)

3. The cup[1] of the True One is naturally perfect; he gives it to drink to the one on whom he looks with grace (N. *Āsa*, 38:2). God the Lover [fills] with the love of God [the one who] night and day sings God's glories with love for God (R. *Ghoria*, 1:2:5). Without love God cannot be obtained (G. *Thirty-three Sawwaiyas*, 18); without God's sweetness[2] there is no liberation for anyone (N. *Maru Solhe*, 8:10). Those who are filled with love for the One disregard human opinion and so are happy (5:319 G)[3]; if you turn to him with sincere love, then you shall win God[4] and be absorbed into the feet [you have] won! (K. *Bawan Akhari*, 36) [He] may be called a [true] lover (who) always remains immersed [in love] (A. *Āsa dī Vār*, 21 Sl.1); so saturate this heart [of yours] in the love of God! (R. *Āsa*, 9:1)

---

[1] The 'cup' is presumably that spoken by the Sūfis; it is filled with the wine of love and is given by the King with his own hand to his favourite courtier.

[2] *rasa*, the sweet juice of a fruit, so: love.

[3] From the Introduction to Guru Govind Singh's 'Purānas'

[4] *Allah*, the usual Muslim name for him

4. The disciple may laugh, the disciple may weep, whatever the disciple does is from devotion to God[1] (R. *Śloka* 14). O heart, let your love for God be such as the lotus has for water; even when dashed about by the waves it blooms in its affection ... O heart, how can you escape [from sorrow] without love? [God] is immanent in the disciples and grants them a treasure of devotion. O heart, let your love for God be such as the fish has for water; the more it has, the more intense its happiness and the greater the peace in its mind and body; without water it does not live for more than a few minutes[2]—the Lord knows its sufferings! (N. *Sri Ashtapadi,* 11:1-2)

5. God never forgets the one who feels the love of God in his heart, and who ever repeats the Name of God in heart and mind (AD. *Gūjari* 4:1). Night and day he remains spontaneously immersed in love and worships the Name of God in his heart (R. *Suhi Chhant,* 4:1). In age after age I have known the One Supreme Lord (N. *Barah Maha,* 15); my heart is inebriated by drinking the sweetness of the Name and remains spontaneously lost in love; day and night I am resolved to fix my love [on God] and to

---

[1] *Sāi,* also a Muslim name.

[2] lit: twenty-four minutes *(ghali)*

hear the uncaused sound[1] (N. *Āsa*, 38:1). To devotees nothing seems sweet but God! (Ar. *Jaitsari ki Vār*, 11)

God keeps his promise to guard the devotee and lover who clings to him; could he be less faithful than his own creature? He draws such ever nearer to himself and adorns them with every virtue and grace. And when they come to him they find in him the most absolute return for their love in an unending bliss which drowns the very memory of the long lonely ages.

This 'reward' of his grace comes to the soul which loves him for himself alone, and finds all joy in him alone, so that the idle chatter of the mob cannot disturb it from its rest in him. The true love of God is that which never slackens; even when it flows underground and unseen it pours on in a steady flood towards the ocean.

The soul may have earthly ease and comfort or it may have ceaseless troubles and have to tread the thorny path of martyrdom—but still it clings to the chosen God of its heart and its love deepens with every event of life. Be it sorrow or happiness, joy or pain, all is joy because it comes from the Beloved; all the soul's actions are suffered with the rapture of knowing it is for him and his glory all is done and ensured.

Such a devotee indeed lives in God, starves without him, bathes in him as the fish in the mighty sea. Nanak himself is one such soul; for uncounted ages he has found his happiness in God and loves to spend his every moment in that adoring love which fills life with immortal sweetness.

---

[1] i.e, *anāhata*, the mystic sound in the *heart-chakra*

43. HOW TO FIND HIM

1. He cannot be realized by cleverness; without hammering how can the value be brought out?[1] (N. *Gaurī Ashtapadi,* 2:1) [One must] beat out egoism, and then shall he meet God[2] (AD. *Gūjari,* 4:4). This heart is freed when it meets the true Guru; … by his word the glamour of worldliness is burned up,… egoism comes out when washed [by him] (AD. *Basantu,* 16:3-4, 17:1). The water [of life] is obtained through the Guru's word when the ego has been driven out (AD. *Mālār ki Vār,* 12 Sl. 2); [the heart] becomes clean, and then the True One is found (N. *Āsa di Vār,* 16 Sl. 2). If a man meets such a true Guru, he will entrust his head to him,[3] and then selfhood departs from within; the Owner of the soul meets him, God comes and continually dwells in his heart (AD. *Anand,* 30:3-4).

2. The restless heart runs off in the ten directions, but it can be stopped [and made] motionless (T. *Dhanasari,* 3:2); today **God** can be met…on restraining the feelings which disturb the heart (F. *Āsa,* 2:1). Think [of God] in your heart again and again, and the affection for worldliness will pass

---

[1] Gold is purified and made more valuable by beating on the anvil; so is the soul's vision purified, made clear, by suffering and pain.

[2] i.e., God is found when the Guru has purged the heart of its egoism.

[3] i.e., devote his life to him

20

away. The immortal God is with you; O my mind, plunge into the love of God![1] (Ar. *Gaurī Ashtapadi,* 6:14) Without the power of a perfect love for the Master,[2] who has won the noble God?[3] (G. *Akāl Ustat,* 245)

3. Law codes and scriptures define merit and sin,[4] but do not know the essence of Reality… in the absence of the Guru…. The world is sleeping in the delusion of Nature, it passes the [whole] night asleep.[5] By the Guru's kindness those persons wake who let God dwell in their heart and utter his nectar hymns. Nanak says: he obtains the Reality who day and night turns lovingly to God and passes the night in wakefulness[6] (AD. *Anand,* 27).

4. The Immaculate is in your very bosom, yet you grow desperate in seeking him elsewhere! (T. *Sorathi,* 3:2) Why leave him who stays near in your bosom and go far away? You shall find close at hand him for whom you search the world (K. *Bawan Akhari,* 16), for he is naturally nearer [than your] hands and feet (Rd. *Sorathi,* 1: 4),

---

[1] *Rachu Rāma ke rangi .*

[2] lit: husband, lord (*pati*)

[3] *Padamapata,* i.e., Lakshmi's Lord, Vishnu, who is God.

[4] *Simriti sastra punna pāpa bicharade*; cf. 62 : 3.

[5] The metaphor of sleep runs back far in religious history.

[6] For vigils of prayer

the Soul of soul in all, ever pervading every breast. By the Guru's grace he is manifested even at home, and [there also] spontaneously pervades [every-thing] .... Then, Nanak, the burning is extinguished (N. *Mālār Ashtapadi*, 1:7-8). As fragrance resides in the flower, as the reflection is in a mirror,[1] so also God dwells within; seek in the bosom itself, my brother! (T. *Dhanasari*, 1:1) He is mad who does not recognize himself[2]; when he realizes the self, then he knows the One (K. *Bilawal*, 2:4).

5. One day...I was going to worship God in a temple,[3] but the Guru explained that God is in my very heart (Ra. *Basantu*, 1:1). God is won by loving the true Guru (N. *Sorathi*, 7:4); now that I have met him by means of the Guru's affection and love, we shall not be separated [again] (AD. *Suhi X*, 1:14). *Why send for pen and ink? Write in your heart. If you remain always in the love of God, your affection shall never be broken off from him. Pens and ink bottle will perish, the writing will go with them, O Nanak, but the love of the True One which he grants from the beginning shall not perish* (2:70 AD.).

---

[1] cf. the striking gnostic saying in GMC 69:2

[2] Ramana Maharshi said: 'What, was there ever a time when you did not know yourself?'

[3] lit: in a [certain] place; *eka divasa...pūjana chalī brahama thai.*

6. Serve God, do no other service; from the service of God is gained the fruit anxiously [desired by] the heart; in any other service life passes in vain (AD. *Gūjari*, 2:1). Some have chains on the necks as they are led off to prison, but they are freed from bonds when they really recognize the True One (N. *Mālār ki Vār*, 21). The Light is in all; now thou art met thereby but beautified by love![1] (N. *Suhi Chhant*, 3:1) Love pleases the Beloved! (N. *Mālār Ashtapadi*, 1:1)

7. Easily shall the disciples who please God in the heart be united to God. The Beloved dwells in present and future; say in what way he can be won [today] ! (AD. *Gaurī*, 17:1) By fear and love, by the offering of devotion day and night, the soul sees God ever present (AD. *Sri*, 21:2); when the Name [once] dwells in the bosom, then the Beloved is [soon] met by the Guru's teaching (AD. *Gaurī Chhant*, 4:2). Having spread the Word abroad, [God] causes you to meet himself in the Guru; having revered[2] the True One [in him] (N. *Mālār ki Vār*, 2), you repeat the [Name of] the Immaculate and cling [to him], O heart (N. *Gaurī*, 15:4); God himself then closely embraces you (R. *Gaurī Karahale*, 1:9).

---

[1] M. translates: by it Thou are known, but thou art found by love.

[2] Or: obeyed

8. The True One unites you to himself and then delights your heart and enfolds in his embrace [the one who] walks according to his pleasure (N. *Āsa Ashtapadi,* 17:2). Nanak, the disciple is as easily united [with God] as water mixes with water (R. *Basantu,* 9:8); it is the Immaculate, the Invisible, who himself unites man with himself (AD. *Gauri,* 17:1). [My] heart has reverenced him, so I have known God (K. *Sorathi,* 11:4).

God is not found by reasoning or logical argument, but through the 'crucifixion' or 'abandonment' of the ego, which the soul can reach when inspired by the presence and teaching of the Guru. This is a baptismal flood which washes away the stain of selfishness, purifies the heart, and so enables it to give a home to Immaculate Divinity.

The heart and mind run here and there away from their real happiness (*Gītā* 6:35), but they can be brought under control and fixed in God. If they once taste his nectar, they can never be lured away from him again—can the drunkard leave his glass undrained? Deeper and yet more deep the heart will dive into that nectar ocean of God's love, finding in it its own fulfilment, its perfect joy and peace after the restlessness of ages. Doctrine and ethics can tell us what to believe and what to do; the scriptures are our guide for actions in the outer world; but who can guide the heart in its deeper diving into God? It is his love that guides and draws on the heart, that reveals to it all himself, planting in it a passionate attachment to his feet.

Where is he, that we may find him? Shall we search the deserts, build palm-leaf shelters on the bank of great rivers, crouch in ice-girt caves upon the lofty mountains of the earth? Is he found by wandering through the markets of distant lands, by holy pilgrimages, by dreadful austerities? Nay, he is at our very side, within that very heart which throbs so restlessly in its yearning, and he smiles out of the eyes of everyone we see. Dive deep, then, my brother, within that little heart of yours, that heart which trembles in desire and disappointment, which longs for perfect friend-ship, for the fullest understanding love! There he dwells, and there he can be found in lonely silences, by the sounding seas, on the wind-swept hill, amid the endless toil of domesticity.

Who is that Self within, whom we feel astir in the silent hours? Who asks this question of himself? Seeing that self, that 'I', we see the very Self of self, the 'I' of every 'I', the God within, from whom all things have come and in whose arms all things are held.

To love that Self, to serve that Self—this alone can make our toilsome life worth living! Those who never drink that nectar of God's Life have lived in vain; they cannot hope for freedom from ignorance and sorrow. And that nectar comes to us in the Guru's chalice; to serve him, the saint, the child of God—is to serve God himself; to love him is to win God's love, which will never fail the heart that longs for him. And he who wins God's love unites with him, and never never again for a moment can he be separated from that Infinite Source of bliss. He blends inseparably with God, like 'the dewdrop in the shining sea', and yet remains the dewdrop for ever mingled with the eternal waters.

44. INTENSE YEARNING FOR HIM

1. Happy night, grow long, that I may fasten my love upon the Beloved![1] Be brief, O wretched sleep, that I may ever touch his feet! I am always longing for the dust of his feet and begging for the Name for love [of which I have] left the world![2] Filled with love for the Beloved and spontaneously inebriated,[3] I have given up great follies; when I met the Beloved on the straight[4] path he took my arm and I was drenched with love. Nanak humbly begs: 'Graciously let me remain clinging to thy feet' (Ar. *Bihagale Chhant*, 4:1).

2. I am thine, thou mine[5] (AD. *Suhi Chhant*, 1:3). Those who have obtained God do not wander about again and again[6] (K. *Maru*, 3:1), so if thou be our friend, do not for a moment[7] be separate [from us]. Thou hast fascinated my soul; when shall I behold

---

[1] This recalls the wonderful duet by Tristan and Isolde in Wagner's great opera beginning: 'O sink down ...'. It is in the 'night', when senses close to this outer illusory world, that the soul communes with the Inner God and realizes him in love.

[2] *Jāchau nāma rasi bairāgani.*

[3] *Pria rangi rātī sahaja mātī.*   [4] lit : true

[5] *Hau terā tū hamārā.* This is a typical example of the extreme economy of words common to all the Gurus; those who know speak little, those who know not babble much!

[6] This is the aim of birth; when it is achieved, how can rebirth occur?

[7] lit: a dawn (*hika bhorī*)

thee, my life? (Ar. *Maru ki Vār*, 2 Sl. 1) Without my Beloved I shall pine to death (K. *Maru Kafi*, 1:2), and on seeing thee I shall blossom like the lotus (Ar. *Āsa*, 74:2).

3. Foolish Nanak has become mad after the King, **he** knows no one but God. When one has gone mad with awe [of God], then he is considered insane; when he knows no other second beyond the One Master, then he is deemed mad when he does this one thing. But when he recognizes the Master's will, in what else is the perfection of cleverness?[1] Then is he thought mad when he holds the Master dear and deems himself unworthy[2] and the rest of the world good (N. *Maru*, 7:1-4). But what care I for the world so long as I please thee? (N. *Āsa Ashtapadi*, 21:1)

4. If thou give happiness, then I adore thee; even in misery I brood on thee!... If thou seat me near [to thee], then I adore thee; even if thou strike and repulse me, yet will I ponder thee... If the world praise, then [am I] like thee; and if it blame, then I cannot leave thee![3] Poor Nanak has become mad after a sight of thee, O God! (R. *Suhi Ashtapadi*, 1:2, 8-9, 12) The pain has become [a very] dying!...

---

[1] *dūjī avar siānapa kāi*.

[2] lit: bad (*mandā*)

[3] I am like God in receiving the praise of his world; if criticism or hate come instead, then to whom can I go for comfort save to him?

Say how [there can be] sleep or hunger without God; raiment does not console the body, ...without God how can happiness be attained? (N. *Barah Maha*, 9-10) Various people have various [friends, but] I have only thee; why do I not die of weeping when thou comest not into mind? (A. *Suhi ki Vār*, 20 Sl. 1)

5. Within [me was] a thirst for the Name of God (R. *Sri*, 3:1); crying 'Beloved! Beloved!' I wandered over the whole world, but my thirst did not go. Nanak, my thirst departed when I met the true Guru; on returning home I obtained the Beloved (AD. *Bihagale ki Vār*, 13 Sl. 2). Yes, when I returned after climbing the mountain in search [of God], I found him in the strong castle[1] which he had fortified (K. *Bawan Akhari*, 20). God, thou art one in every place! (N. *Sri Ashtapadi*, 13:8) God's Name is nectar, the thirst of him who drinks it goes away; ...Nanak, disciples who drink [that nectar] their thirst does not return! (AD. *Mālār ki Vār*, 11 Sl. 1)

6. When the Name is found the heart is satisfied; accursed are beings without the Name![2] (R. *Sri*, 2:1) My friends and companions, let us stay clinging to

---

[1] The 'castle' is of course the heart; cf. St Teresa's metaphor in her wonderful study of mysticism, *The Interior Castle*.

[2] This is not a curse but a mere statement of fact.

the feet of the Lord; in our hearts there is intense love for the Beloved, let us now ask for devotion to God[1] (Ar. *Bihagale Chhant,* 4:2). When we were bound with the noose of worldly glamour, we tied thee with a bond of love. Make attempts to free thyself, Beloved; we got free by adoring thee! O God, thou knowest our mutual relationship, now what wilt thou do with us?[2] (Rd. *Sorathi,* 2:1)

Nanak prays that the mystic 'night' of God's felt presence, when all distractions are forgotten, may be longer and longer, and that less and less time be spent in the sleep of forgetfulness of him amid life's business. He has once tasted that sweetness of God and for his sake turned away from the world's delights; now he would for evermore be free to abide in him. His love is indeed delightful and abide in him. His love is indeed delightful and all-satisfying; so intense and delicious that Nanak cannot for a moment bear to be left alone without his love. He has become mad with love because he can think of, see, hear, feel nothing any more but God in everything and now devotes his whole life solely to his service. Though his true humility ever increases, he has no care for the world's opinion, being absorbed in pleasing his Beloved.

Whether God sends him joy or sorrow, honour or disgrace, he will always cling to him with faithful love. Why is this? If God escapes from him even for a moment he will die in misery; God is his only hope and consolation. How then can he let him go?

---

[1] We already love, now let us serve and eternally adore him.

[2] So M. *Madhave janata hohu jaisi taisi: aba kaha karohu ge aisi*

Long ago he wandered here and there vainly seeking that Beloved and crying aloud in his anguish. Only when he met the saint who was to be his Guru did he learn that such outward search is futile, for the Beloved of each soul dwells in his very home, in the heart. There, then, he sought, and found. He drank deep of that divine nectar, and with the living draught of God his agelong thirst was quenched. And now he challenges God to try to escape from his clinging arms; the devotee has enslaved his Master; tied him with the unbreakable cords of love and adoration. What can God do but give the fullness of his infinite love in return?

CHAPTER SEVEN

Union With The Beloved

One of the Guru's favourite themes is the spiritual courtship and marriage of the soul with God—a theme full of unfathomable depths of meaning which can be even partly grasped only by those who are on the Mystic Path. It is an ancient theme, and in the Near East along one of its Babylonian lines can be traced back to the story of Tammuz. The Sūfīs speak this language; so do the Vaishnavas; so do many Christian saints; and so from age to age have certain of God's chosen 'brides' sung this immortal song in words of thrilling warmth and ecstasy. St Teresa of Avila, the writers of the *Odes of Solomon* and the Manichean Psalms, Sri Jayadeva, Rabia and Āndāl, Mīrā and Hafīz are among those who spoke this mystic language and enriched the literature of our world with gems of devotion. But no recognized scripture in the world so lingers on this theme as the *Guru-Granth Sahib*, which lovingly recurs to it from time to time throughout its many pages.

Here, too, a prolonged study would let us trace the various stages of the mystic path outlined by the great mystics of East and West, with their alternation of ecstasy and 'dark nights of the soul', but I have made no such attempt in this volume, tracing rather the simple progress from a burning thirst for God, to the soul's adornment with his graces, the Guru's intercession, the coming of the Beloved, and the endless of perfect union.

45. THE BELOVED IS NEAR

Having established the nine houses, the highest house, the palace,[1] (is where) God dwells in his own home (N. *Barah Maha*, 2). He is near, do not think him far away; he ever cares for and remembers you (N. *Gūjari*, 1:4). The Spouse is near at hand, O foolish woman; what are you seeking outside? (N. *Tilang*, 4:1) By seeking outside one is ruined[2] (N. *Sri Ashtapadi*, 15:4). Infatuated by the glamour [of worldliness] one thinks he is distant but, Nanak says, he is always present (Ar. *Gaurī Cheti*, 1:4), the reality is in the house [itself]; the self-willed miss it through egoism, the disciple gets it at once (N. *Sri Ashtapadi*, 15:4). Where can one go to be far from him?[3] (Ar. *Sukhmani*, 22:7)

---

[1] Beyond the 'nine houses' of creation is the 'tenth door of the sky' (§ 39:5) which leads to the 'palace' or 'bed-chamber' of the Spouse, the King of Heaven. So too St Teresa's 'seventh mansion', where the Divine Lover waits for his bride, is beyond six 'courts' or 'mansions' to be crossed by her in turn on her inward way.

[2] It is indeed ruin for the bride to retrace her steps and to turn outwards to the 'world' she has already left behind.

[3] This recalls the Psalmist's cry of exultation: 'If I ascend to heaven, thou art there; if I go down to the underworld, there art thou also!'

The senses speak to us only of this 'unreal' world, for they can neither hear nor see nor touch the living God; so we often forget how very near he is to each of us and, driven by our spiritual need, look for him in all manner of places outside ourselves. The lover may be reminded here that her spouse is already at her side; she has only to clarify her vision and she will see him there. When the sense of separation wears thin, the dimness over her eyes will go, and she will see her Lord.

46. THE BRIDE LONGS FOR HIM

1. For the bride the night is tedious; sleep does not come, her woman's soul pines away through grief, saying ... 'How can my eyes see him? (N. *Gaurī Purbi Chhant,* 1:1) In every house the spouse enjoys a happy wife; why have I been forgotten by the Bridegroom?' (N. *Barah Maha,* 4) My eyelids do not close;[1] I am steeped in love for the Dear One, and my heart looks ceaselessly in anxiety for the Lord (Ar. *Āsa Chhant,* 14:2). I have [grown] crazy in the agony of separation from my Beloved (F. *Suhi,* 1:2). Continuously she walks about burning,[2] day and night enduring great pain without the Beloved (AD. *Mājh Ashtapadi,* 4:2).

2. The woman is waiting for [Thy coming on the]

---

[1] *Palaka na lāgai.*

[2] *Anadinu jaladi phirai;* the word 'burning' is apt; this is the real *tapasya* of spiritual life, no futile self-torturings deserve the name.

path; listen, O Divine Spirit![1]... [She cries:] 'Why dost thou not come? (N. *Barah Maha,* 1, 14) Wandering here and there I weep and wring my hands[2]! (Ar. *Āsa,* 15:3) Save for God, to whom can I tell my agony? (F. *Śloka,* 10) My heart greatly yearns for the sight of God like a thirsty man without water (R. *Gond,* 6:1); it is impossible to remain without a sight of God. I have not yet tasted love; my thirst is not yet quenched; my girlhood has gone, and I mourn.[3] Now also I awoke thirsty with hope, yet I have been disappointed and now remain without expectation (N. *Āsa,* 26:3-4). I am wandering in search of that dear charming Darling; show him, my dear! I will give my head for you—give a sight [of him if only] for a very little while![4] My eyes are swimming[5] with the love of that Dear One, they cannot be still even for a moment![6] (Ar. *Jaitsari Chhant,* 1:1)

3. 'Standing in my house I long for thee; in my heart is an excessive eagerness. (N. *Suhi Chhant,* 3:1) If anyone comes and lets me meet my dear

---

[1] *Ātmārāma*

[2] *Bhrami bhrami rovai hātha pacholai.*

[3] *Gayā su jobanu dhana pachatānī.*

[4] lit: for a dawn; the actual moment of dawn in the tropics is very brief.

[5] Or: inundated, drenched; *naina hamāre pria rangā rangāre.*

[6] *tilu,* i.e., a very tiny seed

Beloved, I will sell myself to him [as a slave] (R. *Suhi Ashtapadi*, II, 1:1) In my heart and body is fixed a longing for God (R. *Gūjari*, 4:2); for without my dear God I cannot play the [game of] love' (R. *Āsa Chhant*, 14:6). When the Beloved does not come to her house, how can the wife find happiness? Her body wastes away from the anguish of separation[1] (N. *Barah Maha*, 5).

4. God's arrow of love has pierced my heart; my suffering God the Lord [alone] knows the pain within my heart (R. *Gond*, 6:1); the one whom the Beloved's arrow has smitten knows the burning agony of it[2] (R. *Āsa Chhant*, 8:2). Now I cannot remain without seeing my Beloved; separation from God is a weight within me (R. *Gaurī*, 29:3). I would lay my heart before any who pleased my Darling (Ar. *Jaitsari Chhant*, 1:2), for none seems to me like the Beloved (Ar. *Āsa Chhant*, 4:4). O friend, I love my Beloved, but he cares not at all [for me] (Ar. *Jaitsari Chhant*, 1:3). The one prayer [I use] is for devotion to God (R. *Āsa Chhant*, 8:3), and that I may remain in contact with my Beloved and hold him pressed [to me] in my bosom! (AD. *Sri Rāg dī Vār*, 19 Sl.1)

---

[1] *birahi*, i.e., Skt: *viraham*

[2] cf. Mīra's song:
 'Only the wounded know the anguished pain
 When one is wounded sorely to the heart;
 None but the Lord himself can save me now!'

The young bride mourns that she alone is left unvisited by God while all her comrades enjoy his love. Life without him is dark misery; she does not know how to live through the long 'dark night', filled as she is with a burning thirst for him whom she so feverishly awaits. She has no real friend to whom she can expose her grief, for who can understand love's sorrows who have not been smitten with its arrows? She is desperate with longing, and roams about like a wild thing caged, ready to die even for a mere fleeting glimpse of him; and then she stands eager at the door, looking out along the path by which he will come at last to her, hearing his step in every crackling twig.

She knows her life was made for him, her body exists solely to give him its delight, her heart's only work is to give itself to him—and yet he comes not to her heart and leaves her fruitless. Youth is meant for love, but her youth passes in barrenness and grief. Again and again her hopes leap up as she imagines he has come at last, and then are dashed once more down into despair to find herself mistaken. She knows it useless to tell another of her woe, for he alone can understand her heart who made it for himself, and in his absence she must endure the very agonies of death unconsoled. Yet in the midst of her anguish she asks but one thing—for more and more of this agonizing bliss of love for God, so that in her heart at least she may embrace him constantly and hourly draw nearer to the culminating meeting of full union.

This most beautiful section, so full of passionate feeling, recalls strongly to the mind the throbbing words of Sri Jayadeva in his immortal *Gīta-Govinda;* the cry of St Gemma Galgani is in the same key: 'When, oh when shall I see thee face to face?... Make haste, Jesus; oh, dost thou not see how

21

this heart longs for thee?....Does it not pain thee, Lord, to see it thus languish in desire? Come, come, Jesus; make haste, come near, let me hear thy voice. Oh God, when shall my whole being be satiated with thy light, oh when? ...I thirst for thee, Jesus. Dost thou not see how I suffer?...These flames of love consume my body as well as my heart, and I shall be reduced to ashes!' Yes, the mystics speak one common language. Is there any Tamil Vaishnava who will not now remember Nammalwar's glowing cry for the consoling presence of his Beloved?

47. IT IS HE WHO CALLS AND ADORNS HER

1. Sleeping on a dark night,[1] how can you pass the night without the Beloved? Your bosom burns, your body is burning, your heart and property[2] burn away as sacrifice.[3] When a woman does not enjoy the Spouse, then her youth goes in vain; her Spouse [may be] on the couch, [but his] wife is un- aware [of it] (N. *Sri Ashtapadi,* 2:7-8). The virtuous one enjoys [him by practice of her] virtue (N. *Barah Maha,* 13); Nanak, when the young girl pleases her husband, he will himself enjoy [her company] (N. *Tilang,* 3:4).

---

[1] *Nisi andhiarī sutīe:* M. translates: 'You who are reckless...', but I find no such use for the word *sutīe* elsewhere. The meaning seems clear, and is common to nearly all mystics.

[2] *dhanu:* M. translates 'O woman', as from the word *dhana*

[3] *iali bali jāi.*

2. [She says:] 'I may put on many dresses, but without the Beloved I can win no place in the nuptial chamber. When I am desired by the Beloved I adorn myself with necklaces, pearls, scents, silks and satins (N. *Barah Maha,* 16); nay, he himself decks, himself colours, and he himself gives a look of gracious approval[1] *(N. Tilang,* 3:4). [Beloved,] thy Name alone is the madder that dyes my robe—the colour remains ever fast! (N. *Suhi,* 4:2) I will wear a flower garland as a necklace round the throat; when I meet the Beloved, then shall I make this adornment! (N. *Āsa,* 34:2) Hear, beloved Lord, [with thy] virtues in my fair bosom I please thee and bathe in thy tank! . . . Having become pure, I have come to know the holy bathing-place within'[2] (N. *Barah Maha,* 15).

3. When the lovely bride[3] pleases thee, thou adornest her with thy grace adorned with the Guru's word, she belongs body and heart to[4] the Beloved (N. *Sri Ashtapadi,* 2:1-2). Nanak, that woman meets him when caused to meet him; without the Beloved no sleep comes to her. The bride's

---

[1] Nothing we may do of ourselves can win his favour; when he has adorned us with his own graces he can approve of us and take us to himself.

[2] *Tirthu antari*: i.e., 'the sanctuary of the heart'; bathing in the Name, and so loving God in the heart

[3] *sohagani*   [4] Or: sits close to (*pira kai pāsi*)

soul is unhonoured without her dear lord: how can she get happiness without holding him in embrace? (N. *Gaurī Purbi Chhant,* 1:1-2) She easily gets comfort in the mind if the girl wins God as her Bridegroom in the home! (N. *Barah Maha,* 5) She has all his prudence and ornaments of peerless beauty, O Nanak, that happy wife who is pleasing the Creator (Ar. *Āsa,* 118:4).

4. [She says:] 'I sleep, the Beloved is awake[1]—to whom shall I go to ask [what to do]?[2] (N. *Āsa Ashtapadi,* 2:8) I have searched the four corners [of the world, but] few friends are mine;[3] if it please thee, Master,[4] thou art mine, I thine[4] (N. *Āsa Ashtapadi,* 14:1)'. All are God's handmaids and all say, 'he is mine!' Nanak, it is the one whom he has adorned whom he lets abide in happiness (Ar. *Āsa,* 117:4). Some **he** takes to meet himself others **he** allows to stray away from **himself**[5] (N. *Āsa dī Vār,* 11]; he is known as a disciple to whom he reveals himself [A. *Āsa dī Vār,* 2 Sl. 3). Dear friend, [if you merely] go, how can there be a meeting? If you are adorned with virtue, then he will meet you, and

---

[1] *Hau sutī pira jagata*

[2] Or: consult

[3] M. prefers: ' I found no friend'.

[4] *Je tudhu bhavai sahiba tū mai hau taidā.*

[5] The text has this in the second person; 'thou', etc.

when there has been a meeting he will not part [from you again], if he have [really] met you[1] (N. *Suhi,* 4:2-3).

Her friend pities her misery, for she too remembers when she suffered likewise before the bridegroom came to her; she warns her also that she must remain alert lest he come and find her sleeping, unaware, and pass on his way again. The unhappy girl replies that she has begun with the Guru's aid to learn how to find him within her heart, and that the very sleep against which her friend has warned her is his gift and could not come to her but from his hand.

She goes on to tell how God comes to her in that sleep and decks her, all unseen, with his own virtues so that she may please him and win his love, for nothing she can do of herself can satisfy his perfection. Hope now surges in her heart, for she knows how beautiful she is becoming under his adorning hand, and she resolves to go forth to meet him in all the graces he has given her through the Guru's teaching.

It is true that all God's children have equal claims upon him, but he draws into the intimacy of perfect communion only those whom he himself has beautified with virtue, to whom he has revealed himself as the source of all goodness and all beauty. And he will never let go of those whom he has thus drawn to himself and favoured with his glance.

---

[1] The word 'meeting' does not imply merely the outer contact, but rather a close and intimate union. Once united with God, the soul does not slip away from him again.

48. HOW TO WIN HIS LOVE

1. If a woman become gentle[1] and if she become like a thread, she shall take and string in the mind a jewel[2] of inestimable worth (N. *Wadhans,* 2:2). Having dropped egoism, let her adorn herself thus … with fear and love, and then shall the Spouse enjoy his young wife on the couch. Nanak, then will she please her Husband's heart and leaving self importance[3] be united with her Master (N. *Āsa,* 26:4). Women adorned with love for the dear person cannot be held back from offering devotion [to him] day and night; their dwelling [will be] in his chamber[4] made ready by the Word. They will make prayer (their) service to the True One and (so) be beautiful walking straight beside the Master according to (His) will (N. *Mājh ki Vār,* 22).

2. She walks so as to please the Spouse and so always enjoys his embrace (AD. *Mālār ki Vār,* 6 Sl. 1); O Spouse, if she only remains attached to thee, then the bride will enjoy thee (N. *Wadhans,* 2:4). Nanak, blessed is the happy wife who loves her husband! (Ar. *Sri,* 23:4) My

---

[1] M. translates 'virtuous' (*karanī*).

[2] This is the mystic 'pearl' of the Gnosis God's heart.

[3] *chodi vadāī.*

[4] *Mahala manjhi nivasu.* cf. Manichean Psalms: 'Take me into thy chambers that I may chant with them that sing to thee.'

Beloved is playful;[1] when a woman has intense affection for the Beloved, [he is] kind [to her] with delight and love (N. *Āsa Chhant,* 1:1). That woman is very dear [to him] in whose heart there is devotion for the Beloved; ...Nanak, the All-Blissful delightedly enjoys the love of her who has a loving friendship for God.[2] ...[When she] knows Him by his grace, she meets and is absorbed in his glories (N. *Barah Maha,* 13-14, 7).

The soul who would win God's love must make herself so small that she is like a slender thread on which to thread his heart, so that he may wear it on her breast. All the coarseness of the ego must be refined away and the spirit become subtle (*tanumānasi*), so that she may capture him and hold him fast. Then she will find him in her arms, and there will be no more hindrance to her perfect enjoyment of his love. Day and night will then be filled with exquisite delight as she blends her person with that of her Beloved so long desired.

Ever watchful of his pleasure, she does all to please him and remains always obedient at his feet like the perfect wife; he in his turn lavishes on her the richest affection of his heart, for none can be so dear to him as the perfect devotee who is filled with reverent love.

49. A VIRTUOUS BRIDE'S JOY

1. She who is dear to her Spouse is a happy wife (N. *Tilang,* 4:4); through the Beloved's affection

---

[1] *raliālā*, i.e., delightful, full of love's sweet ways

[2] *Hari siu priti saneho*

and love she is the beautiful Queen of all (AD. *Āsa Ashtapadi*, 8:4); beautiful, fair of form[1] and accomplished, it is she who is called 'clever' (N. *Tilang*, 4:4). With both hands folded she stands and utters sincere prayer;[2] in love with the Darling, she dwells in awe of the True One; imbued with love, she delights in bliss.[3] She is called the handmaid of the Dear One and answers to the name of Darling[4] (N. *Sri Ashtapadi*, 2:2-3); thus she is saturated with love-bliss, intoxicated with intimacy, night and day immersed in love (N. *Tilang*, 4:4). Her true love is not interrupted, and the True One brings about close union [with her][5] (N. *Sri Ashtapadi*, 2:3).

2. Her heart is filled, drenched with the Word—I ever surrender to her! Such a woman will never end

---

[1] Or: nature (*Sarūpa*)　　　　　　[2] *Sachu kahai aradāsi.*

[3] A line full of music: *lālī ratī sacha bhaī vasi bhai ratī rangī rasī.* Besides their supreme spiritual genius the Gurus have a wonderful gift of poetry.

[4] *Lālī*

[5] The bliss of this 'meeting' is well paralleled in the Manichean Psalms: 'Christ my Bridegroom has taken me to His bridal-chamber, I have rested with him in the land of the immortals.' St Gemma is in a like mood: 'As long as I had so many desires my soul was without rest; now that I have only one I am happy. ... Here, Jesus, here in my heart I will raise thee a pavilion of love. Thou alone must enter into it. I will keep thee always with me, always here a prisoner .... I am awaiting the grace to be entirely transformed into him, and I am consumed by the desire to be able to plunge into the infinite abyss of divine love. ...I would wish to be all dissolved in the midst of the flames of thy love!' Western mystics almost all speak thus.

up as[1] a widow if she be assimilated to[2] the true Guru; her Beloved will be a source of bliss ever new and constant[3] bodily—he neither comes nor goes, but always delights in the true happy wife who obeys [his mere] glance. The woman makes truth the parting [of her hair], love her dress and ornaments, the implanting of God in the mind [her fragrant] sandal wood, the tenth gate her abode. Having kindled the lamp with the word, [she wears] the Name of God as a garland on the breast; fairest among women, [she wears] on the brow the jewel of love; her beauty and intelligence are attractive [and she is] unequalled in her true love.[4] She knows no man save the Beloved; her affection and love are for the true Guru [alone] (N. *Sri Ashtapadi,* 2:3-6).

3. Lowering clouds have spread and rain has delighted all; love makes [me] happy in heart and body; Nanak, nectar words rain down, and the [Beloved] comes graciously into my house! (N. *Barah Maha,* 4) At the meeting my friends asked, 'What is the Spouse like?'[5] but being filled

---

[1] lit: sit down as

[2] Or: intent upon

[3] lit: true; i.e., reliable. God is always there with his lover, even physically present, though invisible.

[4] The full esoteric significance of this beautiful description of the bride adorned for her spouse would take many pages to expound.

[5] cf. Canticles 5 :9, an almost exact parallel

with the sweetness of love I could not say anything! (Ar. *Āsa Chhant,* 10:3) He graciously came to my house; then my girl friends met and arranged for the marriage;[1] as I watched the play, bliss came in to my heart, the Bridegroom came to wed me! (N. *Āsa,* 10:1). When he embraced me[2] sorrows fled away and my life, heart, body all bloomed anew![3] (Ar. *Āsa Chhant,* 10:2) [My friends,] having left all other maidens the Beloved [is now] my Lover! (Ar. *Suhi,* 4:3) Sing, sing, O maidens, with wisdom and thought! To my house has come the Life of the world as bridegroom; ever since my marriage came about through the Guru, whenever I met the Bridegroom then I knew [him whose] Word is pervading the three worlds (N. *Āsa* 10:1-2). The Dear One has come near and set me on the couch; I no longer listen to what others say (Ar. *Āsa,* 55:2).

4. So long as the 'I' existed then thou wast not; now thou art and 'I' am not![4] (Rd. *Sorathi,* 1:1) Egoism has gone, and the heart rejoices (N. *Āsa,* 10:2). Thou art the jewel of a very profound deep [sea];[5] Thou the Beloved, I the Bride! (Ar. *Suhi*

---

[1] So M. reads *kāju.*

[2] *Anga sangi lāge;* lit: limbs pressed together, or the like.

[3] lit: became green

[4] *Jaba hama hote taba tū nāhī aba tū hī mai nāhī.* cf. GP 28:1

[5] Or: a very deep and profound jewel

Chhant, 4:2) Thou art indeed love-bliss,[1] thou art glory, thou art beauty, thou art love! ... Nanak, he is the nearest of the near! (Ar. *Gaurī*, 156:1, 3) Thou, [O God, art] in my heart! (Ar. *Āsa*, 30:1) Sing God's sweet praises, [O my] life, sing thou the sweet praises of God! ... Come, my beloved God, night and day with every breath I meditate [on thee]! (Ar. *Gaurī*, 172:1, 167:1) Paying no heed at all to my merits and defects, thou hast in a moment pardoned [me]! (Ar. *Wadhans Chhant,* 1:4)

5. Nanak, that is the [real] gift which comes to us [when] the Master is pleased (A. *Āsa dī Vār*, 23 Sl. 1); he arranges his own affairs, there is no one else to do it—which affairs are [the giving of] truth, contentment, kindness and faith; a few disciples will understand.[2] Nanak suggests: he is the one Beloved of all; she on whom he looks graciously becomes his happy wife (N. *Āsa*, 10:3-4).

Now all her sorrows flee away, for she is his chosen bride blessed abundantly with the permission to stand at his side, ready always to give him little services and to utter from time to time her little cries of love and need. In his near presence she acquires more and more of beauty and of all good gifts, his intimacy a ceaseless source of blissful union with him.

---

[1] Or: delight

[2] It is only those who try to live the life of a true Sikh or disciple who can understand the nature of God's gifts of those virtues which beautify the soul for him.

Never can such a bride lose her eternal Spouse, for her whole heart is ever overflowing with requited love and with joy in her own opportunity for instant and glad obedience at her Beloved's slightest wish. The Beloved dwells now on her very bosom and covers her with his own infinite loveliness, so that he delights in her as she in Him; knowing how utterly she is his, he gives himself as utterly to her. How can she tell another of the charms of that darling of her heart? Those who know love for themselves will know his charms who himself is Love, but others cannot learn from words. They must taste the honey for themselves to know what sweetness is. So great is her joy in him that she is silent now upon his loveliness and can only exclaim in rapture how he has come at last to her as Spouse. In his embrace she has forgotten the long agony of loneliness; the Guru brought about that meeting; and now the two are one. What more can she say? Even her ears cannot hear their questions, for she is already lost in bliss!

She knows only that this blessed union arose when she so forgot herself as to see only him; so long as she thought of her own misery she had no room in her heart for him, but when she remembered only him she found him at her side, in her arms, and knew him to be her all in all. And now her joy bursts forth in rapturous jubilation; she calls on all to share her ecstasy by joining in her adoration of her beloved Lord. Stepping in his infinite condescension into her lowly cottage, he has raised her to his couch and filled her with songs of bliss. None could do this but he; no friend could bring about this perfect 'marriage of the soul', for the Guru who arranged it all was himself but the Bridegroom in disguise. And now the humble village girl has become a queen, the Queen of Heaven.

50. THE SPIRITUAL MARRIAGE

1. I will take a fan and wave it over my Dear,[1] for…the Spouse has taken me and made me Queen …What do I know of how I have pleased the Spouse [even though] I am helpless, poor and unhonoured? (Ar. *Āsa*, 95, 2-3) I will prepare the bridal tent of reality[2] in the lotus of my heart (K. *Āsa*, 24:1); the Lord fulfils my desire who have sought shelter with the true Guru (R. *Gūjari*, 4:2). I was stricken with hunger for God, and now my heart is satisfied with God's Name; God is my relative and will at the last be my Friend (AD. *Gūjari*, 2:2). God the King is [indeed] my true Friend; the Guru met me and my heart revived, the hopes in my heart and body were fulfilled. …When I met God, the heart expanded (R. *Gaurī*, 29:3). [My] Dear …has taken away the burning of my heart; it is well that I have obeyed the saying of my Dear (Ar. *Āsa*, 95:1). [Now] have I obtained my Beloved, and I have made [my dress of] red colour[3] [because] we friends have met after so very long a time (Ar. *Āsa Chhant*, 4:4).

2. Nanak, having taught me love, the true Guru has caused me to meet God and I dwell in his fear

---

[1] *Le pakhā pria jhalau pāe.*   [2] *tata barāti*

[3] Red is an auspicious colour for marriages, much used in North India; of course it here has no reference to the orange robes of renunciation.

(N. *Sri Ashtapadi*, 2:8); the Beloved is unchangeably dear to me, steady and clever, the wise Arranger,[1] while the whole world is fickle. ... Nanak, my Guru has brought me into union [with God], I a [mere] girl have obtained the Spouse in my home! (N. *Barah Maha*, 13, 16) Nanak, God is my Friend, I am not of the world![2] (N. *Āsa Chhant*, 1:4) God is my love and standard,[3] God is the only subject of my talk! By the Guru's grace my heart is drenched with love—thus is my service repaid! (AD. *Gūjari*, 2:1) My eyes are wet with God's nectar and my heart is dyed with the love of God the King! (R. *Āsa Chhant*, 8:1)

Queen of Heaven! Bride of God! This is the destiny of every human soul, once freed from the heavy clouds of egoism and filled with the love of the adorable Lord of all. And now she delights in his service while ever wondering at his measureless condescension which has raised her to his arms. She was lowly, unknown and miserable, crying in the dark; now she is Queen, honoured by all and filled with overflowing joy! God is her all, she has found in him her every need, she knows him as the fulfilment of her heart's desire. She testifies to us that it is because she obeyed the Guru's word and put away her petty selfishness that she is now robed in auspicious colours, the 'Robe of Glory', for her wedding with the Lord.

---

[1] Or: Creator (*bidhātā*)

[2] *Thākura mīta hamāre, hama nāhī lokāne*

[3] Or: rule of life (*rīti*)

Her only fear now is lest in some way she fail to please her Beloved, and yet she knows well that even then his love would be changeless, infinite; never again can she lose him. She rejoices that through the Guru's kindness she has won him for all eternity, her heart is simply saturated with love, and she can no longer for even the fraction of a second look at or think of anything but God, her One Beloved Spouse.

The interested reader would be struck to see how very closely akin the thought of the Sikh Gurus often comes to the nearly contemporary Spanish mystic, St Teresa, when speaking of this sublime crowning of human life. It fills the heart of all lovers of mankind with joy to realize how God calls men and women out of all nations on the earth into this sweet intimacy with him which can only be spoken of in shadow with the language of human love and marriage. This mystery has enriched all the higher religions of earth.

51. THE BLISS OF ETERNAL UNION

1. One who has destroyed egoism has sewed a garment;[1] through the Guru's speech she has won the fruit of her lord's honeyed talk[2] (N. *Suhi*, 4:4). Easily burns the lamp kindled by essential Reality; love-sweetness is the oil of the lamp, [and when] the girl has met the Beloved **she** has been overwhelmed

---

[1] This 'garment' is the soul's 'robe of glory', the 'wedding garment', without which none can enter before the King on the 'wedding day'. It consists of the King's own virtues with which he has adorned the soul, cf. GP. 28

[2] The nectar converse of the soul with her Lord comes to her ears only when they have been purified by listening to the Guru's words.

with ecstasy[1] (N. *Barah Maha,* 12). One who meets in the heart keeps meeting [again and again]—and that is to be called the [real] meeting;[2] by words only there will be no meeting even if she desires it intensely. Metal melts into metal, love runs to love[3] (N. *Tilang II,* 1:7-8). Nanak, one united [with God] by means of the Word never becomes separate [again] (N. *Sri Ashtapadi,* 5:8). And when thou [art with me] then what more [need]?[4] (N. *Mājh kī Vār,* 17)

2. Good are **all times** when the True One spontaneously comes to meet us;[5] when the dear Lord is met, everything runs smoothly[6]—The Creator knows all things and she whom he has adorned is dear to him. I who have managed to meet him am happy in his love; delightful is the couch in my home when the Beloved makes love—the happy fortune [written] on a disciple's brow! (N. *Barah Maha,* 17)

---

[1] When God lights the lamp of the heart with oil of love, the darkness of ignorance which has hidden him from the soul is all dispelled.

[2] 'God is Spirit, and they who worship him most worship him in spirit and in truth' (Jn. 4:24); no external prayers or rites avail with him. The contact is ceaselessly repeated until *sahaja* dawns.

[3] i.e., we can meet with God only in so far as we are like Him. The text here runs: *dhātu milai phuni dhātu kau liva livai kau dhavai.*

[4] A typical piece of Guru Nanak's terseness: *jā tū tā kiā hori.*

[5] The text here reads: *bhale ghali mūrata pala sāche āe sahaji mile.*

[6] lit: 'is arranged'

3. There is a true paean in my house, for the Lord has come, my Lover! Inundated with the delights of love-making, I have exchanged hearts with God; I have given my own heart and taken God as Spouse. As he wishes, so does he make love [to me]! (N. *Āsa Chhant,* 1:4) I remain happy in great blessedness, for the Beloved is kind and ever gives me new delight! (Ar. *Jaitsari Chhant,* 1:4)

4. Girl friends, gather and sing with delight a song of joy; my lover has come to my house! Heart and body are sprayed with nectar, and the jewel of love is within [my heart] (N. *Suhi Chhant,* 2:2-3). If he set his foot on me, I shall blossom like the lotus! (Ar. *Maru ki Vār,* 13 Sl. 1)

5. At the union of husband and wife a song of joy is sung, a joyful song [upon God's] glories is sung; the bride rejoices in love, her heart is ecstatic.... With folded hands that girl prays: 'Let me be steeped night and day in love's delight' (N. *Gaurī Chhant,* 1:4), [and he replies:] 'If you continue to be mine, then all the world shall be yours!' (F. *Sloka* 95) Nanak, now the Beloved makes love to the girl, my desire is fulfilled! (N. *Gaurī Chhant,* 1:4) Day and night the Beloved delights [in me]; God is my Husband, [and I am] eternally a bride! (N. *Barah Maha,* 17) Nanak,

22

the man [of God] has found lasting wedded bliss![1] (Ar. *Āsa*, 53:4)

No more storms of anxiety and longing! The Bride is now eternally with her adored Husband and holds him tenderly in her heart, whence he can never more escape! How can they be separated indeed who have now merged in *one*? Who can put apart the two whom God Himself has joined—the human soul transformed by love and the eternal God of Love himself? And 'in him are all the lesser loves'; the Bride finds in her Spouse all that can delight and fill her heart.

Always together—and yet to this perpetual unspeakable bliss is added mystically the joy of incessant reunion. Again and again that ecstatic delight recurs; the loving soul is saturated in the raptures of God's embrace, sweeter each time than it was ever yet before! No longer now is she herself, she has become as it were a part of God, his heart in her, her heart in him, and both filled to overflowing with love's delight! It is a joy ever new and changing and yet always the same, for love is but love though it assumes a myriad forms with every fleeting mood.

And now the blissful Bride calls again to her friends and fellow-lovers of the One Lord to share her song of joy in the Marriage with her Spouse and in the ineffable ecstasies which follow it in the heart's sweet intimacy. It is an eternal song they sing, for unending is that union and infinite the bliss the song vainly tries to utter forth.

---

[1] The last quotation is: *thiru sohāgu Nānaka jana pāyā.*

CHAPTER EIGHT

The Guru's Descent

After very briefly recalling the stories of the nine earlier bodies through which the One Guru, Nanak, has manifested to his disciples, Guru Gobind Singh, the 'Tenth King', tells us how God called him and commissioned him to establish a new and distinct religion on earth, and how he is resolved faithfully to carry out that divine work. In a few swift phrases he then summarizes the essential teachings of the Gurus, to which the Sikhs must always adhere, and at the end he leaves as his successor among them the Holy Book of the Gurus' hymns and the Church of the bravest of their followers.

52. GURU-PARAMPARA

1. Born in the line of those Vedis, NANAK RAI conferred happiness on all his disciples and helped them in this world and the next. He established religions in the Dark Age and showed the way to all holy men. Sin never troubles those who follow in his footsteps; from those who embrace his religion God removes all suffering and sin; never do pain

and hunger disturb them, nor do they fall into the noose of death (G. *Vichitra Nātak,* 5:4-6). Guru Nanak made a prostration to the disciple while he was himself alive, the Master gave the mark[1] [of guruship] while he yet lived;...Nanak proclaimed the accession of ANGAD[2] was the reward of service, he had the same light, the identical way of life, the Master [merely] changed the body.[3] ...Nanak having exchanged bodies with his scion, he sat upon his throne (SB. *Rāmkali ki Vār,* 1:6-7, 2:8-9, 3:5).

2. Thus Nanak assumed the body of Angad and made his religion current in the world. Afterwards he was called AMAR DĀS, as one lamp is lit from another (G.*Vichitra Nātak,* 5:7); the same mark, the same throne, the very same court (SB. *Rāmkali ki Vār,* 6:19). Lehnā [Angad], having made the religion of the Church[4] [firm], handed it over to the worthy Amar Dās (*Rām Dās Sawwaiye,* 30). When the time came to fulfil the blessing (G. *Vichitra Nātak,* 5:8), while the True Guru was still incarnate, he himself crowned the successor, and all the disciples, relations, sons and brothers fell at the feet of RĀM DĀS;....all fell at the feet of the true

---

[1] The mark was the *tilak,* a red spot on the centre of the forehead.

[2] In the original the Guru's first name, Lehnā, is used.

[3] *Joti ohā jugati sāi sāhi kāyā pheri palatīai.*

[4] *panthu*

Guru in whom the Guru's self had been infused (*Sadd,* 4:5-6, 6:3). As Guru Nanak had embraced Angad, so did Guru Amar Dās to Guru Rām Dās (*Rām Dās Sawwaiye,* 55). Then Rām Dās became the Guru; Amar Dās gave him the guruship according to the ancient blessing, and himself took the road to paradise (G. *Vichitra Nātak,* 5:8).

3. [O Guru Rām Dās], thou art Nanak, thou art Lehnā, Guru Amaru[1] art thou, I consider! (SB. *Rāmkali ki Vār,* 7:8) Thus the holy Nanak was revered as Angad. Angad was recognized as Amar Dās, and Amar Dās became Rām Dās; the disciples saw this but not the fools;[2] these thought them all different, while some few persons realized they were all one. Those who understood this gained perfection, for without understanding perfection cannot be attained. When Rām Dās was blended with God he gave the guruship to ARJAN (G.Vichitra Nātak, 5:9-11); to uplift the world, Guru Rām Dās established the Light in Guru Arjan[3] (*Arjan Sawwaiye,* 16). The whole [human] race comes and goes but thou thyself art new and

---

[1] A short form of the name Amar Dās.

[2] Failure to recognize this 'apostolic succession' led to an estrangement from the actual Guru and thus to the individual dropping from the brotherhood altogether. Spiritual life then naturally retrograded.

[3] *Rāmadāsi gurū jaga tārana kau gura joti Arjuna māhi dhari*

ever whole, Arjan, seated on the Guru's throne (SB. *Rāmkali ki Vār,* 8:4-5).

4. When Arjan was going to God's City he appointed HARI GOBIND in his place, and when Hari Gobind was going to God's City he set HARI RAI in his seat; afterwards his son HARI KRISHAN became the Guru. After him came TEG BAHADUR, who protected their caste marks and sacred threads and showed great courage in the Dark Age.[1] When he was putting an end to his life for the sake of holy men, he gave his head but uttered not a groan, he suffered martyrdom for the sake of his religion; he gave his head but swerved not from his resolve. Men of God would be ashamed to work the tricks of conjurors and cheats.[2] Having broken his potsherd on the head of Delhi's king, he departed to paradise. None came who performed such deeds as **he;** at **his** departure there was mourning in the world, there was grief throughout the world but joy in paradise (G. *Vichitra Nātak,* 5:11-16). [Before] he departed he said to his disciples: The Name remains, the good man remains, and Guru GOBIND remains![3] (T. *Ślokas* 56)

---

[1] He protected Hindus from Moghul and Panjabi Muslim persecution and at last deliberately offered himself as a martyr; see Introduction, pp 73-74.

[2] The Emperor of Delhi asked him to work miracles to show the truth of his mission, but with dignified contempt he refused to do such things.

[3] *nāma rahiu sādhū rahiu gura Gobinda.*

In this passage, largely taken from the autobiography of Guru Gobind Singh and filled out with a few isolated texts from different parts of the Holy Granth, the doctrine of the essential unity of all the Gurus with Guru Nanak is taught. Each of the ten before his passing away ensured the continuity of training by themselves appointing their successor; in a large public gathering of disciples each in turn enthroned the chosen heir and offered him the traditional gift of a coconut and five coins. There was a slight variation in the case of the last, who instead of selecting an individual human Guru to manifest the divine spirit transferred the afflatus to the *Granth Sahib* and to the *Khālsā* (i.e. Church) as it meets in official status and issues *a gurmata* (decree). From Nanak himself, the first form of the Guru, who taught the whole truth, down to the beloved martyr-hero Teg Bahadur, and through him to his son Guru Gobind—all alike were equally inspired, ensouled, by the same great Teacher. Those who understand this truth are on the path to the true understanding of religion as revealed to the Sikhs.

53. THE TENTH GURU

1. God brought me into the world as I was doing austerities on the Hemakuta Mountain,[1] **where** I performed such penance that I was blended with God.[2] My father and mother[3] had also worshipped the Unseen and striven in many ways to unite themselves with him; the Supreme Guru was

---

[1] The actual place is said to be in Sapta-sringa, at Hemkund or Lokpal, not far from the path to Badrinarayan.

[2] Or: till diversity was changed into one form

[3] Their names were Guru Teg Bahadur and Mata Gūjari.

pleased with their devotion to him (G. *Vichitra Nātak*, 6:1-4).

2. The Supreme gave the command[1] and I was born in the Dark Age; I had no desire to come, my mind being fixed upon God's feet. God pleaded earnestly with me and sent me into the world with the mandate:...'I have cherished you as my son and appointed you to spread my religion.[2] Go into the world, establish virtue[3] and keep the people from evil.' I stood up with folded hands and, bowing the head, replied: 'The Religion shall prevail in the world when thou lendest thine aid.' (G. *Vichitra Nātak*, 6:4-5, 29-30)

3. To this end he sent me [here]; so I took birth, I come into the world. As the Lord spoke to me, so do I proclaim to the world; to none do I bear enmity. Whoever calls me the Supreme Lord shall fall into the pit of hell;[4] know that I am but God's servant and have come to behold the drama of creation.

---

[1] Or: when the Supreme made known his will

[2] *panthu*

[3] *dharama*

[4] Guru Gobind must have had definite reason for warning against such a tendency to deify him; little truly spiritual was added to Christianity or to other creeds when the Founder's spiritual oneness with God was misunderstood as a claim to unique divinity; cf. GI 37 and 27. The prophet Muhammed also denied such ideas with reference to himself and made such denial a proof of the true prophets of God.

What my Lord told me, that I repeat in the world;[1] I shall not be silent for the fear of men.[2] As God spoke, so do I declare; I will pay heed to none [but God]....I do no worship to stones, nor do I imitate the rites of anyone;[3]...I meditate upon the Name of the Infinite and so attain to the Supreme Light. On no other do I meditate, the name of no other do I pronounce (G. *Vichitra Nātak*, 6:31-39).

4. For this sole reason, to establish virtue, was I sent to the world by the Divine Guru;[4] ... no one understood the Supreme Being or understood the true principles and practice of virtue. The doctrine of no other is of any avail, ... there is no benefit in any other teaching, fix this in your minds. ... Nothing but virtue shall avail at last. ... When I obtained the sovereignty I promoted virtue to the utmost of my power; ... knowing me to be his slave, [God] has aided me, he has given me his hand and saved me (G. *Vichitra Nātak*, 6:42, 45, 48; 8:1,14:2).

---

[1] cf. the faithfulness of all true prophets. The text reads: *jo nija prabha mo so kaha so kahiho jaga mahi.*

[2] In Gurumukhi: *kahio prabhu so bhākha hun, kisu na kana rākha hun.*

[3] Owing to the conflict with Muslims, a tendency to confuse Sikhism with Hindu 'idolatry' doubtless caused this declaration from the Guru.

[4] cf. the passage from the same source: *ehai kāja dharā ham Janamam / samajha leo sādhū saba mananam / dharama chalavana santa ubārana / dusata sabhana kau mūla upārana, //* (6:43), i.e., 'For this purpose I took birth—understand all pious folk—to uphold righteousness and exalt the saints, to tear up all the wicked by their roots.'

So too, not less than his nine predecessors, was Guru Gobind a reappearance of the same great Guru—in another form and mood as required by the changing times. He came partly to earn the respect of the Muslim rulers of that day, so that they might learn to leave his followers, the Sikhs, in peace. He came with the sword, in warrior garb and desperate campaignings, so that many were deceived and thought he changed the truth revealed by Guru Nanak; but he came with the same message of pure religion, even though he added to it the needed truths of fortitude, a readiness to sacrifice life gladly for the cause, a manly independence and a strong resistance to injustice and to all wrong. He strove, and with God's good help he carried his arms to success, though to the outward superficial eye his life might seem a failure like that which ended on the hill of Calvary. It was only in later years that men could see how well he did the work God gave to him, how firmly was laid the foundation for the brave and noble nation of the Sikhs.

54. THE GURU'S LAST WORD

1. A death[1] of truth, and falsehood prevails; [because of] the blackness of the Dark Age [men are like] demons (N. *Āsa dī Vār*, 11 Sl. 1). *Yet for the love of such creatures did the Guru take birth to save them. He has taught them the true Name, and very fortunate are those who have accepted and valued his teaching, for by it they are enabled to*

---

[1] *kāla:* M. reads this as 'dearth', Professor Jodh Singh as: 'Truth is scarce.'

save themselves and others from the perils of the world-ocean[1] (5:243 G).

2. By egoism is one bound, by the Guru's words set free[2] (Ar. *Mājh Ashtapadi,* 2:6). *As when rain falls after a drought there is plenty, so the Guru, seeing human beings in misery and longing for happiness came to give it them and to take away their sorrows by his teachings* (5:243 G). [Now] has the Supreme God our Lord sent the Cloud[3] and made it rain on sea and land in all Earth's ten directions.... The Cloud pours rain in every place; ... yes, rain has fallen, and it was God who made it fall.... Comfort has come [to man], all thirst is quenched, there is joy everywhere![4] (Ar. *Mājh,* 34:1, 32:1, 34:1) *And us the rain stays where it falls, so does the Guru's teaching ever remain with his disciples*[5] (5:243 G).

3. The true Guru meets him for whom it was written of old, [to him] the Lord comes (R. *Gaurī kā*

---

[1] This, with most passages of this section in italics, comes from M.'s account of the passing away of the Tenth Guru, which may derive in part from the *Prem Sumarag* used in para 7, quoted by Teja Singh in his useful little book *Sikhism* (p. 32).

[2] *haumai bādhā guramukhī chūtā:* the Guru's usual economy of words. We may read, 'the disciple escapes'.

[3] *Pārabrahmi prabhi meghu pathāyā*.

[4] This resumes the theme in GGS 1, but carries a slightly more hopeful colour—'all thirst is quenched'.

[5] Because he has infused his spirit into them

Vār, 7 Sl. 2); sweet is the Guru's nectar speech![1] (AD. *Mājh Ashtapadi*, 7:1). Now is the egg of illusion broken, light has shone out in the mind; the Guru has cut the fetters from his feet and made the captive free![2] (Ar. *Maru*, 14:1) Say, Nanak: When through the Guru the illusion is lost, Allah and Parabrahman are [seen as] one[3] (Ar. *Rāmkali*, 45:5); temple and mosque are the same,[4] worship and prostration[5] are the same —all men are one, but various are the forces (leading them)[6] (G. *Akāl Ustat*, 86). Do not say the Vedas or [other religious] books[7] lie; he who does not study them is lying (K. *Prabhati* 4:1). Allah and Abhekh[8] are the same, Purāna and *Korān* are the same—one only in their essence as One

---

[1] *Amrita bānū gura kī mīthi.*

[2] This verse was taken by M. as a motto for his fine volumes.

[3] *Kahu Nānaka guri khoe bharama / eko Alahu Pārabrahama.*

[4] *Dehara masita soi.* This word is a Punjabi corruption of Arabic *masjid.*

[5] *Pūjā au nivāj; pūjā* is understood as the worship of God through rites performed before a visible emblem of him, such as an image, the sun, flame; it is a purely Hindu word. *Nivāj*, or *memāz*, is the fixed ritual of prostrations to God performed according to Koranic rules and before no visible symbol, but directed vaguely towards Mecca (cf. GI 93:1).

[6] *prabhāu;* M. reads this passage: 'It is through error they seem different' but this is certainly too free; the text is: *aneka ko prabhāu hai.*

[7] *Kateba;* this word (Ar. *kutub*) is generally used for the sacred books of Muslims, Jews, Christians, but we need not thus strictly limit it; the literal meaning is just 'books'.

[8] *abhekha:* lit: 'without *vesha,* or *rūpa*', i.e., the Formless One.

alone made them all (G. *Akāl Ustat,* 86). The Master of Hindu and Muslim is one; what can a Mulla do, what can a Sheikh do?[1] (K. *Bhairo,* 4:3)

4. Many gods and primal youths, many Krishnas and Vishnus [have taken] birth![2]... Many were terrible[3] or small[4] in appearance, many Rāmas and Krishnas of peerless beauty! ... The Maker [*Karta*] and the Noble [*Karīm*], Providence [*Razak*] and the Merciful [*Rahīm*] are all the same;[5] through carelessness or superstition do not imagine any difference at all [between one and] the other (G. *Akāl Ustat,* 39-40, 85). The Hindu worships in the temple and the Muslim in the mosque; **Nanak**[6] serves the same God where neither temple is nor mosque (Nd. *Gond,* 7:4).

---

[1] I am indebted to Professor Jodh Singh for the rendering of the second half of this sentence. He explains that even the learned Muslim cannot controvert this fact that there is one Lord for Hindu and for Muslim alike.

[2] *Kaī deva ādikumāra / kaī Kisana Bisana avatāra.* While freely using the holy names of Hindu deity which have such sweet association, the Gurus were quite clear that all such 'avatars' were simply men chosen by the One God to do his work on earth and that to worship them is to betray the truth.

[3] *raudra,* like Hiranyakasipu's slayer Narasimha, who came to save Prahlad

[4] *chudra,* like the dwarf Vamana who liberated Bali from his pride

[5] While *Karta,* the Creator is a typically Sikh Name for God, *Karīm, Rahīm* and *Razak* are more familiar to Muslims. The Guru did all that was humanly possible to draw these two great religions closer together, cf. the Names of God in Islam.

[6] In the original, of course, Nāmdev's name stood here.

5. I do not fast by [Hindu] vow, nor do I observe the Ramadan,[1] yet I serve him who will save me at the last; the one Lord is my Allah, the judge of both Hindu and Muslim.[2] I do not go on pilgrimage to the Kaaba or worship at [Hindu] shrines;[3] I serve the One and no other besides. I do not offer [Hindu] worship, nor do I cause [Muslim] prostrations to take place; taking the One [who is] formless into the heart, I bow [to him there]. I am neither Hindu nor Muslim; body and life belong to Allah-Rāma![4] Nanak says 'I have made this declaration: when I meet Guru or Pīr,[5] I recognize my own Master'! (Ar. *Bhairo*, 3:1-4)

6. Ever since I have touched thy feet I have cared for no one else; Rāma's Purānas[6] and Rahīm's *Korān*[7] express many views, but I accept none of

---

[1] *Varata na rahau na maha ramadana;* for the Muslim month of fasting see GI 88.

[2] lit: *turaka.* Even today in many parts of India Muslims are called Turks.

[3] *Haja kabai jau na tiratha pūjā.* The Kaaba is the great black stone in Mecca, believed to be possibly a meteor, which is the Muslim 'centre of the world' and the goal of the 'hadj', or pilgrimage.

[4] The Guru shows his perfect catholicity by thus combining the two holy names adored by Muslim and Hindu. This passage, originally written by Kabīr, was bodily incorporated by Guru Arjun in his own poems.

[5] *pir,* a Muslim saint or religious teacher, equivalent to 'guru'

[6] Most of the Purānas deal with the avataras of Vishnu, one of whose best known names is Rama.

[7] The *Korān* is a message from Allah to man, and he is therein continually named '*Ar Rahmāni Ar Rahīm*'.

them (G. *Rām Autar*). Millions of men may read the *Korān*, they may read innumerable Purānas, but it shall be of no use to them in the future life and the power of fate shall still rule over them[1] (G. *Vichitra Nātak*, 6:47). God is not found in the Vedas or [in other] Scriptures;[2] know this [well that] God is in the heart of man (G. *Vichitra Nātak*, 6:61), the Giver of all, Knower of all, and Guardian of all (G. *Akāl Ustat*, 190), One in the heart and One in every place [besides]! (Ar. *Gaurī*, 8:4)

7. *The Sikhs who love the true Guru are beloved by him in turn* (5:243 G); O Nanak, it is he whom the Guru meets who dwells in his heart (Ar. *Gauri ki Vār II*, 13 Sl. 2), within the disciples of the Guru the true Guru abides (R. *Gaurī ki Vār*, 33 Sl. 2). The Guru is the Sikh and the Sikh the Guru when he spreads the teaching of the One Guru[3] (R. *Āsa Chhant*, 2:8). *Wherever there are five Sikhs assembled who abide by the Guru's teachings, know that I am in their midst;*[4] (5:243 G) *let him who wishes to see me go to an assembly of Sikhs*

---

[1] This is not an attack on sacred books but on bibliolatry, relying on adherence to one rather than another to supply the lack of virtue and devotion.

[2] *Beda kateba bikhe Hari nāhī.*

[3] *Gurū sikhu sikhu gurū hai eko gura upadesu chalāe.*

[4] cf. the promise of Jesus to his disciples (Mt. 18:20)

and approach them with faith and reverence; he will surely see me amongst them (Prem Sumarag). Henceforth the Guru shall be the Khālsā and the Khālsā the Guru; I have infused my spirit, heart and body, into the Granth Sahib and the Khālsā.[1]*...O Khālsā, remember the true Name; ...I have attached you to the skirt of the Immortal God and entrusted you to him—ever remain under his protection and trust to none besides (5:243-244 G).*

8. *O beloved Khālsā, let him who desires to see me look into the Guru-Granth. Obey the Guru-Granth, it is the Guru's visible body; and let him who longs to meet me search diligently its hymns.... Read the Guru-Granth, or listen to it; so shall your hearts receive consolation, and you shall certainly obtain a dwelling in the Guru's heaven (5:243-244 G).*

9. At dawn repeat the Lord's Name and brood upon the Guru's feet (Ar. *Maru ki Vār* II, 16 Sl. 1); as a mother is wrapped up in her child, so does the knower [of God] take the Name (Ar. Sorathi, 83:3). Remember that Beloved day and night, for where that memory is your fear of men departs (K. *Rāmkali,* 9:5-6). *Those who remember the true*

---

[1] Here we have a conception closely parallel to that of the Christian Church as the 'Mystical Body' of Christ; the Guru is in a sense actually incarnate in the body of the faithful.

Name make their lives fruitful, and when they depart they enter the mansions of eternal bliss (5:243 G); by remembering God you will attain to union [with him][1] (K. *Rāmkali,* 9:7). God and God's servant are both one; do not think there is any difference between them (G. *Vichitra Nātak,* 6:60); the saints and God are one[2] (K. *Suhi,* 5:4).

In this fallen age men are indeed often like demons, and yet God loves them even in their wickedness and to save them he sends the teacher of the Truth, who sings in their ears and sows in their hearts the all-redeeming Name.

It is egoism, selfishness, which causes all earth's misery, and the Guru's message destroys that egoism and set men free. In our chosen age God has once more sent that Guru, and his teaching now pours out upon the drought-parched earth like the soft refreshing rain at the close of summer heat. Everywhere the Truth is now revealed, and all who care may know how to be free from sorrow; God has also built a Church, written a Holy Book, in which to store that Truth so that it may at all times be available for every seeker while the world endures.

The Truth has made us free; it has shattered the dark illusion of the ego which held us bound to misery; it has brought us to the vision of the Lord. And we, coming out of every nation on the earth, have found that each has the same one Infinite Lord; it was our egoistic pride alone that made us fancy only our own creed was true and all other men were deceived by false religions—but now we see that all alike are

---

[1] *Hari simmaranu pāīai sanjoga.*

[2] Could we end this chapter better than by Kabīr's thrilling words: *'santa Rāmu hai eko'*? They sum up the essence of the whole book.

God's children and led by him along their own paths into the unity of his one true Universal Church. There is no false religion as such; Islam and the Sanatana Dharma, Christianity, Buddhism, the Parsee teachings of Zarathushtra, the lost creeds of Mani, Pyramid, Egyptians and the Gnostics—all are God's own truth, decked in varying colours for men's different tastes; all alike lead his many children home to his feet.

How many creeds there have been on earth! How many prophets and wonderful avatārs of God have laboured to save erring men from their darkness and their sin! How many names they have used for God, each to appeal to the heart of different souls and peoples! Some worship him in one way, some in another; some through art or science, some with lights and incense, some in the silence of the heart or the sweet songs of mighty congregations, some through the courage of explorers or men of war! Yet all are his children, seeking him in various ways, led by him through different paths to the ecstasy of mystic union at last; their feeble voices of prayer and praise are equally sweet in that Father's ears, whatever words or actions they choose to show their love for him.

The Sikh is not a Hindu or a Muslim; he is the disciple of the One Eternal Guru of the world, and all who learn of him are truly Sikhs and must not corrupt his teachings with the confused utterances of men who live among them and around. Sikhism is no disguised Hindu sect but an independent revelation of the one Truth of all sects; it is no variant of Muslim teaching, save in that it too proclaims the love of God and the need for men to hold him always in their heart. It, too, is a distinct religion like the other great religions of the world.

Those who have once seen God have no eyes for any

other, have no ears for any lesser truth; their whole being is absorbed in the Light they have once perceived. Though the ways of seeking him are taught in many holy books, he cannot be found in any book, in any outer thing—for he is in the heart of man, that holiest of temples built by his own holy hand and sanctified by his perpetual presence there, even as he is indeed in all the universe besides. But those who rely superstitiously on their adherence to a special sect or creed or scripture will have to seek him there in the heart itself some day; salvation depends on deeds and on devotion and not on external observances or loyalties.

Where the pupil is, there too is the Teacher, and nevermore will the Sikhs be alone or deprived of that holy Guru. For he who cannot lie has given the promise that he will always be where only five are faithful to his teaching and that he will manifest to them through all the councils of his faithful Church. And where only one single Sikh is found? There too is he, abiding in the heart, and residing also in the hymns sung by him through the hallowed bodies of the Ten—now gathered for the delight and enlightenment of all the ages in the *GURU-GRANTH SAHIB*. In the holy presence of the Guru's Book, the Guru himself is manifest.

Those who love that Book, who cling devotedly to the God whom it proclaims in words of matchless beauty, who seek to spend their every moment at his feet, will be free from every fear, will enter the heaven of God's own presence and there attain to everlasting union with the Beloved Lord.

———————

PART TWO

CHAPTER NINE

Japji—the Guru's Hymn

We close our Gospel of the *Guru-Granth Sahib* with this great hymn wherewith the *Guru-Granth* itself commences; it is one of the world's noblest religious and devotional writings, of which Puran Singh writes in such glowing terms (see Preface). It is the common view of Sikh scholars that this hymn contains the essence of the whole teaching of the Guru, and it is the pious practice of all Sikhs to start each day with its recitation.

After a noble account of God himself, the Guru shows us how all happiness, all wisdom, all spiritual progress on earth, all worldly success, really derive from obedience to and love of him. He then teaches us how great is the saint and devotee amid the countless types of living beings made by God—on whose infinite greatness he again touches lightly. The whole adoration of the universe which he has made rightly goes to him. Then the Guru in a few powerful words sketches the five 'planes' of spiritual life, and closes with the reminder that truth and sincerity lead to the One True Being in whom is all eternal bliss.

55. THE ETERNAL UNKNOWN

1. One Supreme Being, the true and eternal Name, the Creative Person[1] fearless and without enmity, the timeless Form unborn and self-existing,[2] the Enlightener [known] through grace;[3] true in the beginning, true in the night of ages, he is true even now, and will be true [eternally, says] Nanak.

2. By thinking comes no thought [of the Real], even if I think tens of thousands of times; by keeping silent the real Silence does not come, even if I remain long entranced; the hunger of the hungry does not pass, even though I be burdened with many worlds.[4] Even were there thousands and tens of thousands of clever speculations, not even one could finally succeed [in reaching him]. How then to attain the Truth? How can the veil of falsehood[5] be rent asunder? By walking so as to satisfy the [Divine]

---

[1] *Purakhu*: this is explained by Sikhs as 'the Pervading One'.

[2] *Saibham*, i.e., who gives out light independently

[3] *Gura prasādi*; or: 'enlightener through grace'

[4] Nothing can satisfy the soul's hunger, even if a universe be given. It is only the Infinite can fill the human heart and leave no want.

[5] *Kūlai*, i.e., the unreal, illusory view of things

Will which is written [in the heart],[1] says Nanak (N. *Japji* 1).

The great Hymn opens with the 'Mūlamantra' we have already met in §2:3, wherewith the Holy Book of the Sikhs commences, placing thus as its very foundation the Holy Name and attributes of God.

Nanak proclaims that so great is this God he cannot be found by reason or speculative thought, nor even through silent meditation as believed by the philosophers—the yearning for that perfection which is in him alone can only be satisfied by obedience to his will as expressed in the conscience of each soul.

56. THE GLORY OF GOD'S WILL

1. At [God's] will[2] forms come into being; that Will cannot be uttered in words. At his will living souls come to be and at his will they grow great;[3] at his will [they become] noble or mean, at his will they receive the sorrow or happiness decreed [as a result].[4] Some get pardon[5] by his will, others at his will are always straying; all are within his will, not one is outside [the sphere of

---

[1] God can be found only through the path of surrender and obedience, by means of devotion and good action. The conscience is the guide.

[2] Or: command; and so throughout this section

[3] lit: greatness meets [them]: *hukamī milai vadiāī*

[4] Noble acts earn happiness, mean acts sorrow; this is the Law.

[5] Or: grace (*bakhasīsa*)

his] will.[1] Nanak, if one understands this will, then he will never speak of the ego[2] (N. *Japji* 2).

2. Those who have the power [of song] sing his power; some sing his gifts, realising [in them] signs [of his goodness]; some sing his glories and the greatness of his beauties; some sing a philosophy hard to follow. Some sing, 'After creating it he turns the body into dust';[3] some sing, 'Having taken souls away he gives [them back] again';[4] some sing, 'He seems to be far away'; some sing, 'He sees [us, being] very near indeed'.[5] No end comes for the telling of those who tell of him, millions and millions have tried to tell in millions of ways; the Giver keeps on giving while the receivers grow weary—from age to age they eat and eat. The Ordainer keeps the world's work moving,[6] yet, Nanak, he is blissful and free from anxiety (N. *Japji*, 3).

---

[1] I do not think it is possible to read this section as a glorification of human freewill, as one scholar has done; this does not cohere with the character of the whole passage.

[2] Realising how God's Will *is* always done on earth as it is in Heaven, man understands how puny his petty desires and efforts are, unless confirmed by being in line with that almighty Will of God.

[3] The doctrine of Christians, Muslims, etc.—also of materialists to some extent

[4] The doctrine of reincarnation, as taught by most Hindus, Buddhists, etc.

[5] God transcendent, and God immanent; he is both of these.

[6] A rather free rendering for *hukamī hukamu chalāe rāhu.*

That will, the following of which leads us to God, is the omnipotent power which made the universe, fashioned our own souls, and guides eternally all things through time and space. It is by his will alone that some souls find him and others seem doomed to endless wandering through the deserts of despair; it is by his will that some become saints while others seem more like demons. He who knows God's will by constantly revering it realizes that man's petty self has no power to do more than bow before it, and then his conceit withers out of sight.

Infinite is that will of God, ineffable and transcending thought; yet the longing for him which he has placed in every heart tries to express its wonder and admiration; each soul speaks of it feebly enough, but as eloquently as the powers he has given each allow. Souls speak differently according to their views and natures; at times they seem to contradict each other, yet all alike try to tell of the glory of the same Infinite Being beyond all being. They try to tell of him and fail because of the limitations of their vision and their words; but all the time He IS, and unshaken by the weakness of his mortal creatures he is ever good to them and ceaselessly gives them lavishly all they need. He never wearies of doing good; it is they who sometimes grow tired of receiving his benefits.

57. LOVE AND GRACE

1. Eternal is the Master, changeless the Law,[1] and infinite Love is his language; begging we say, 'Give! give!' and the Giver makes his gifts. What [can we] offer in return[2] so that we may see his court? What words are we to utter with the lips so that he may hear and love us? In the nectar hour [of dawn] brood upon the greatness of the eternal Name; from his grace comes the Robe, through his kindly look Liberation and the Door;[3] Nanak, thus know that the Eternal himself is in all (N. *Japji*, 4).

2. He cannot be installed [in temples], nor was he [ever] made; he is of himself immaculate;[4] it is the one who clings to[5] him who has obtained honour.[6] Nanak, let us praise the Treasury of

---

[1] *sachā sāhibu sachā nāi ;* this word *sacha,* cognate with Skt. *satyam,* has its dual sense of reality and truth, eternity and changelessness. This verse may be taken as: 'True is God and true (his) Name', but most Sikh scholars prefer the reading 'Law' in this place. It amounts to the same thing, for the *Name* is God manifest in his law.

[2] lit:'What can we place again before him?' *(pheri kī agai rakhīai)*

[3] An important verse: *karamī āvai kapalā nadarī mokhu duāru.* Some take it to mean: 'By [good] action a better birth comes, but the gate of liberation through grace'. I suggest the *kapalā* is rather the robe wherewith the spouse adorns his bride, for virtues come through God's kindness too. *Mokhu duāru* is presumably a case of *hendiadys,* i.e., 'liberation [and] the gate' for 'the gate of liberation' (cf. § 59:4).

[4] *āpe āpi niranjanu soi;* 'stainless', 'unconditioned by *māyā*'.

[5] *seviā:* serves, remembers, delights in

[6] Or: greatness *(mānu)*

Goodness, let us sing and hear [his praise] and keep his love in the heart; he will remove our sorrow and take us into the abode of happiness.[1] The Guru's word is music, the Guru's word is scripture, the Guru's word is all-pervading;[2] the Guru is the Lord, the Guru is the Protector of Souls and the Creator, the Guru is Mother Parvati.[3] Even if I know him I cannot describe him for he cannot be told. O Guru, grant [me] this one understanding, that I may never be able to forget the One Giver of all souls! (N. *Japji,* 5)

3. I would bathe in the holy waters[4] if I [could thus] please him, but without pleasing him what is the use of that bathing?[5] I look at all the [visible] creation made [by him]; what can be gained without his grace? Gems, jewels, pearls[6] [appear] in the understanding if even one teaching of the Guru be attended to; Guru, grant [me this] one

---

[1] So Prof. Jodh Singh

[2] A striking verse; it runs: *gurumukhī nādam guramukhī vedam guramukhī rahiā samāi.* There are many ways of translating it; we may prefer to read 'The disciple [becomes] ....' in each clause.

[3] *Isaru...Gorakhu...Baramā...Pārabati māī;* I have preferred to translate most of these names rather than preserve the somewhat deistic Hindu flavour of the original. Guru Nanak was no worshipper of Siva, Gorakh, Brahma or Parvati.

[4] *tīrathi nāvā*

[5] The path is one of effort and obedience, not of mere rites.

[6] Or: rubies

understanding, that I may never be able to forget the One Giver of all souls! (N. *Japji*, 6)

4. If [a man] lived through the four ages[1] or even ten times longer and were known in the nine parts [of earth],[2] were everyone to follow him and he to win a good name and obtain glory and fame in the world—unless [God's] gracious glance came to him, then no one would enquire after him,[3] he would be held a worm among worms and a guilty offender. Nanak, [God] makes virtues in the virtueless and grants [more] virtue to the virtuous; no one is to be seen who can make any virtue for him[4] (N. *Japji*, 7).

Like a father to his child, so does he give to us; what can we give to him who already has, is, all? How can we worthily praise him whose nature far transcends our boldest dreams of perfection? There is nothing we can do to increase his endless glory; it is for us simply to bask in its radiance, to delight in meditating on his love and greatness, which give us all the virtues, all the graces, all the beauties we may possess —and through whose kindness we enter at last his eternal Kingdom.

---

[1] The Satya, Treta, Dwapara and Kali Yugas, totalling 4,320,000 years.

[2] Or: continents (*navā khandā*); we now speak rather of five.

[3] i.e., care for him; cf. §§ 31:6, 32:2 and 35:2.

[4] Note the Visishtādvaita meaning here given to *nirguna;* the passage reads *niraguni gunu kare gunavantiā gunu de/tehā koi na sujhaī Ji tisu gunu koi kare.* The word does not primarily mean 'qualityless'.

God is not an image we can fashion and instal in a temple for our worship, nor is he born as a human child; he alone IS, beyond all time and space, everywhere and always. Our rituals and bowings, please ourselves and, as outer acts of submission to God's will, they have their own place in our training to be saints—but they leave God unmoved on his eternal throne. He feels no anger at those who withhold from him such acts of worship, but rather pities them for the loss of the happiness interior surrender would ensure to them. It is love for him which is our only real path to joy, for he alone can be our spiritual teacher. Can the tiny child understand everything his teacher says? So is he too beyond our thought or understanding, and it is for us only to hold him lovingly in our heart and to remember him at all times.

Outer sacramental rites are of little or no real value unless they correspond to the inward reality. All blessings, all graces, all virtues come not from ceremonies but from God's kindness, which adorns the loving soul with every beauty. It is this clinging love which is the essence of God's teaching to the heart and which blossoms out in every beauty.

Immortality and universal sovereignty, fame and power are worth nothing at all unless they be gifts of God's grace to lead the soul towards his feet. It is he alone who gives us what we need, and to snatch at other things is gross impiety. He gives us all, and there is none of us can add to his infinite wealth of goodness by a single prayer or gift.

58. THE FRUITS OF DEVOTION

1. By listening[1] [to the Name one becomes] an adept, a saint, a god, a master;[2] by listening [one becomes] the Earth, the [supporting] Bull,[3] the Sky; by listening islands, spheres and underworlds; by listening immune to time;[4] Nanak, devotees ever blossom [in joy,[5] for] by listening their sorrow and sin are destroyed (N. *Japji*, 8).

2. By listening [one becomes] the Lord, Creator and King [of Gods],[6] by listening praises come in the mouth of the vile,[7] by listening the secrets in the body [are learned] through the practice of yoga,[8] by

---

[1] *suniai:* The word implies far more than merely 'hearing' God's Name uttered by the lips, it connotes the eager watching for signs of God's will and ceaseless holding of heart and mind as in his presence, ready to anticipate his least suggestion and to carry it out in life. This is the stage of *sramana*.

[2] *Siddha pīra suri nātha.* The *'siddha'* is one who has carried his yogic practices through to perfection, the *pīra* (or guru) one qualified to teach spiritual life to others, the *'sura'* is the immortal deity, and the *'nātha'* one who has mastered the law of life.

[3] Popular mythology of that and earlier times held that this earth was kept in its place on the back of a huge bull—that animal being a symbol of strength; the absurdity of this idea is well shown up by the Guru in § 60.

[4] Or: death

[5] *vigāsu*, Skt. *vikāsa*, increase, spread, blossom; it is used for any great exultant joy which 'expands' the heart.

[6] *Isaru Barama Indu; i.e.*, 'Iswara [Śiva], Brahmā and Indra'; see note to § 57:2.

[7] i.e., even wicked men are led to worship God. But Teja Singh reads this: 'he will begin to dislike the offering of praise to them', while Sahib Singh and Mohan Singh agree with our reading.

[8] *Suniai joga jugati tani bheda.*

listening the scriptures, codes of law and revelations [are understood]; Nanak, devotees ever blossom [in joy, for] by listening their sorrow and sin are destroyed (N. *Japji*, 9).

3. By listening generosity, contentment and wisdom [arise],[1] by listening [comes] the merit of bathing in the sixty-eight [holy places], by listening they obtain the credit of reading and reading, by listening they easily attain to deep contemplation;[2] Nanak, devotees ever blossom; [in joy, for] by listening their sorrow and sin are destroyed (N. *Japji*, 10).

4. By listening they achieve the ocean deeps of goodness,[3] by listening [they become] sages,[4] saints and kings, by listening even the blind find the road [to God], by listening they come [to understand] the depths of the world-ocean [of life];[5] Nanak, devotees ever blossom [in joy, for] by listening their sorrow and sin are destroyed (N. *Japji*, 11).

All progress comes to us through devotion to the will of God and continual dwelling in the memory of his Name; the weak and sinful become righteous, the

---

[1] *Satu, santokhu, giānu*

[2] *Suniai lāgai sahaji dhianu..*

[3] *Sara guna ke gaha*, lit: grasp the qualities of the ocean.

[4] *Sekha*, the familiar Arabic word *'sheikh'*, wise man, old man.

[5] *hātha hovai asagāhu;* M. reads 'the hand becomes irresistible', but Sahib Singh shows how it acquired the meaning we have adopted.

ignorant become wise, the mortal attain to immortality, the human change to the divine, purity and all virtues arise in the heart, the mind gains the power to dive deep into the sources of all true wisdom, the heart learns how to penetrate the secrets of saintliness. Yes, obedience to the divine will because of love for him transmutes man into God himself and destroys every trace in him of frailty and wretchedness. How then can such a man be other than eternally happy?

59. THE FRUITS OF OBEDIENCE

1. The state of the obedient[1] cannot be told; if anyone [tries] to tell it he repents later on; [there is] no writer with pen on paper to sit down and make a study of the condition of the obedient—so unconditioned is the Name, as anyone knows who looks carefully into his heart[2] (N. *Japji*, 12).

2. By obedience[3] intelligence and clear thought[4] arise in the mind, by obedience an awareness[5] of all the worlds, by obedience one suffers no

---

[1] *manne;* this word is cognate with Skt. *manana,* and is held to mean the paying of close attention to what is heard (from God) and the steady effort to put his will into practice. The second stage of meditation.

[2] *Aisā nāmu niranjanu hoi / je ko manni jānai koi.* The word *niranjamu,* lit: unstained, immaculate, is taken to mean *'untouched by māyā'.*

[3] *mannai,* i.e., by the aforesaid act of carrying out, keeping 'God's commandments' after the careful consideration of what they are.

[4] *Surati...budhi.* The former is the power to form wise decisions, the latter the ability to distinguish instantly between right and wrong, important and unimportant, etc.; it is rendered by S. as 'wakefulness' (*jāgrata*).

[5] *sudhi,* i.e., one comes to know what happens in other worlds and planes.

calamities,[1] by obedience one does not go in death's company—so unconditioned is the Name, as any-one knows who looks carefully into his heart (N. *Japji,* 13).

3. By obedience no obstacles are found on the path, one proceeds openly with honour by obe-dience, by obedience one does not walk on bye-lanes, by obedience [he becomes] united with righteousness[2]—such is the unconditioned Name, as anyone knows who looks carefully into his heart (N. *Japji,* 14).

4. By obedience they gain the door of Liber-ation,[3] by obedience the family is supported,[4] by obedience the teacher is saved and saves the disciple, Nanak, by obedience they do not wander as beggars[5] (in the world)—so unconditioned is the Name, as anyone knows who looks carefully into his heart (N. *Japji,* 15).

It is impossible fully to narrate the glories of such obedience to God with faith or of the devout contemplation of his Name; they can be known only through ourselves

---

[1] lit: 'one does not eat blows in the mouth', i.e., has no insulting trouble.

[2] *Dharma seti sana bandhu:* thus becoming one with the Path itself, after which no wandering astray is possible, no sin can arise.

[3] *Mokha duāru;* cf. note to § 57:1.

[4] *Paravārai sadhāru;* Teja Singh points out that spiritual support is meant here and not the mere provision of worldly needs.

[5] *Bhāvahi na bhikha;* i.e., they wander no longer into rebirth seeking God, for they have already found him.

experiencing them in our own lives. This much can be said, that they arouse understanding and courage in the heart, destroy the fear of death and suffering, remove all spiritual hindrances, enrich the soul with honours and steadiness and all kinds of good qualities, lead it to perfection, and then bring it as the saviour of its fellows. Such is the power of 'repeating the Name' with faith and love, that is, of practising the presence of God in a spirit of adoring aspiration, putting the revealed God first as the ruling power in our hearts and lives, in everything we say and do.

60. ALL CREATURES OBEY GOD'S WILL

1. The elect[1] are trusted, the elect are leaders, the elect receive honour in God's court, the elect shine in the gate of kings;[2] contemplation is the only teacher of the elect.[3] If anyone speaks or makes [deep] consideration [he knows that] the Maker's works are not to be counted. The [supporting] 'Bull' is Righteousness the son of Kindness, who maintains patience by means of rectitude[4]—if

---

[1] *pancha:* lit: 'the five'. In a village the five chief men formed a sort of village council, the *panchāyat,* and so the word gained the sense of chosen leaders. Sikh commentators explain that the 'elect' are those who day and night always keep God lovingly in their minds. The stage of *nidhidhyāsan,* contemplation.

[2] *Panche sahahi dari rājānu.*

[3] They need no outer teacher but find all truth within.

[4] *Santokhu thāpi rakhiā jini sūti:* 'rectitude' or 'the order of nature'.

anyone understands this, then he becomes enlightened.[1] What a weight upon the 'Bull'! More worlds, more and more beyond! What kind of support is under all that weight? (N. *Japji*, 16:1-12)

2. [There are] creatures of [many] species, kinds and names; all have been written with a flowing pen, but few know how to write the list, and if the list were written how vast it would be! How great God's power and beauty of form, how great his gifts, who knows how to guess? So great a universe from one Word, whence hundred of thousands of rivers have been formed! What power have I to imagine thee! I cannot even once surrender [truly to thee]! What pleases thee, that work is good; O Formless One, thou abidest everlastingly![2] (N. *Japji*, 16: 13-24)

3. Countless persons pray[3] and countless [do acts of] love, countless worship and countless [perform] austerities, countless read scriptures and Vedas aloud, while countless yogis remain mentally detached, countless devotees ponder on God's glories and his wisdom. Countless are the generous and countless the givers, countless the heroes facing

---

[1] *Sachiāru*, i.e., imbued with the eternally true.

[2] This refrain, repeated four times, once with the omission of the first clause, runs: *kudarati kavana kaha vicharu/ varia na java eka vara / jo tudhu bhavai sai bhalikara/ tu sada salamati nirankara//*

[3] *Asankha japa;* or: countless repetition (of the Name)

steel, countless the silent ones[1] concentrating love [on thee]! What power have I to imagine thee? I cannot even once surrender [truly to thee]! What pleases thee, that work is good; O Formless One, thou abidest everlastingly! (N. *Japji*, 17)

4. Countless the fools totally blind, countless the thieves robbing others' property, countless those who depart after a violent reign, countless the slayers who commit murder, countless the sinners who depart after committing crimes, countless the liars who wander in falsehood, countless the barbarians who devour filthy food,[2] countless the slanderers taking a load upon the head![3] Lowly Nanak[4] expresses this opinion: 'I cannot even once surrender [truly to thee]! What pleases thee, that work is good; O Formless One, thou abidest everlastingly!' (N. *Japji*, 18)

5. Countless the names and countless the places,[5] countless the worlds altogether out of reach; 'Countless', they say, but on their heads is a load

---

[1] *Monī*

[2] *Asankha malecha malu bhakhi khāhi.*

[3] Cf. §§ 4 : 2, 36 : 1.

[4] *Nanaku nichu;* cf. § 3 : 3. It is only his humility that makes the Guru use this language; he does not wish to seem self-righteous in criticizing others.

[5] *Asankha nāva asankha thāva.* Teja Singh points out that the Guru here teaches God has many, not 99 or 108 or even 1000, names (cf. GH 9:4), and that to him all places are sacred, not only places like Mecca, Banaras, Jerusalem, Rome or Talwandi.

[for the word is inadequate]. Yet by words [we speak his] Name, by words his praise, by words his wisdom, hymns and depths of goodness; by words are the writing and speaking of the Utterance, and the destiny is expressed on the head in words. But nothing is on his head who wrote this[1] and as he ordains, so exactly do [souls] receive. As much as he has made, so much is the Name;[2] there is no place without the Name.[3] What power have I to imagine thee? I cannot even once surrender [truly to thee]! What pleases thee, that work is good; O Formless one, Thou abidest everlastingly! (N. Japji, 19)

It is the saints who as God's messengers carry the burden of the universe, who rule the worlds from within, and are trusted by their Lord. In that universe there are numberless worlds—how could they all be upheld by the fabled bull of old mythology, any more than by the earlier tortoise? No, the real 'Bull' which supports the worlds is only that eternal Law of infinite justice born of mercy, the law of karma; this maintains all creation, and it is through the study of its workings that the soul can win to real wisdom and the understanding of God's infinite will. That will is not arbitrary or haphazard, but it is the creative

---

[1] cf. *Ar. Bawan Akhari,* 54; all but God is describable by words.

[2] A clear definition of the 'Name' as the whole creation which reveals God; other passages show that it includes also revelation through scripture.

[3] As God is everywhere revealed, so we can everywhere find him. This important passage reads; *jeta kita teta nau / vinu nāvai nahi ko thau//*

keynote of the universe sounding on the keyboard of each soul; it is the *āsha* taught by the Prophet Zarathushtra through the great *ahuna-vairya-mantra,* the Law of Righteousness, the Great Plan, which gradually raises every individual through fluctuating fortunes to the height where ego cannot survive; it falls away, and leaves him free to enter God's holy court.

Who indeed can number the countless beings of innumerable kinds that God has made? How infinite must he be who with a single utterance of his will produced all these! Imagination falls back baffled from all attempts to realize his greatness, and cannot for a moment pay him worthy homage; it is enough for us to accept gladly whatever he may send to us, knowing it must be always for our good.

Endless beings adore him and try to do his will, each in his own way, spiritual or material; many are devoted to study or to ceremonial rites, many turn to silent contemplation, while others lavish gifts upon the needy in his name and for his sake, many bravely suffer martyrdom for him, while others only 'stand and wait', the unknown faithful ones who keep God's flag flying in the privacy of their own homes.

But without the 'villain' there can be no long play, so many maintain the drama of life by opposing these righteous souls, by their own wicked deeds of violence and filth they corrupt the world; these too serve him by drawing into play the patience and hidden virtues and courage of his saints.

Even the word 'countless' conveys no real sense of the number of beings in God's universe; no word can convey such a thought, yet we must use words to suggest ideas and feelings to each other, even though they be altogether inadequate. We use words even to speak of God, who is beyond all that any words can suggest, who cannot be limited by anything that words convey. He IS; and he is the giver of all, the absolute sovereign of all, who governs all by his will silently revealed by creation, and which we call the 'Name', eternally omnipresent.

61. GOD'S NAME ALONE CAN PURIFY

1. If the hand, foot or trunk of the body are dirty, they are washed with water and the dirt is removed; when the clothes are soiled with dirt, soap is applied and they are washed clean;[1] [so if] the mind is defiled by contact with sins, they can be washed away by the love of the Name. 'Meritorious' and 'sinner' are not [mere] words; whatever acts you may perform you record and take long [with you][2][3] you yourself sow, you yourself also eat; Nanak, at God's command you come and go (N. *Japji*, 20).

2. If anyone has [visits to] holy places, austerities, kindnesses and charitable gifts, he [has only] tiny merit;[4] [if he] listens to, honours and loves [the Name] in the heart, he bathes thoroughly in the holy

---

[1] *Mūta palūtī kapalu hoi / de sābūnu laīai ohu dhoi !/*

[2] *Kari kari karanā likhi lai jāhu.* We notice how often the Guru recurs to the law of karma; both Hindus and Musilms at the time relied too much on ceremonial purity and external credalism, and it was necessary to insist on the purely ethical nature of the hereafter as taught by Zarauthushtra.

[3] As *sanskāras,* which may produce another birth in the world

[4] *Tila kā mānu,* i.e., 'the honour of a til-seed', which is very small

waters within.[1] [O God,] all goodness is thine, I am nothing; unless thou make virtue [in me] there can be no devotion[2] [to thee]! Hail to thee, Creative Power, Word and Creator, eternal Beauty in whose heart is always love![3] (N. *Japji*, 21: 1-8).

Material things can be cleansed with soap and water, but what can these do to wash away the stains of sin from the heart? The only remedy for impurity is purity; the only purifier of the heart is God himself, revealed and glorified by his holy Name, just as the only solvent for the fat of wickedness is the soap of piety. It is folly to undervalue virtue or to make light of sin; sin is not a mere abstraction but a heavy load which, pressing on the soul, prevents its ascension to God's Court. The foul and filthy cannot enter there—if they were taken in they would hurl themselves out again at once, unable to bear its radiance and its awful purity—and those who play with sin slam its door upon their own faces. Who but themselves can be blamed for that?

Material remedies cannot avail for spiritual needs, nor can outer deeds of piety wholly wash away the inner corruption past sin has caused. It is only the 'water of life' which wells up within the heart from the infinite source within—the constant loving thought of God, the fount of holiness—that can really purify within. God is Spirit, and only Spirit can purify our spiritual bodies. Of ourselves we are indeed nothing, and that is the climax of human knowledge; but with

---

[1] cf. § 47 : 2.

[2] It is God's grace which alone can call a soul to devotion.

[3] *Suasti āthi bānī baramāu / sati suhānu sadā mani chāu//* The word *āthi* is understood as *māyā-prakrti*, to use a Skt. expression.

God we can do all things, and the greatest thing anyone can do is to make an act of whole surrender to his love (*Islam*). No sin can survive that surrender, the heart is washed wholly clean by the tide of faith and love.

62. GOD'S GOODNESS

1. Which was the moment, which the time, which the date and which the day of the week,[1] which was the season and which the month wherein the [universe] took shape?[2] The pundits did not get the [exact] moment or it would have been written in a Purana; the Qāzīs did not find out the time or they would have recorded it in writing in the Korān.[3] No yogi knows the date or the day of the week[4] —no one knows the season or the month; the Creator who made the universe, he himself alone knows. How can I speak of,[5] how can I praise, how describe or know him? Everyone tries to talk, each wiser than the other, says Nanak. Great is the Master, and

---

[1] *Suvelā,* auspicious time for starting something; *vakhatu,* the Arabic word *waqt,* which means simply 'time'; *tithi,* the Skt. word for the day of the month; *vāra,* the Skt. word for the day of the week.

[2] *Akāra;* i.e., (visible) form

[3] The Guru suitably uses the Skt. word when speaking of pundits and Purānas, and the Arabic word when speaking of qāzīs and the *Korān.* Of course the *Korān* was not written by 'Qāzīs' but dictated by the Prophet when in the 'mood' of inspiration, and later compiled into a book by the learned.

[4] To yogis all kinds of wonderful powers and knowledge are attributed, but not even the greatest yogis has given us this information.

[5] *Kiva kari ākha.*

great the Name whose making [is whatever] exists! Nanak, if anyone thinks 'I myself [know]', when he has gone forward he does not shine there[1] (N. *Japji*, 21: 9-18).

2. Underworlds [below] underworlds in thousands, skies [upon] skies![2] Indeed the Vedas say only one word:[3] 'We are weary of seeking their limits!' [Other] books speak of eighteen thousand,[4] whose root is the One eternal Creator. Could there be a list, they would write [it down], but they would perish in the writing.[5] Nanak, they say 'Great!', but he alone knows himself! (N. *Japji*, 22)

3. The praisers praise but have gained no such[6] realization [of him]; rivers and streams enter the sea but do not know [what it is]. Kings and emperors of

---

[1] There have been those who pretended to such high knowledge, but in the next world when men are seen as they are we shall know them to have spoken in the pride of their own ignorance.

[2] This saying is said to have roused the ire of certain orthodox Muslims who thought Nanak was contradicting the *Korān*, which speaks only of hell, earth and heaven; the Guru is said to have given them a vision of some of these many 'planes' or worlds.

[3] Or: fact (*vāta*)

[4] This number is quoted by T. as given in Bh. Kahna's *Gaurī* hymns. I do not know of any place where it is in the 'western scriptures' referred to, we are told, by the word *kateba* here. It is not in the *Bible* or *Korān*, but may be in some lost apocryphon.

[5] *Lekhai hoi vināsu.* They would not live long enough to finish.

[6] i.e., such as to know how great he is

the oceans may have mountains of property and wealth,[1] but are not equal to the ant whose heart forgets thee not! (N. *Japji*, 23)

4. No end [of his] praises, no end of telling them; no end of his works, no end of his gifts; no end by seeing, no end by hearing, none can find the end of plans in his mind.[2] No one can see[3] an end of the created universe, nor see the limits of that end. How many have been distressed in [trying to] make out the boundary, but they could find no end to him— no one can ever know that end! The more you say, the more there is [unsaid]! Great is the Master, lofty his abode, and higher than the high is his Name; were any other to be so great, he would be able to know the height of him.Himself alone is so great, so he himself alone knows; Nanak, gifts[4] are from the kindness of the Gracious One! (N. *Japji*, 24)

5. So many are his kindnesses that they cannot be written, but the great Giver has not a particle of desire.[5] How many peerless warriors ask [of him]! How many whose number is not to be thought of !

---

[1] *Samunda sāha sulatāna girahā setī mālu dhanu.*

[2] *Antu na jāpai kiā mani mantu.*

[3] *Japji;* it is S. who thus translates this word by *dissadā;* T. reads 'find out', which is substantially the same.

[4] Including the gift of knowing him whom we cannot of ourselves perceive

[5] i.e., for gratitude or acknowledgement

How many break by needlessly ruining [themselves]![1] How many receive and receive, and then deny! How many fools [merely] eat and eat! How many are always stricken with sorrow and hunger—but even these are also thy gifts, O Giver! Freedom from bondage comes at thy pleasure;[2] no one can say more. If any fool tries to speak [of another way], then he knows how many [blows] he endures on the face! He himself knows [our needs], he himself gives—[though] very few even admit this. Nanak, he to whom [God] grants the gift of praise is a king of kings! (N. *Japji*, 25)

No human mind can reach behind the hour of its creation to know exactly when and how it was; so God's secrets are not revealed even in the world's noblest scriptures, they are known to God alone. For all man's airy philosophies, for all the words he pours out in lecture halls, he knows very little of the truth; those who claim to know it in all its fullness only deceive themselves and will be exposed in the next world as the impostors they really are. God alone knows all.

There is no limit to the worlds, nor could any complete list be made of them all; though the Puranas may tell their number, theirs is but a symbolic guess. Infinite is his creation—who then can say what he himself must be? It is enough for us to adore, we can no more hope to comprehend than the salt doll can understand the nature and the size of the sea it enters. However great the greatest of mankind, they are

---

[1] *Kete khapi tutahi vekara.* T. has 'wreck themselves with self-indulgence'.

[2] There is no way to liberation save through God's grace and guidance.

but insects before the humblest soul who is really devoted to the Lord.

The more we speak of him, the less we know, for we surround ourselves with a dense fog of egoism; those who know are awed to reverent silence in his presence. God's 'boundlessness' is but a word to us, for to understand it we must see the bound and know that he goes beyond; but where is the boundary for him to go beyond? He is in all, endless and eternal, infinite and unthinkable. Only those on a level with its top can see the height of a tree, and only those like God could measure his greatness; but there is *none* like God, He IS, alone and secondless. What little we can know of him is only what of his mercy he reveals to us. It is when he takes us to himself and sets us free from human limitations that we shall know him as we know ourselves.

He has nothing to gain from us, no defect to be made good, no desire to be gratified; he just gives, unceasingly, to all who turn to him. He feels no pain when the recipients ignore him and deny his gifts, for he is equally in them as well. He gives all, both joy and sorrow, each as may be best for each of us; and as soon as we can bear to be wholly free he releases us from the bonds of ignorance. It is only he who gives; there is no other mediator, there is none but God to whom we can turn. He knows our real needs far better than we ourselves can know them, and he gives before we even ask. Nothing can make us happier than to be grateful to this all-generous Lord of ours.

63. HIS GLORY EXCELS ALL THOUGHT

1. Priceless[1] is goodness,[2] priceless the trading [in it], priceless are the dealers and priceless the storehouse of it, priceless the bringers of it, and priceless the takers away,[3] priceless those in love and priceless those absorbed in it (N. *Japji*, 26: 1-4).

2. Priceless is the Law[4] and priceless the Court, priceless the scales and priceless the weights, priceless the pardon[5] and priceless the sign of it, priceless [God's] mercy and priceless the decree[6] —beyond all pricelessness and indescribable; guessing and guessing, men remain lost in ecstasy[7] (N. Japji, 26:5-10).

3 The texts of Vedas and Puranas[8] talk[9], scholars

---

[1] The keyword of the first two paragraphs is *amulu,* and of the third is *ākhahi.*

[2] *guna,* one of the many words for which no single English equivalent is satisfactory; it connotes qualities, good qualities, virtues, glories.

[3] Guru Nanak shows in his hymns many such memories of the days in his own youth when his parents tried to drive him into commercial business.

[4] *dharamu,* i.e., the law of righteousness, ethics, religion, duty

[5] *bakhasīsa,* to be distinguished from *karamu* in the next verse; it stands rather for 'acquittal', while the latter implies 'forgive- ness', 'mercy'.

[6] *furmānu,* i.e., the sentence of the court, in this case favourable

[7] Amulo amulu ākhiā na jāi/akhi ākhi rahe liva lāi//

[8] Most scriptures contain hymns and laws like the Vedas, and histories and parables and doctrines like the Puranas, so these two words may stand for all the world's scriptures.

[9] The keyword of the first two paragraphs is *amulu,* and of the third is *ākhhi.*

talk and Indras[1] talk, Gopis talk and Govindas talk[2], Lords[3] talk and Adepts talk, how many created Buddhas[4] talk! Demons talk, gods talk, divine men, silent sages and servants![5] How many talk or try to talk! How many talk and talk till they die![6] Wert Thou to make as many more as have [already] been made, even then not even one would be able to utter it all! [God] becomes as great as he pleases; Nanak, only the Eternal knows [how great he is]; if any babbler begins to talk, then write [him down as] the fool of fools[7] (N. *Japji*, 26:11-26).

Blessed indeed is devotion and blessed those who gain it, those who share it with others, all who have anything to do with it. For the devotee enriches, saves the world; the very sound of a hymn to God, even from afar, uplifts the hearts of all who hear.

Perfect indeed is the justice of God's law which upholds his universe; we can rely with absolute confidence on that judgement which awaits each human soul—for each will get exactly what he has earned, or needs, of joy or sorrow. And who

---

[1] *Indras*; the word may be taken as a symbol of worldly rulers.

[2] *Gopis* and *Govindas* i.e., the givers and receivers of devotion

[3] *Isara*, Skt. *Iśwara*, i.e., the rulers of world systems under the One

[4] *Buddha*, i.e., enlightened men, real Gnostics of the highest order

[5] *Ākhai suri nara muni jana seva..*

[6] *Kete kahi kahi uthi uthi jāhi*, i.e., get up and go off.

[7] *Je ko ăkhai bolu vigālu / ta likhiai siri gavara gavaru.* Guru Nanak, like many of our own day, grew weary of the philosophy spinners who spend their time in idle words instead of living and doing some good in the world.

can tell how precious, how delightful that moment of his grace, when he pardons all our sins and pours his love into our hearts to make us wholly his; the very thought of that perfect blending of justice and mercy cannot but throw us into a trance of wondering love! Again and again his creatures try to express what they perceive of him and of his vast universe, but it is all in vain. They may pass whole lives in the effort, but he remains ever beyond the reach of language, and it is only foolishness for the finite to try to define the indefinable, the infinite—folly and the grossest of impiety.

64. THE SPLENDOUR OF HIS MAJESTY

1. What[1] is that door,[2] what is that house where sitting thou watchest over all;[1] many and countless tunes are there played by so many musicians— how many singers sing according to the [various] types and modes[3] [of music]! (N. *Japji,* 27: 1-3).

2. To thee wind, water, fire do sing,[4] the king of justice sings at the door [of thy court], the recorders[5] sing who know how to write all [acts and thoughts], and as they write and write Justice

---

[1] The word *kehā* suggests an exclamation of wonder: almost, 'How wonderful is that door, that house!' *So daru kehā, so gharu kehā, jitu bahi saraba samāle.* The last word suggests 'protectest' (*sambhāl karnā*).

[2] It is the 'tenth door of the sky', which leads to God's heaven.

[3] *rāga.... rāgini;* the former almost corresponds to the Wagnerian motif.

[4] The keyword of this section is *gāvahi,* they sing.

[5] *Chitu gupatu,* i.e., Chitragupta, the *karma-lipika* of Theosophists. The name is suggestive of 'hidden or secret mind', reminding us that the inmost motives have most effect on character and so on destiny.

considers! *Īśvara* and the Creator sing, the goddesses, always adorned with beauty;[1] [many] divine kings seated on thrones[2] among the gods sing at the door!

3. Adepts sing in their ecstatic trance,[3] good men sing in meditation,[4] zealous ascetics sing in their perseverance,[5] unyielding heroes sing to thee! Pundits and great seers[6] sing while reading the Vedas from age to age; beauties sing who charm all hearts in heaven, earth and the underworld; the jewels[7] made by thee sing together with the sixty-eight holy places; mighty warriors and heroes sing to thee, the four 'kingdoms'[8] [of living beings] sing; the planes, systems and universes[9] which thou art ever making and sustaining. [More than this], to

---

[1] *Gāvahi Isaru Barama devī sohani sadā savāre.*

[2] lit:: on Indra-thrones.

[3] *Gāvahi sidha samādhī andari.* Samādhi is the state of absolute moveless poise, wherein all fluctuations of the mind cease and the consciousness is merged in the blissful object of its devotion.

[4] *Gāvani sādha vichāre;* the *sadhu* is one who practises spirituality and engages in frequent meditation upon the Real.

[5] *Gāvani jatī sati santokhī:* the *jati* is one who exercises strong self-control and by various mortifications subdues the passions and the mind.

[6] *rakhīsara*, i.e., lords of Rishis

[7] The jewels are the virtues which arise in the mind through the brooding on God's holy Name.

[8] i.e., those born from seed, sweat, mud and eggs

[9] *Khanda mandala varabhandā;* or: continents, worlds and universes

thee sing those who please thee, devotees saturated with the sweet love of thee, and how many more sing they do not come to my mind—what is Nanak to think?[1] (N. *Japji*, 27:8-16)

4. He and he alone is ever true, the eternal Master of eternal Name; he indeed is and ever shall be, he goes not, nor shall go,[2] who has created all creation, who produced nature, making and making, [with its] many colours, kinds and types;[3] as he makes and makes he watches his own handiwork so that he [may see and enjoy] its greatness. What pleases him, that he will do, [our] order can do nothing. He is the King, nay, the very King of Kings; Nanak, [it is right] to remain resigned[4] [to him]! (N. *Japji*, 27:17-21)

In fancy Nanak now throws himself before God's judgement seat, before the gate of his 'diwan', where he attends to petitions and administers the universe. The perfection of his law and the immanence of happiness in all—as a blissful play—is delicately suggested by the music there, the 'harmony' of the spheres spoken of by Hermes. All around is the rejoicing of sweet melody, for all there is peace, and in the absence of injustice no fear can arise. God knows all, and

---

[1] *Hori kete gāvani se mai chiti na avani, Nānak kiā vichāre.*

[2] *Hai bhī hosi jāi na jāsi;* there is nothing here about God being born or not born, it speaks only of his eternity.

[3] *Rangī rangī bhātī kari kari jinasi māyā jini upāi.*

[4] *Nānaka rahanu rajāī.* The summation of all true religion, 'Islam', surrender, ātma-nivedana.

25

he is on the throne, and he is perfectly good. The angel-recorders of men's acts and thoughts assess, the 'King of Righteousness' (Rājā Dharamu), i.e., Death, is judge and perfectly administers God's laws, while the whole universe rejoices in the doom of evil, the apotheosis of God's devotee. How can poor Nanak describe that scene? The whole universe, with all its gods, is there.

He who made all and knows all, rules all and does all, nor is there anything he has not willed in all this vast boundless universe. Our happiness, our righteousness, our glory lies in simply accepting his sweet will as manifested in whatever comes to us, glad equally in joy and pain.

65. ADORATION TO THE ETERNAL

1. Make perseverance your earrings, effort your bowl and pouch, contemplation your ash,[1] readiness for death your quilted coat,[2] perfect chastity your body, and faith your staff; let universal brotherhood be your Ai-order[3]—for to conquer in the heart is to

---

[1] The yogi would do well to make contentment, endurance, patience his adornment; honest hard work should replace in his life the beggar's bowl, and the constant contemplation on God the mere outward sign of renunciation and of 'death to the world' symbolized by the ashes smeared on his body.

[2] T. reads this 'gaberdine', a long flowing robe worn by a yogi to appear like his own shroud; it was made of different patches of cloth, thickened by cotton-wool as in the *razai* of North India.

[3] *Āī-panthī;* the *Āī-sect* was considered the highest order of *sannyasis* noted for toleration; instead of taking pride in his order the real yogi will look on all men as his equals and mingle freely with all. (The phrase here is *sagalā jamātī,* and compares with the teaching in §§ 27:2, 28 and 30)

conquer the world.[1] Adoration, adoration to him, the immaculate.[2] Source, beginningless and endless,[3] in age after age the one same Form![4] (N. *Japji*, 28)

2. Make wisdom[5] your sweetmeat,[6] kindness the steward,[7] [hearing] the sound of music in every bosom;[8] let him be the Lord to whom all belongs, and wealth and psychic powers be titbits for others;[9] both attraction and repulsion[10] so act on things that the written destiny comes [to each]. Adoration, adoration to him, the immaculate Source, beginningless and endless, in age after age the one same Form! (N. *Japji*, 29)

3. One Mother united [with God] became

---

[1] *Mani jītai jagu jītu;* one of Guru's precious epigrams, containing in the fewest possible words the greatest possible wisdom-revelation.

[2] *Anīlu,* colourless, and so pure, unstained.

[3] *Anāhati,* imperishable, undying.

[4] This refrain, which recurs at the end of each paragraph in the section, runs thus: *ādesu tisai adesu / ādi anīlu anādi anāhati / jugu jugu eko vesu//.* The word *ādesu* is explained as a greeting equivalent to prostration and implying a willingness to obey any order given by the greeted..

[5] Or: Gnosis, i.e., the direct realization of God, which implies love.

[6] *bhugati;* lit: what is enjoyed, i.e., food which gives pleasure

[7] Or: treasurer, storekeeper (*bhandārani*)

[8] The horn sounded by yogis to announce their coming is to be the sound of the 'voice of the silence' heard in every living being, i.e., the realization of God as immanent in all, (*ghati ghati vājahi nāda*).

[9] *Āpi nathu nāthā sabha jākī ridhi sidhi avarā sāda.*

[10] lit: joining (and) separation (*sanjogu vijogu*)

25a

pregnant and gave birth to three sons:[1] one the Householder, one the Provider, one the Judge.[2] As it pleases him, so he directs according as his decree may be; he watches [all, yet] the look of grace does not reach them[3]—very marvellous is this! Adoration, adoration to him, the immaculate Source, beginningless and endless, in age after age the one same Form! (N. *Japji,* 30)

4. His seat and storehouse are in every world, whatever he has found there was found at one time;[4] making and making, the Creator watches [his creation][5]—Nanak, eternal is the work of the Eternal! Adoration, adoration to him, the immaculate Source, beginningless and endless, in age after age the one same Form! (N. *Japji,* 31)

Surrender to God is the only *real* yoga, which unites our will to his and makes us one form with him, and not the assuming of showy outward signs and insignia. Let us then replace these with inward virtues of the heart: with endurance, honest work, mental effort, the readiness to meet

---

[1] *chelo;* the word usually means 'disciple'.

[2] *samsārī ...bhandārī ... lāe dibānu.* Siva is here described as the one who 'summons the court', i.e., brings all things to account and closes the record.

[3] i.e., He sees them, yet they do not see him.

[4] So most commentators; T. reads: 'He put in once for all whatever he had to place in them.' The meaning is similar.

[5] The Guru often insists on God's work being unending, so those who seek union with him cannot look for eternal idleness hereafter.

life's 'end' at any moment, purity and confidence, together with the humility of being absolutely accessible to all as an equal and a friend. For this is the greatest victory man can win, and these are the real *siddhis* or perfections for which he must strive; self-conquest is the highest of dominions, the hardest and the most delightful to achieve.

Nanak now turns from the homeless ascetic to the householder's kitchen: the true knowledge of God is to be served out to all as the sweetest titbit of the feast for guests, while outsiders may seek the childish bauble of psychic powers if they will. It is right there should be these two parties in the world, the spiritual and the worldly; the law of harmony is a delicate balance between the two, attraction and repulsion together hold the worlds in place and make evolution possible on them; between them the 'devas' and the 'asuras' churn the ocean of milk whence arise nectar and so many other things, both demoniac and divine. It is kindness and compassion for others which awakens in the heart God's soft voice, and this leads us at last to full surrender and so to union with him.

Māyā-śakti is the 'mother' of our triune universe which is symbolized by Brahma-Vishnu-Śiva, Creator-Maintainer-Absorber, and the three qualities of *rajas-sattva-tamas*, activity-rhythm-passivity. It is Brahma who builds the 'house' or 'heart', it is Vishnu who pervades all and gives all, and Śiva who assures perfect justice to all; and these three are really only 'sons' or 'disciples' of the real God who is above and beyond them all, ruling through them all the worlds, and calling one here, one there, into union with him.

Indeed, all his worlds are even now in him, and he dwells in them—as the sea is in each wave and each wave in the sea; for he is everywhere, incessantly at work, omniscient, omnipotent. And they who enter into union with him will share for all eternity in that ceaseless work, having at their disposal the same infinitely extended power as he. Wise indeed are they who see him and adore him as the ever-changeless, in whom all else exists in ever-changing forms, who pattern their own being so that they may truly reflect him, and enable them to share his infinite bliss of endless work for the upliftment of all that is!

66. ALL POWER IS IN HIM

1. [A man says] 'If from one tongue a lakh[1] were to come into being, and from the lakh twenty lakhs were to appear—I would call lakhs and lakhs of times on the one Name of the Lord of the World; in this way would I climb the bridegroom's [five] stairs[2] and become one [with him]; on hearing talk of the sky, a longing comes even to worms!' Nanak, he is obtained through grace; false are such boastful falsehoods![3] (N. *Japji*, 32)

2. In speaking [we have] no power, no power in keeping silence,[4] no power in asking, no power in giving, no power in living, no power in dying, no power [in getting] kingdom or wealth which thrill the heart, no power [in attaining] intelligence, wisdom or meditation, no power to reach the escape

---

[1] *lakh*, the common Indian word for a hundred thousand; a hundred lakhs make one crore *(koti)*

[2] *Etu rāhi pati pavaliā chaliai;* this 'ladder' or 'staircase' consists of the five stages of spiritual life, whereof the lowest is on this physical world.

[3] *Nadari pāiai kūli kūlai thīsa.*

[4] *Akhani joru chupai naha joru:*cf. § 55:2.

from the world; he in whose hand the power is, is he who makes and watches all; Nanak, no one is noble or mean [by his own effort alone] (N. *Japji*, 33).

3. Nights, seasons, dates, days of the week; wind, water, fire; the underworlds—amidst these has he established the earth as an inn,[1] wherein there are living beings or habits and colours whose names are many and endless. According to the actions these perform, so is the verdict; he himself is just, and true [is his] court; there the elect are glorified and through his look of grace win the mark of favour; there the imperfect and the mature are distinguished[2] [from each other]. Nanak, on going there it comes to be known [what each one is] (N.*Japji*, 34).

At this stage the devotee may burst out in a song of ecstasy that even if he had millions and millions of tongues he would devote them all to the ceaseless adoration of that wonderful God, Vahīgurū, keeping his Name ever on them all. So he would pass easily upward through the five stages or planes of the spiritual path to union with him, all by his own effort and devotion. It is natural for man to long for this; does not every creature, even the lowliest, desire to rise to higher things—the caterpillar dreams of wings that it may fly—and what is higher than the Lord?

But Nanak pulls us up sharply here. There is only one way to reach God, and that is through his grace. Man in his foolish

---

[1] *dharamasāla*, properly used for a building set apart for the free use of travellers and pilgrims for a night or so.

[2] *Kacha pakāī othai pāi;* lit: the raw and cooked there are found out.

pride thinks he can do everything by himself; he invents so many creeds, relies on sacrifice, on intercession, on gifts, austerity, intellectual subtleties—but none of these can take the soul to God; any doctrine, and philosophy, which omits the omnipotence of grace is false.

Of ourselves alone we can do nothing at all; even in this world of ours we depend absolutely on God. How then could we imagine we could come to his transcendent world and merge with him by our own effort? Can the man fallen into mud pull himself out by tugging at his own hair? He alone has power, he alone can do what He will, He alone can save the fallen.

This earth of ours on which we live today in physical bodies is the plane of law and righteousness, a *dharmsāla* indeed—and also in its second sense an inn, for none of us stay here long; we come, meet strangers here, and pass upon our way (cf. §22:1). Those who act righteously in that brief sojourn, as guided by conscience and the Guru's teaching, are approved by God in the 'judgement' after death and receive his award; in that court all will know the real character of every soul, for no deception avails against the spirit's penetrating gaze. This physical world, the *dharama-khand,* lies between the subtler elemental world and the grosser planes of *pātāla;* it is ruled by time and space under the control of the Lord and his saints, the 'elect'.

67. THE PATH TO THE REAL

1. Such is the law of the plane of law;[1] now speak[2] of the action of the plane of wisdom. How

---

[1] *Dharama khanda kā eho dharamu.*

[2] *Ākhahu;* some read this as 'I will tell'.

many winds, waters, fires! How many Krishnas and Sivas![1] How many creators shaping forms of [various] beauties, colours and shapes![2] How many fields of action,[3] how many mountain summits [of contemplation], how many teachings from Dhruva![4] How many planets[5] and moons, how many suns, how many habitable spheres![6] How many Adepts and Buddhas, how many Masters, how many goddess-robes![7] How many gods and demons, how many sages, how many kinds and oceans of gems! How many races,[8] how many languages, how many emperors and kings![9] How many [kinds of] contemplation,[10] how many servants [of God]—Nanak, no end to them! (N. Japji, 35)

---

[1] *Kete Kāna Mahesa. Kāna* stands for *Kanhaiya,* a name of Sri Krishna, and *Mahesa* is the Skt. *Maheswara,* the Great Lord.

[2] *Kete Barame ghalati ghalīahi rūpa ranga ke vesa.*

[3] *Karama bhūmi:* i.e., lands of action, or grace, i.e., worlds

[4] *Kete Dhu upadesa:* Dhruva was a five-years-old boy whom Nārada taught full devotion to the Lord; he assumed rule over the polar star, round which the universe revolves. Thus the Guru here means: 'How many teachings of divine wisdom which control the worlds and guide its beings!'

[5] lit: *Indras (inda);* i.e., worldly divine kings; so I have understood the meaning as 'planets', a word which seems to fit in the context.

[6] *Mandala desa;* i.e., spheres (and) lands; I have taken it as hendiadys for 'inhabited spheres' because *desa* (Skt. *deśam*) implies habitants.

[7] *Devī vesa:* S. has proved that *kete* here goes with *vesa* and not with *devi,* so *devi* must be used almost adjectivally.

[8] *khāni;* or *mines,* i.e., sources from which human souls are quarried.

[9] *Kete pāta narinda;* some read this 'How many royal dynasties'.

[10] *ketiā suratī:* S. shows this to be fem. plu. We may prefer 'How many [kinds of] intelligence!'

2. In that plane of wisdom, wisdom is supreme; there is the joy of music, of spectacles and plays.[1] But beauty is the note of the plane of effort, and there most exquisite forms are fashioned—the facts of that state cannot be told, if anyone [tries to] tell he afterwards repents. Intuition and understanding are moulded there, and discrimination [awakes] in the heart;[2] it is there the awarenesses of gods and adepts are formed (N. *Japji*, 36).

3. The keynote of the plane of grace is power; no one is there[3] save warriors mighty and brave, in whom God is everywhere pervading.[4] Sita upon Sita is there in glory,[5] whose beauty cannot be described. They will never die nor be misled [by *maya*] in whose hearts God dwells; many worlds of devotees live there rejoicing [because] the Eternal is in their heart (N. *Japji*, 37:1-10).

4. In the plane of reality dwells the Formless One; making and making, he watches with

---

[1] *Tithai nāda binoda koda anandu;* S. understands *kautak* for koda, while T. reads it as *koti* 'crores', M. and U. agree with T. Prof. Jodh Singh reads: 'and numerous forms of happiness.'

[2] *Tithai ghatiai surati mati mani budhi.*

[3] *Tithai horu na koi horu:* it may be better to read this: 'There is no other thing there [save power]'.

[4] *Tina mahi Rāmu rahiā bharapūra.*

[5] It has been pointed out that here the Guru shows the greatness of women, for where the perfect man is named, women too have a rightful place.

delightful look of grace. Planes, worlds and universes are there—if one were to [begin] telling them, then, [he would find] no end of them! Worlds upon worlds of living forms—exactly as his command [may be] so exactly [is their] work![1] He watches, and is pleased while making meditation [on them all]; Nanak, to describe [such things] is as hard as iron![2] (N. *Japji*, 37:11-18)

Nanak sketches the way home through the four inner planes of life. First, the plane of wisdom, known to many of us as 'the Hall of Learning', the subtle world of profusion which fills with delighted wonder so many souls who enter it through the gate of death. It is the source of countless inspirations, of archetypal forms, of primal beauties, of melodies destined to enter musicians' minds on earth and there to find a partial incarnation as immortal music among men; it is the realm of unnumbered beings built of 'astral' or radiant matter, the 'spirits' of the departed and of the unborn. Here are the elementals and the deities men worship at village shrines, the nature spirits that enform great mountains and rushing streams, the 'invisible helpers' whose work was so well described from observation by C. W. Leadbeater, the builders of form and fairies, the 'spirit-guides' and controls, initiates, Masters and adepts labouring among men on earth. Here through the manifold forms assumed by life the soul gradually learns to see the One, and so, in a realm palpitating with all human joys and delights, is slowly purged of ancient ignorance.

---

[1] *Tithai loa loa ākāra jiva jiva hukamu tivai tiva kāra.*

[2] i.e., extremely hard to tell, *(kathanā karalā sāru)*.

We pass on with our guide to the next higher realm, the plane of happiness or of effort, the *Sarama-khand,* where dwell the proto-forms of matchless beauty which have been the model for the workers in the lower plane. Hence originate the ideals and archetypes which workers in that *gyana-khand* transmit to artists on the earth—who try to translate those dreams of perfect form into great poems, noble buildings, symphonies or social reforms. Very subtle and easily moulded by thought is the matter of this plane, the 'mental plane' of the Theosophists, and very great the joy of those who dwell thereon. The close association between joy and beauty is well brought out by Ruskin's saying: 'Whatever is pleasurable, therefore, is also beautiful.' And on this plane of effort, which leads to so great effects, it is natural that the dwellers there find it is a plane of happiness as well.

Further in, or up, we come to the plane of grace or action—the meaning *karama-khand* is disputed. Here there is no longer any concern for the fruits of action or success but solely for disinterested duty. This is wholly selfless, and so it is Godlike and draws us very near to the glory of the all-pervading Rāma and the beauteous Sita—types of perfected beings whose 'life is hid in God', whose efforts can never be in vain or perish, nor can they be deceived by the false appearances of *māyā*. Thus their actions are filled with omnipotent grace, everything they do is filled with the love and power of God. This is the realm of those who are merged in God, the Great Ones who from time to time come forth to liberate men from the miseries spawned by ignorance, who are always labouring for us from their mountain summit of achievement.

The plane of truth or eternal reality (*sack-hand*) is God's own home, where he alone abides in eternal bliss, because all who reach that plane are one with him. In that eternity the past, present and future blend into an all-present Now; there is neither space nor time there, all is he alone. He is the absolute *Brahman* of whom the Hindus speak, the Formless One, whose qualities are so far beyond human thought that no word could be imagined to descirbe them, so we call him the *Nirguna,* 'without qualities'. None can enter his court save those who have been 'at-oned', made one, with him, for here there can be no 'otherness'—here he IS; and from here he watches from his seat in the heart of every living thing all that he has made. This is indeed a paradox, but how else can we speak of the infinite at all? There is no *time* for the plane of truth, for it has been, is and always will be *now:* there is no *space* for the plane of truth, for it is not here or there but everywhere, within as without, being co-terminous with the Infinite himself!

And so the soul rises, climbing the five steps of this 'ladder' with the Guru's aid to his real home (cf. § 26:1). By the faithful and brave doing of his *duty* on earth he earns the right to knowledge and *wisdom,* and so is enabled to make happy *efforts* in the helping of others. By this means he wins the *grace* of the saint, and so is lead by him to union with the Beloved whom he has sought so long as the final *Truth.*

68. TRUE RIGHTEOUSNESS

1. Self-control is the smithy, patience the smith,[1]
Understanding the anvil, wisdom the tools;[2] the fear
[of God] is the bellows, burning austerity the fire,

---

[1] *Jatu pāhārā dhiraju suniāru.*

[2] *Arahani mati vedu hathīāru.* Note that the 'wisdom' in this passage is not gnosis (*giānu*), but rahter 'thorough knowledge' (*vedu*).

and love the crucible wherein you melt the nectar[1]—in this true mint the [Guru's] word can be coined,[2] [and this is] the work of those on whom [falls] the grace of his glance. Nanak, from grace upon grace comes bliss[3] (N. *Japji*, 38).

2. The Breath [of life] is the Guru, Water the father and great Earth[4] the mother; Day and Night[5] are the two nurses male and female[6] —the whole world plays [in their lap]! Justice reads out in [God's] presence the good and evil deeds [of men], and each according to his own actions [shall be]—some near [to him and] some far off. Those who have brooded on the Name and achieved by effort, Nanak, are bright of face; how many are freed along with them! (N. *Śloka*)

Nanak, in a few strong phrases has limned out the distant paths ahead of all, but he closes his great hymn by bringing us back to the practical side of life, which is not an empty dream of philosophy but a hard fight for right. He now gives us a few hints on the discipline needed by the aspirant before he can expect to tread that path to the very end: he lists the

---

[1] *nectar:* i.e., of God's Name

[2] The reader will, no doubt, enjoy working out the details of this striking metaphor.

[3] *Nadarī nadarī nihāla.*

[4] *Dharati mahatu:* in the latter word there may be an allusion to Skt. *mahat,* one of the stages in evolution.

[5] i.e., life and death, light and darkness, joy and sorrow, etc.

[6] *Dui dāyi dāyā.*

qualifications which make up that discipline and must first be acquired. (1) Chastity and self-control of body, mind and desires; (2) steady perseverance in effort, for the fickle and faint-hearted cannot travel far; (3) pure reason, which must lie behind all true thinking and so illumine the mind with a sight of truth; (4) the essential truths of all religions; (5) a fearlessness which is born only from reverence for and faith in God; (6) the austere fire of renunciation and spirituality; (7) the immortalizing love of God; (8) the divine Name, which is the Guru's enlightening 'Word', wherein the soul is melted into the form of the King, just as the metal of a coin is stamped with the sovereign's head. These are the qualities needed by the 'metal'; but it is the authority of the King alone which permits the coin to be struck, and that is Grace; as his grace pours down upon the soul it rises through the planes to him.

The Japji concludes with a single *sloka* or stanza added by Nanak himself to remind us that good actions too are needed by man in his upward climb. Not works alone, not grace alone, but Grace enabling works! And all the forces of nature aid the man of grace who strives to live according to God's Word. The child of soul (*water*) and body (*earth*), man has the breath of life breathed into him by the Guru; that breath is fostered by time as he repeats the Name by day and night, and so he is enabled to use his opportunities for right action; he thus wins the great reward, earlier or later, here in this life or in the next. Those who thus find the Lord become the teachers of others in their turn, for they share his eternal work of uplifting souls; they themselves 'shine as the stars of heaven', and they spread radiance on the faces of all who came in touch with them.

Prayer

O true and eternal King, in thy presence [we offer] the prayers of Sodaru and Rahiras; pardon our mistakes, [overcome our] difficulties and defects of letters; let the glorious name of Guru Nanak rise, and in thy good pleasure [may there be] the good of all ! (*Ardas*)

Bibliography

1. GURMUKHĪ TEXT ALONE

ĀDI SRI GURŪ — Pub. by Bhāi Pratapsingh
GRANTH SĀHIBJĪ   Pritamsingh; carefully
checked by the Kartarpur
copy of the *Granth Sahib*;
1430 large pages in heavy
type.

Sundara Gutaka — Pub. by Bhai Catarasingh
Jivansingh

Akāl Ustat — Pub. by the Khalsa Tract
Society

2. GURMUKHĪ TEXT WITH PUNJABI COMMENTARY

Dasama Grantha satīka — Bisan Singh
Vārān Bhāi Gurdās satīka
Saloka Bhagat Kabīra jiu ke — Khalsa Tract Soc.
Bārah Māhā Tukhāri bhāva,
prakāsani ūkā sahit
Srī Jāpu Sāhib
Rahiras

ṭīkā Japujī Sāhib, 1946   — Mohan Singh
saṭīka Āsa dī Vār   Sahib Singh
Jāpu Sāhib saṭīka, 1949
Jāpu Sāhib saṭīka, 1950
saṭīka Sukhamani Sāhib, 1945
Saloka Guru Angad Sāhib, 1948
Shekh Farīd jī dī Bānī, saṭīkā, 1946
Bhattān de Sawwaiye saṭīkā

3. ENGLISH TRANSLATIONS

The Sikh Religion, (6 vols.),   — Max Arthur Macauliffe
1909 (cited as M.)
The Japji and Discourses   — Mehta Udhodas (U)
on the Bhagavad Gītā, 1932
The Japji, 1924   — Teja Singh (T)
Asa di War
The Psalm of Peace
(Sukhmani)

4. ENGLISH BOOKS ON SIKHISM AND ITS HISTORY

Catechism of Sikh   — Awatsingh
Religion, 1932   Mahtabsingh
Sikhism, a Lecture   — Annie Besant
Shri Guru Arjuna Dev,   — Brijendra Singh
the Poet and the Organizer
The Religion of the Sikhs,   — Dorothy Field
1914
Something about Sikhism,   — Harbans Singh
1929

Guru Nanak and His Sikhs	— Kamla Akali
Guru Nanak as an Occultist, *1926*	— H.C. Kumar
The Life and Work of Guru *Gobind Singh, 1909*	— Bh. Lakshman Singh
Sketch of the Sikhs, 1812	— Lt. Col. Malcolm
The Transformation of *Sikhism, 1912*	— Gokul Chand Narang
The Book of the *Ten Masters, 1926*	— Puran Singh
Sikhism, a Universal *Religion*	— Rup Singh
The Philosophy of Sikhism	— Dr Sher Singh
The Oxford History of India, *1920*	— Vincent A. Smith
Guru Nanak's Religion in *His own Words*	— Teja Singh
Sikhism, its Ideals and *Institutions, 1938*	

5.   OTHER BOOKS

India, Burma and Ceylon, *1933*	— Murray's Handbook
Pub. by G.A.Natesan	— Nāmdev, Sketch of His Life and Teachings
Pub. by G. A. Natesan	— Ramanand to Rām Tirath
selected by Munshi *Jagannath Sahai,* *(Lakhnau 1926)*	— Ānandasāgar, prathama bhāg (Kabīr Ravidās)
One Hundred Poems of *Kabīr (with Introduction by* *Evelyn Underhill), 1923*	— Dr Rabindranath Tagore

Tisara Bhāg, Kabīrdās ke Bhajana	— Manaharana Bhajanavali
Bhakta Bālak, (Gorakhpur, 1930) (Dhannaji)	— Hanumān Prasād Poddār